THE ENTREPRENEURIAL LIBRARIAN

THE ENTREPRENEURIAL LIBRARIAN

*Essays on the Infusion of Private-Business
Dynamism into Professional Service*

Edited by Mary Krautter,
Mary Beth Lock *and* Mary G. Scanlon

McFarland & Company, Inc., Publishers
Jefferson, North Carolina, and London

LIBRARY OF CONGRESS CATALOGUING-IN-PUBLICATION DATA

The entrepreneurial librarian : essays on the infusion of private-business dynamism into professional service / edited by Mary Krautter, Mary Beth Lock and Mary G. Scanlon.
p.   cm.
Includes bibliographical references and index.

ISBN 978-0-7864-6468-5
softcover : acid free paper ∞

1. Library administration.   2. Organizational change.   3. Entrepreneurship.
I. Krautter, Mary, 1954–   II. Lock, Mary Beth, 1962–   III. Scanlon, Mary G., 1955–
Z678.E58 2012   025.1—dc23   2012001220

BRITISH LIBRARY CATALOGUING DATA ARE AVAILABLE

Cover image © 2012 Photosani

Front cover design by Rob Cheney (http://robcheney.com/)

Manufactured in the United States of America

McFarland & Company, Inc., Publishers
Box 611, Jefferson, North Carolina 28640
www.mcfarlandpub.com

Table of Contents

Acknowledgments

The editors would like to acknowledge Dean Rosann Bazirjian of the University of North Carolina at Greensboro Libraries and Dean Lynn Sutton of Wake Forest University's Z. Smith Reynolds Library, who initiated the first Conference for Entrepreneurial Librarians: *Inspiration, Innovation, Celebration* held June 3 and 4, 2009. Their conversations about the need for entrepreneurial approaches to librarianship resulted in a collaboration between Z. Smith Reynolds and UNCG librarians that has spanned several years and included a second conference, *From Vision to Implementation*, a webinar, and plans for a third conference. The three editors were all members of the original Planning Committee formed in 2008 and have been collaborating on this project as part of our commitment to the principle that entrepreneurship enriches and advances the practice of librarianship. We want to thank all of the librarians who helped plan the conferences and who have supported us in the writing of this book: UNCG's Rosann Bazirjian, Kathy Crowe, Mike Crumpton, Kimberly Lutz, Barry Miller, LaTesha Velez, and WFU's Wanda Brown, Ellen Daugman, Derrik Hiatt, Vicki Johnson, and Carolyn McCallum. We also thank the many presenters at the two conferences and the webinar whose innovative approaches, shared with our conference attendees, were lively contributions to the conversation on entrepreneurship.

We want to thank our respective libraries for their support. We particularly want to thank our family members, George, Katie, Sarah, Cedric, Bun, Madeleine, Richard, Nicholas, Gerianne, Kelsey, Matthew, RJ, and Adriene for their patience and love. Most of all we want to thank the authors who provided the material for this book and worked so diligently with us in the editing process—three rather exacting, or dare we say demanding, editors who much appreciate your cooperative spirits!

Introduction

MARY KRAUTTER, MARY BETH LOCK
and MARY G. SCANLON

Background

The importance of entrepreneurship in the world economy is firmly established; hundreds of books have been published on all aspects of the topic from practical explanations of how an entrepreneur might start a business to historical accounts of past entrepreneurs. Entrepreneurial tendencies are sometimes found in surprising places. Titles such as *Unlikely Entrepreneurs: Catholic Sisters and the Hospital Marketplace 1865–1925* (Wall) re-examine historical events in light of what we now know about entrepreneurial practices, and books such as *Pricing without Fear: A Sewing Entrepreneur's Guide* (Wright Sykes) apply entrepreneurial principles regarding marketing, consumer behavior, and business planning to enterprises in narrow specific markets.

In 2003, Jerome A. Katz documented the robust growth of entrepreneurship education programs in colleges and universities in the United States, noting that a 1947 class at Harvard Business School can be identified as the first entrepreneurship course in the United States. Katz has developed and Saint Louis University hosts a website listing colleges with majors in entrepreneurship (a total of 224) and Ph. D. programs as well as a list of Entrepreneurship Centers <www.slu.edu/x17964.xml>. The prevalence of entrepreneurship programs in higher education clearly indicates that it has evolved into a mainstream phenomenon.

The old image of an entrepreneur as a scrappy, independent risk-taker has been replaced by the reality of individuals incorporating innovative ideas in more traditional settings. One of the most compelling examples of this evolution is the widely recognized practice of social entrepreneurship. Organizations such as the Schwab Foundation for Social Entrepreneurship, described *in The Power of Unreasonable People*: *How Social Entrepreneurs Create Markets that Change the World* (Elkington and Hartigan), advance the notion that planning a project benefiting society has distinct parallels with starting a for-profit business. The "unreasonable people," the social entrepreneurs thus described, are developing enterprises, each with a social mission and in a spirit of advocacy. Their unreasonableness stems from their refusal to take the reasonable stance that some problems are too big to be solved.

If one adheres to the stereotypical notion of a brash businessperson taking risks and using innovative techniques, the idea of an entrepreneurial librarian may seem incongruous. Librarians typically work in bureaucratic organizations and, while they much lament the stereotype of Marian the Librarian with her timid and retiring nature, to the general public such an image may seem ill-suited to risky and creative ventures.

These stereotypes are continually proven untrue. Marilyn Johnson's 2010 *This Book Is Overdue! How Librarians and Cybrarians Can Save Us All* features a caped librarian on the

1

cover, charging into the stratosphere, sensible shoes propelling her over a cascade of volumes left behind for the new library cyberworld. The librarians portrayed by Johnson are not the repressed Marians of bygone days, but savvy, blogging, computer-wielding information warriors, fighting for intellectual freedom and striving to forge a navigable path through the information jungle. Indeed, the inherent notion of libraries is entrepreneurial in its promotion of a model of sharing resources for the public good. How appropriate that Benjamin Franklin, a successful businessman and an innovator in countless endeavors, should have conceived of the subscription library, an idea carried to fruition in the Library Company of Philadelphia and considered to be the forerunner of the modern public library. Sharing information and empowering users is inherently a bold notion, and librarians embrace the techniques that make this possible. In this volume, we offer a view of librarians who crusade to bring about social change, who design entrepreneurial new services, who create new fundraising programs and who incorporate innovation and an entrepreneurial spirit into a variety of endeavors, even while providing traditional services. Entrepreneurial librarians are flourishing in the digital age, embracing technology with creative energy which leads them to redefine and reinvent systems and services. Some librarians pursue entrepreneurial activities by developing and implementing their ideas within their institutions, while others have stepped outside the doors of the library, starting new businesses which serve the library market.

Genesis of the Book

Our own interest in entrepreneurial librarians began in early 2008, when the library deans at the University of North Carolina–Greensboro, Rosann Bazirjian, and Wake Forest University, Lynn Sutton, collaborated to co-produce a conference with this theme. The steering committee, which consisted of librarians from both institutions, began planning a conference which was held in June 2009, *Inspiration, Innovation, Celebration: An Entrepreneurial Conference for Librarians,* whose goal was to provide a forum in which librarians could discuss entrepreneurship. The conference celebrated innovation and allowed attendees to learn from each other's successes. Several of the presentations from that successful first conference were published in the September 2009 issue of *Against the Grain* (Bazirjian). In the subsequent iteration of the conference held in March 2011, *The Conference for Entrepreneurial Librarians: From Vision to Implementation,* a different philosophy prevailed: true entrepreneurship in libraries, focusing on providing programs that developed ideas and programs with actual or potential commercial applications. The two keynote speakers for this conference, Mary Ellen Bates and Tim Spalding, are entrepreneurs who have built information businesses of very different types; their stories are shared in this volume through interviews.

The book's editors met as members of the conference steering committee. After observing the entrepreneurial activity associated with the two conferences, we felt there was strong interest in the subject, as well as valuable ideas that needed exposure. We find the time is right to document the current state of entrepreneurial initiatives in libraries.

The concept of the entrepreneurial librarian has been well recognized in library literature. One of the earliest examples is from 1987, when *The Journal of Library Administration* published a double issue entitled "Creativity, Innovation, and Entrepreneurship in Libraries," which covered such topics as developing new services, managing innovative information technology, and initiating fee-based information services. There has also been international recognition of the importance of entrepreneurship in libraries, including Axtell's conference on entrepreneurial libraries which was held on 6–7 November 2008 at Nacka's Dieselverk-staden Library in Stockholm and included librarians from the Nordic countries, the UK and Canada (Dhanjal).

While not the first to link the idea of entrepreneurship to librarianship, Guy St. Clair's *Entrepreneurial Librarianship: The Key to Effective Information Services Management* (1996) is one of the key works in the field. St. Clair credits Peter Drucker with the development of his own ideas about the application of entrepreneurial ideas to the field of librarianship. St. Clair advocates that those "who work in information services should recognize the value of the entrepreneurial approach and link it to the strategic planning and planning management that are basic to the success of the organizations we work for" (xix).

Stan Skrzeszewski's *The Knowledge Entrepreneur* (2006) details methods by which librarians can apply entrepreneurship in their professional lives. He calls for knowledge workers, including librarians, to "become engaged in entrepreneurial activity involving the creation and use of new knowledge for community, organizational and personal development and the development of new products and services" (viii).

As the 2009 *Risk and Entrepreneurship in Libraries* states: "Transformative actions are urgently needed if libraries and the practice of librarianship are to continue" (vii). In his introduction to the book, Marshall Keys discusses the role of risk as an essential part of the entrepreneurial approach and emphasizes the difficulty of being entrepreneurial in a traditional organization, particularly in bureaucratic hierarchical settings. Keys provides a template for potential entrepreneurs and many of the authors in this collection have adopted the practice he describes. In this same book, Joyce Ogburn articulates her vision of the entrepreneurial librarian focusing on the need to accept risk and "craft a new future while remaining true to the library's mission to find, preserve and make available the many stories of research, cultures, and people's lives and imagination" (43).

Models of Entrepreneurship

As in the business world, entrepreneurship in libraries follows several models: intrapreneurs, entrepreneurs, and social entrepreneurs. Intrapreneurs create ideas and projects intended primarily for internal use. Entrepreneurs are those who develop their ideas into commercial entities with the possibility of financial risk and reward—often acting independently or starting new organizations. Social entrepreneurs develop organizations or programs for the purpose of promoting causes; they may promote these through advocacy, education or fundraising. Many of the entrepreneurial librarians in this volume work in traditional, non-profit settings, but they have taken the techniques that allow independent businesses to succeed and created successful and creative programs that advance the missions of their individual institutions.

Intrapreneurship

While forming a company that provides services to the library market is one manifestation of entrepreneurship in libraries, there are also numerous examples of other entrepreneurial activities within libraries. Our collection of essays emphasizes entrepreneurial librarians who have innovated out of necessity, providing creative answers within the traditional framework of the library. *Library Journal* highlights entrepreneurial ideas in its annual list of Library Movers and Shakers—honoring librarians dedicated to innovation and creativity. While entrepreneurship usually implies starting a business, librarians who start new programs within their libraries need many of the same skills and apply the same principles to achieve success. An example of a hybrid model comes from Tim Bucknall of University of North Carolina at Greensboro Libraries, who led a team to develop Journal Finder, a program that improves access to electronic journal holdings; the product became so sought after that it was licensed to other libraries and eventually acquired by WT Cox Subscriptions.

Another example is LibraryH3lp "an integrated IM/web-chat help system designed specifically for libraries." <libraryh3lp.blogspot.com> It was jointly developed by Pam Sessoms, (a presenter at the second *Entrepreneurial Librarian* conference and librarian at the University of North Carolina–Chapel Hill) and her partner and husband Eric Sessoms, a software developer. The program was initially intended for the Triangle Libraries Network to provide features and functions customized for chat in a library setting, but now it is marketed to other libraries as well.

ENTREPRENEURSHIP

Entrepreneurship has its roots in a strongly capitalistic approach—taking a risk in starting a business with the goal of yielding profits. Certainly, such approaches have been successful in companies that serve the library market, and some of these have been initiated by librarians, sometimes starting in a non-profit setting and later branching out to the commercial world.

The history of entrepreneurial librarians is comprised of those who built library-related projects into commercial enterprises. Frederick Kilgour, who embodied the spirit of entrepreneurship, advocated for library automation while he was head of the Yale Medical Library (OCLC, 2006). The Ohio College Association hired him to develop a computerized library system which became Ohio College Library Center (OCLC), the nonprofit organization that remains one of the most influential forces in libraries worldwide.

Peter McCracken says "librarians are full of great ideas and these ideas can easily become full-fledged companies" (17). There are countless examples of librarians who have changed the profession by developing and marketing new products. Slaven Zivkovic developed Springshare's LibGuides, a system that allows librarians to exercise their creativity in producing research guides within a flexible and affordable web-based system; it is currently being used by over 1,200 libraries. Duncan Smith established NoveList, an online reader's advisory service which was acquired by EBSCO. Peter McCracken, co-founder of Serials Solutions, a journal-linking service, is another entrepreneur who has used his knowledge of libraries to develop a commercial enterprise. Librarians have also created research-based businesses; one of the most successful of these is Mary Ellen Bates of Bates Information Services, and this volume includes an interview in which she describes her career as an independent researcher.

SOCIAL AND CULTURAL ENTREPRENEURSHIP

In addition to the models of entrepreneurship associated with businesses, there are alternate models in which an entrepreneurial approach advances the mission of libraries and aligns them with social or cultural enterprises. Jelke Nijober points out in "Cultural

Entrepreneurship in Libraries" that in the Netherlands, libraries must "be more market-oriented and less dependent on traditional subsidies from local and national government" (435). Nijober discusses library partnerships which creatively integrate libraries into community life in new ways.

In a very similar model, one of this book's authors, Melody M. Allison discusses librarians as social entrepreneurs, using business practices and entrepreneurial techniques to promote social causes. Ms. Allison explores her transition from interested parent to activist, advocating change in her community and in the roles of librarians. This model is also related to the ideas of Taylor Willingham, who advocates the library as an agent of civic involvement, an active participant in the process of engaging the public in civic issues.

The Entrepreneurial Organization

While most entrepreneurial activity begins as an individual activity, organizations can also be entrepreneurial in their ways of thinking and behaving. Tough economic times have led to downward budget pressure on most public libraries; in response, libraries have become more creative in demonstrating their value to the government bodies which fund them. The entrepreneurial library is looking for other funding sources to meet its needs. Adam Corson-Finnerty, former Director of Special Initiatives and Board Communications at the University of Pennsylvania Libraries, and presenter at the first *Conference for Entrepreneurial Librarians* has been an advocate of entrepreneurial approaches to fund-raising in libraries and other non-profit organizations. Public library systems can also become entrepreneurial, as Clay and Bangs describe in an article on the Fairfax, VA, public library which established an unusual public-private partnership for fund-development.

What the Reader Will Find in This Book

The purpose of this book is to document the current state of entrepreneurship in libraries in its many forms. By capturing examples of librarians' endeavors we will have established, for this moment in time, a record of the breadth and depth of these endeavors. We hope this record will serve several purposes: to document the current situation; to celebrate these entrepreneurs; and to inspire future entrepreneurial pursuits among librarians.

The book is organized into sections with the first section offering some foundational principles of ethics and management that entrepreneurial librarians should consider. The three sections on differing approaches of entrepreneurial librarians include intrapreneurship, where services, products or programs are developed and kept within their institutions; entrepreneurship, where services or products are developed into commercial entities with the potential for financial risk and reward; and social entrepreneurship, in which services, programs or products are developed to promote causes. Each of these sections will provide representative examples of successful endeavors in its area. The book's authors tell their stories about different types of programs and services, united by the entrepreneurial spirit. They have taken risks in developing programs that enhance the missions of their organizations; one of the common themes is that they have been unafraid to fail, going beyond the traditional programs and services of libraries to craft new and different services.

The first section of this volume, "Foundational Issues," contains an essay exploring a central theme of this book. Kristen Whitehair provides an ethical framework for entrepreneurial projects and a moral foundation for issues that must be addressed as librarians become more entrepreneurial. Whitehair reviews the *ALA Code of Ethics* in light of entrepreneurial programs in libraries and carefully addresses issues of dealing with limited resources while still preserving the core values of librarianship. Each project described in this volume addresses to some extent the theoretical and philosophical questions raised by Whitehair.

Andrea D. Berstler incorporates the idea of using a strategic plan to promote libraries in an entrepreneurial way, employing such plans to gain support for libraries and market their programs. Berstler, a public library director, addresses issues of promoting the public library to perhaps its most important constituency, local government funding agencies, but also discusses using strategic planning in the creation of highly visible programs that make clear the value of the library in the community. Her ideas on treating libraries as a business can be useful in any setting in managing projects and approaching funding agencies.

"Section II: Intrapreneurs" presents essays about innovations developed as librarians look beyond their daily responsibilities and initiate programs that extend traditional services and roles. Entrepreneurial programs can be of almost any type; the innovative approaches and techniques borrowed from the business world are evident among these intrapreneurs. Joe M. Williams and Stephen H. Dew describe a project at the University of North Carolina at Greensboro Libraries in which librarians provide a campus-wide publishing service for open access journals. University librarians have consolidated their position as leaders in technology as well as strengthening ties to faculty who create and contribute to these journals. In addition to supporting faculty as they develop open access journals, Dew and Williams have also started their own open access journal devoted to the topic of learning spaces, an extension of the original project.

INSIDE Idaho, a project described by Bruce Godfrey and Gail Z. Eckwright, began as an intrapreneurial effort within the University of Idaho Library. INSIDE Idaho was an early effort to improve access to geospatial data within the university community and more widely with users outside of that community. Unique research needs were met by this project, particularly those of rural users. As Godfrey and Eckwright point out, this project has elements of social entrepreneurship, in its effort to provide information equally to all Idaho patrons and also in several sustainability applications developed by the project.

Christy Groves and Heather Lambert from Middle Tennessee State University discuss a technologically-based project which extends library services in new ways. Information Commons have become prevalent in libraries and such projects very often incorporate entrepreneurial techniques. The library at MTSU developed a multi-media technology lab and help desk, and then used social media techniques such as crowd sourcing to improve it. They have used marketing techniques to brand and promote it, generating demand from both students and faculty. The success of the Digital Media Studio is enhancing the library's value on campus, and making technology tools more accessible to students.

Entrepreneurs in library-related businesses, while not the primary focus of this book, bring an important perspective that we wanted to present. In "Section III: Entrepreneurs," we have captured two compelling interviews with entrepreneurs so that their voices could be heard. Amy Archambault interviews Mary Ellen Bates, who became a successful independent information specialist by offering personalized services after realizing that she wanted to be her own boss. In an interview with our contributor Jeff Tiberii, Tim Spalding discusses his online service, *LibraryThing*, that makes it possible for individuals to catalog their own books in a social network environment, discovering connections with other people based on the books they've read in common.

Another of the essays in this section closely follows the model of an independent research service; Peter Hesseldenz runs a research service for small businesses on a university campus, and his institution is considering transitioning this service to a fee-based model. Thus, this program that assists entrepreneurs may become more entrepreneurial, and issues of funding and marketing will need to be addressed as if it were any other small business. Hesseldenz also addresses the ethical issues involved in entrepreneurial services, in particular the inherent dilemmas for librarians who provide both free and fee-based services. How shall the library decide where to allocate scarce resources: to its traditional patrons or paying customers?

While librarians often are averse to fundraising, some of our authors have designed unique programs that serve a purpose beyond simply finding new dollars in a tough environment. The 5K race described by Susan Sharpless Smith and Erik Mitchell does raise funds to support a student-centered program, but it does more than that: it also builds a sense of community within Wake Forest University and beyond, bringing to campus those who might not otherwise have a connection to the university and providing them with a positive experience that strengthens their interest in and ties to WFU. Smith and Mitchell went beyond their own experiences at Wake Forest University Library to survey other libraries which have conducted similar 5K events and the authors share general conclusions about the benefits and possible complications in hosting such fundraisers.

In "Section IV: Social and Cultural Entrepreneurs," we present librarians whose programs are powered by ideals of reform and promotion of social issues. Shakeela Begum and Manuela Boscenco tell the story of a fascinating foray into fundraising at British Columbia University Library where images from their collections of rare and unique materials are shared through sales of products such as notecards and reproductions of artworks, as well as through a website which helps drive traffic to the library's Development Office to enhance donor awareness. Increasing the accessibility of the images is one of the major goals of the project. The dollars raised by this project have become almost incidental to raising the visibility of the collections throughout their university and to the outside world, in particular to potential benefactors who become aware of the treasures housed by the Libraries.

Sharon K. Curtis, Doralyn Rossman and Molly C. A. Anderson from Montana State University have provided a detailed analysis of using a return on investment approach to deal with a common library dilemma — discarding unneeded library materials in a time-efficient and cost-effective manner. This classic business perspective allows for an impartial look at library functions. These authors take into account not only the practical and financial sides of such an enterprise but also examine how such projects can be in accord with library values. Using the return on investment model, they were able to determine more concretely the benefits of various options for disposing of withdrawn material. Their approach is well worth considering for other library projects, creating a method by which librarians can view activities in a businesslike manner and determine the true cost of library programs.

Green librarianship is one manifestation of social entrepreneurship and Anne M. Less, Beth Filar Williams and Sarah B. Dorsey share their own experiences and those of others in promoting sustainability throughout the library community. As green initiatives have taken hold in the world of business, so too have they manifested themselves in the already inherently "green" business of the library world. Less, Filar Williams and Dorsey report on the history of the green movement in libraries and how initiatives have been developed, creating a sustainable community of committed, environmentally-minded librarians.

Yet another look at social entrepreneurship is provided through Amy Archambault's interview of Martha Thomas Larson, who originated the Greensboro Public Library's Financial Literacy program, developed with the worthy goal of increasing teenagers' ability to manage their finances and develop skills to help them become financially stable throughout their lives. This program goes beyond the more passive role of providing information; it educates teens in an effort to improve their lives.

Finally, Melody M. Allison argues that all librarians can be social entrepreneurs, applying the techniques and methods of entrepreneurship to a social mission. Certainly the mission of librarians to share information and the ability to research does promote the social good. Allison carries forward this ideal, describing her fight against the use of pesticides in schools and the crusade that led her to the field of librarianship. Eventually she turned her attention to promoting awareness of the issues surrounding gender bias in medical research and practice. Allison's journey has convinced her that librarians make ideal social activists. The socially aware librarians represented in this section have become leaders in bringing their own activist passions to their libraries.

These entrepreneurial librarians describe programs which are creative and innovative, advancing the roles of libraries into new territory. Libraries nationally are facing tough economic times — the message that we need to prove our value comes from inside the profession and from external funding agencies. Clearly, these librarians have created invaluable programs in the entrepreneurial spirit, clarifying and expanding the position of libraries in their promotion of the public good. Going forward, librarians will have greater need to pursue similar ventures in their own libraries. The editors hope these contributions will provide a road map and inspiration for future endeavors.

Works Cited

Allison, Melody. "Women's Health: Librarian as Social Entrepreneur." *Library Trends* 56.2 (2007): 423–448. *Project Muse*. Web. 18 August 2011.

Bazirjian, Rosann. (Ed). *Against the Grain*, 21.4 (2009): 1–40. Print.

"Creativity, Innovation, and Entrepreneurship in Libraries." *The Journal of Library Administration* 10.2/3 (1989): 1–195. *Taylor and Francis*. Web. 21 August 2011.

Clay, Edwin S. III, and Patricia C. Bangs. "Entrepreneurs in the Public Library: Reinventing an Institution." *Library Trends* 48.3 (2000): 606–618. EBSCO Academic Search Premier. Web. 5 May 2010.

Corson-Finnerty, Adam. "Money, Money, Money: New Sources of Income for Academic Libraries." *Inspiration, Innovation, Celebration: An Entrepreneurial Conference for Librarians*. Greensboro, NC. 3 June 2009. Address.

Dhanjal, Catherine. "The Entrepreneurial Library." *Library Hi Tech News* 26.1/2 (2009): 6–9.

Elkington, John and Pamela Hartigan. *The Power of Unreasonable People: How Social Entrepreneurs Create Markets that Change the World*. Boston: Harvard Business Press, 2008.

"Frederick G. Kilgour January 6, 1914 — July 31, 2006: Librarian, Educator, Historian, Entrepreneur." *NextSpace: The OCLC Newsletter* 3: n. page (2006). Web. Retrieved from http://www.oclc.org/next space/003/1.htm

Katz, Jerome A. "The Chronology and Intellectual Trajectory of American Entrepreneurship Education." *Journal of Business Venturing* 18.2 (2003): 283–300. *Science Direct*. Web. 31 July 2011.

McCracken, Peter. "Peter McCracken on Library Entrepreneurship." *Library Journal* 134.16 (2007): 17. Print.

Nijboer, Jelke. "Cultural Entrepreneurship in Libraries." *New Library World* 107.9/10 (2006): 434–443. *Emerald Library*. Web. 23 August 2011.

St. Clair, Guy. *Entrepreneurial Librarianship: The Key to Effective Information Services Management.* London: Bowker-Saur, 1996. Print.

Skrzeszewski, Stan. *The Knowledge Entrepreneur.* Lanham, MD: Scarecrow Press, 2006. Print.

Wall, Barbara Mann. *Unlikely Entrepreneurs: Catholic Sisters and the Hospital Marketplace, 1865–1925.* Columbus: Ohio State University Press, 2005. Print.

Willingham, Taylor L. "Libraries as Civic Agents." *Public Library Quarterly* 27.2 (2008): 97–110.

Wright Sykes, Barbara. *Pricing without Fear: A Sewing Entrepreneurs Guide.* Chino Hills: Collins Publications, 2005. Print.

Section I
Foundational Issues

1— Navigating the Ethical Waters of Entrepreneurial Librarianship

An Ethical Risk Analysis

Kristin Whitehair

"Libraries are complex environments of competing demands."— Richard Rubin

Introduction

Libraries are facing financial challenges on many fronts. Most public libraries rely directly on tax revenues to fund their operations, but the recent recession has negatively impacted their funding: declining real estate values have diminished property tax receipts and unemployment and stagnant salaries have led to a decline in sales tax receipts. Academic libraries are in an especially difficult situation: in addition to the pressures caused by decreases in tax revenues, academic libraries are also facing dramatic price inflation for electronic resources. While each library's situation is unique many types of libraries are facing reduced resources and increased costs. Standard operating models are not sustainable in this environment because financial resources are shrinking as demand and costs for services are growing.

Current Situation

With shrinking resource pools and increasing demands for information and services, libraries are looking for a new operating model to meet these challenges. The entrepreneurial operating model is especially attractive for library managers and leadership; with its focus on increasing revenues by expanding services and products, entrepreneurialism seeks to directly address the issue of reduced resources. Since an entrepreneur "is one who organizes a new business venture in the hopes of making a profit..." the focus on generating revenues appears to offer promise to managers with reduced resources ("Entrepreneurship"). In contrast, traditional academic libraries are not expected to generate revenue.

Moreover, entrepreneurialism is highly valued and widely respected by the general public (Osborne and Gaebler xx). With calls for the public sector to operate more like the private sector or a business, entrepreneurial initiatives are being implemented in libraries. While entrepreneurialism is the primary business model employed in the private sector, entrepreneurial efforts in libraries require substantial changes in the standard library operating model. The traditional library operation model focuses on service and relies on support from a parent institution or organization to finance operations. In comparison, entrepreneurism requires an abrupt change with the library focusing instead on generating profit. This chapter explores the ethical considerations that the entrepreneurial business model may pose for libraries.

Importantly, an official guideline already exists to guide ethical decision-making in libraries. The ALA Code of Ethics provides foundational ethical guidelines for all types of libraries (Preer 21, see Appendix). While the ALA Code of Ethics creates a solid basis for making ethical decisions, further exploration of ethical issues emerging in entrepreneurial librarianship is needed. This need for additional study is rooted in the non-traditional nature of entrepreneurial activities which focuses on profit compared to long-standing practice in libraries and the larger public sector which focuses on service. In short, the driving force behind entrepreneurism conflicts with that of non-profit institutions such as libraries.

This chapter will focus on entrepreneurial librarianship in public sector libraries. After defining key terms applied to libraries, the chapter will outline areas of increasing ethical risk for entrepreneurial efforts in libraries. Lastly, it will propose five frameworks to guide ethical decisions in an entrepreneurial public sector environment. This is an exciting time for libraries and for the populations they serve. As our libraries adapt to this new environment with increasingly limited resources, it is critical to adapt traditional library ethics to the new environment in a way that preserves the core values of the profession.

Literature Review

The chapter draws from two bodies of literature. First, library literature exploring ethics in libraries provides valuable background for the ethical risks that are emerging. American Library Association documents provide primary evidence of historical ethical values and shifts in values. While numerous articles and books in the body of library literature address topics related to library ethics, Preer's 2008 *Library Ethics* provides the most thorough and up-to-date exploration of library ethics. Preer synthesizes modern issues and historical values to produce a highly practical text based in solid theory.

The second body of literature is not library-centric. Instead it focuses on the intersection of private and public sector values. The seminal text addressing this issue is the work of David Osborne and Ted Gaebler. In *Reinventing Government: How the Entrepreneurial Spirit Is Transforming the Public Sector* a comprehensive analysis of this change is presented. Osborne and Gaebler argue that the public sector is incorporating entrepreneurialism in numerous and diverse ways. Their descriptions and analysis of the public sector offer a broader perspective identifying higher level trends. *Practical Ethics in Public Administration* by Dean Geuras and Charles Garafalo complements Osborne and Gaebler's work by providing ethical frameworks to be used in public sector decision making.

The background used in framing arguments in both of these bodies of literature is composed of historical ethical debate. Primary sources providing justifications and description of ethical lenses provide the foundation for this chapter's examination of ethics such as the work of Immanuel Kant and Machiavelli.

Defining Ethics and Entrepreneurialism

This chapter uses Richard Rubin's definition of ethics described in "Critical Issues in Library Personnel Management." According to Rubin "ethical issues are those involved in deciding what is good or right in terms of the treatment of human beings, human actions and values" (1). A critical element of this definition is that it distinguishes between legal obligations and inner motivations and values.

Elizabeth Buchanan's definition complements Rubin's definition of ethics. In *Case Studies in Libraries and Information Science Ethics* Buchannan argues

> Ethics is related to morals, moral systems, and human conduct. As a brand of philosophy, it systematically examines and studies such concepts as "right" and "wrong." Ethics deals with what we should and should not do, what acts are "good" and "evil." It examines such concepts and constructs as responsibility and rights. As the basis for ethics, morality is a set or system of rules, principles, or values (cultural, professional, religious, *et cetera*) that prescribe behavior and how we evaluate those behaviors [9].

The operational definition used in this chapter views ethics as distinct from the law. In fact, "[e]thics and law are not always in sync: law provides a structured context to which individuals look for a reasonable solution" (Buchanan 75). Legal guidelines do not suggest actions based on morality; instead, they provide a system for rational decision making.

A challenge in examining this topic is that the practice of ethics is unclear and often hidden (Buchannan 12). Most ethical decisions are made by individuals in private, and only the most egregious transgressions are communicated to individuals outside the institution. With the private nature of ethical decisions, it is difficult to gather in-depth information to better inform our understanding of the process of ethical decision-making.

Additionally, the subjectivity of ethics complicates defining this topic and conducting a broad study of the field. In examining ethical questions it is often necessary to identify the underlying reasoning or justification for actions taken or not taken, which helps reveal the concepts prioritized and favored by the actor. Overall, the field of ethics suffers from the lack of a singular source or basis of ethics. Rubin states that "[e]thical issues are less clear because the concept of ethical behavior varies from person to person or group to group and no one body of knowledge is accepted as authoritative" (Rubin *Critical Issues* 2).

Central to the conversation about ethical risks of entrepreneurial efforts within libraries is the meaning of entrepreneur. An entrepreneur "is one who organizes a new business venture in the hopes of making a profit ... [o]ne engages in entrepreneurship when one begins to plan an organization that uses diverse resources in an effort to take advantage of the newly found opportunity" ("Entrepreneurship" 445). Important to the discussion is the last clause of the definition which addresses initiative and risk. These concepts lie outside the norms held by library managers, as they tend to be relatively risk-averse, while risk is an essential element of entrepreneurialism (Bozeman and Kingsley 110).

Among the potential risks entrepreneurs face is failure. When organizations shift to more entrepreneurial models, they must acknowledge this risk and allow for it; permission to fail is essential since entrepreneurial efforts are often a series of attempts. Earlier unsuccessful attempts inform future efforts (Osborne and Gaebler 135). Thus, entrepreneurial ventures operate outside of long-standing expectations, traditions, and organizational structures in public sector organizations such as libraries.

Public management scholars David Osborne and Ted Gaebler also note the role of risk in entrepreneurial efforts in the public sector. As risk is found with nearly all change, this is especially true for entrepreneurial endeavors in potential markets for the firm's good and services (xx). Risk is present in several forms including financial, political, and ethical risks.

The allocation of economic resources shifts when entrepreneurialism is embraced by government (Osborne and Gaebler xix). General qualities of entrepreneurial government include promoting competition, empowering citizens by increasing their control, measuring performance using outcomes, and being goal and mission driven (Osborne and Gaebler 20). As entrepreneurial initiatives are explored and changes are made in the organization there are implications for the entire organization.

Entrepreneurial operational methods cannot simply be plugged into existing public sector or library operating models. Osborne and Gaebler argue that public sector organizations cannot be operated like businesses because they are "fundamentally different institutions" (20). Profit is not the motivator in the public sector that it is in the private sector. Additionally, private sector organizations operate in much more competitive environments, while public sector organizations often operate monopolies. While public sector organizations are fundamentally different from their private sector counterparts, both can embrace entrepreneurialism (Osborne and Gaebler 22). Transitioning to an entrepreneurial model requires significant attention, planning, and adjustment of institutional policies to properly manage competing business models.

The Historical Foundations and Current State of Library Ethics

Several areas of librarianship have received significant attention from ethical studies of the field; these issues include privacy, intellectual freedom, access to resources, and provision of information that may be harmful (Rubin *Critical Issues* 2). However, ethical risks are present in nearly all library operations including those that are less public. In Rubin's studies of ethics in library operations several critical elements were identified as contributing to the creation of ethical problems. These stressors in the library's environment can be divided into four main categories: the principal of survival, social unity, social responsibility, and individuality (Rubin *Critical Issues* 2).

Ethics is recognized as a critical element of professional librarianship. Since the founding of the American Library Association (ALA) in 1876 the concept of ethics in library science has evolved. ALA documents demonstrate that historically the issue of ethics has garnered significant attention. The evolution of ethics advanced by the ALA demonstrates how ethics have grown out of library practices (Preer 1). Initially, the profession's core values were expressed in the ALA Motto which identified the central issue of balancing the cost of providing services with the benefit of serving the widest potential audience (Preer 51).

Building on the ALA motto, the ALA's *Library Bill of Rights*, adopted in 1939, was modeled after the U.S. Bill of Rights. In its six stated rights, it provides a solid foundation outlining the rights of library users. For example, the fifth right states "[a] person's right to use a library should not be denied or abridged because of origin, age, background, or views" (American Library Association, Library Bill of Rights).

In 1997 ALA adopted a Code of Ethics rooted in its desire to obtain professional status for librarians (Preer 5). The *Code of Ethics* and other documents produced by the ALA aimed to reinforce the professional nature of librarians' work, focusing initially on "the librarian's multiple relationships" (Preer 27). With advancing technology and changing roles for all types of librarians, ALA's founding ethics have not changed, but their interpretation has been modernized. Continuing ALA's trend of adapting ethical statements to address issues of the day it is likely that its future statements will address changes in the larger public sector including new business models. The pressure to do so will stem from the broad-based public support for incorporating private sector practices into public sector operations.

Reinventing Government

The growth of entrepreneurialism in the public sector is part of a larger movement often termed the "reinvention of government" (Heeks 9). Since its emergence in the 1980s, "reinventing government" has evolved to encompass new meanings, but it has largely focused on three broad aspects of public sector organizations: inputs into the systems; processes within the systems; and outputs of the system (Heeks 10). Entrepreneurialism is a major influencing factor in the larger movement to reinvent government in all three of these areas.

Entrepreneurialism seeks to increase resources in the system, and implement dramatic changes to the processes within the system to maximize outputs. In the public sector, standard sources for acquiring resources (financial inputs) include tax receipts and user fees. Funding for libraries is usually attained through one of two means: an allotment by the parent organization or institution, or from library-specific taxes. As tax revenues have declined in the latter half of the last decade, so have the resources provided to libraries. A critical motivating element of entrepreneurialism, then, is the opportunity to obtain incremental resources using new methods. From the perspective of library managers the ability to obtain increased resources is an especially attractive characteristic of entrepreneurism.

Secondly, incorporating the entrepreneurial model requires changes to processes within the system. For entrepreneurial librarianship to flourish, managers need increased flexibility to "shop around for the most effective and efficient service providers" (Osborne and Gaebler 35). This need for increased flexibility often strains traditional bureaucratic systems. Highly bureaucratic measures intended to ensure standardization and proper use of resources can represent obstacles to entrepreneurship which hampers public managers' ability to quickly implement change. A balance is needed between bureaucratic measures protecting public sector values and cumbersome regulations.

Additionally, entrepreneurialism requires the ability to make quick adjustments to market fluctuations; to adjust to these changes entrepreneurial librarianship requires a transfer of power to middle-level and front-line staff. As power is shifted from the top levels of the organization to the middle and lower levels, individuals are forced into new roles where they are empowered with the ability to make decisions directly impacting service to users and organizational policy, thereby maximizing outputs.

But without significant policy and structural changes, the activities of these newly empowered staff largely fall outside traditional institutional constraints. In the absence of institutionalized policies and procedures to guide action, ethical decisions will be largely guided by individual beliefs and opinions. If the organizational structure is designed to assert power from above, these structures are not well suited to allow for power stemming from the lower ranks, such as front-line service workers.

Lastly, outputs of an entrepreneurial system are drastically different from traditional outputs; public sector outputs often include services and products otherwise unavailable to the public. In the traditional model, government action is often called in to address market shortages. For example, a university library provides access to unique resources; there is no alternative in the marketplace that provides access to rare and archival resources. Additionally, if these items were available as commercial alternatives, the price to purchase all those resources would be much too high for most students and faculty. With desire for a level of academic research above what the market equilibrium would produce, academic libraries developed and continue to be supported. Essentially, when the private market doesn't satisfy the market demand for library resources and services at the desired level of production, members of the public have called on the government to produce this public good by funding public and academic libraries; yet even at the government supported rate of production, the market equilibrium price that libraries could charge for services excludes many people from accessing the resources. For example, an entrepreneurial program charging for a specific library service may be too expensive for all interested people to afford.

Moreover, traditional measures of library outputs are not linked to profit. For example, the number of volumes in the collection, number of people visiting the library, and number of reference transactions are difficult to incorporate into an entrepreneurial model. In an entrepreneurial model, outputs are used to garner increased inputs that will continue the cycle. In the private sector outputs are marketable and profit is the measure for success. To adapt this business model to libraries, outputs need to be redefined based on the goals, mission, and needs of individual libraries. As entrepreneurial models are incorporated careful attention is needed in defining outputs.

Clearly, significant change to system inputs, processes, and outputs is required to successfully incorporate entrepreneurialism into libraries. These changes involving various types of partnerships can take many forms. Elements often found in public sector entrepreneurial initiatives include: public-private partnerships; quasi-public corporations; public enterprise; rewards; changing public investment policy; technical assistance; information; referrals; volunteers; impact fees; catalyzing non-governmental efforts; convening non-governmental leaders; voluntary associations; and demand management (Osborne and Gaebler 31). With this level of cooperation between private and public sectors there rarely is a clear distinction between these two types of organizations. While some libraries have already begun incorporating some of these elements, for a full transformation to an entrepreneurial model, transformation of inputs, processes, and outputs is required.

The move toward entrepreneurial models in libraries is occurring within the larger context of the public sector. Seeking a new operating model is a critical part of this shift. It also includes structural changes to bureaucratic institutions. Overall, this movement toward a reinvented government, often referred to as New Public Administration, is not limited to libraries. Before the movement toward the New Public Administration, government was largely seen as "slow, inefficient, impersonal..." by the American public including government employees (Osborne and Gaebler 14). The modern environment for both public and private organizations has changed dramatically. Osborne and Gaebler describe this emerging environment:

> Today's environment demands institutions that are extremely flexible and adaptable. It demands institutions that deliver high-quality goods and services, squeezing ever more bang out of every buck. It demands institutions that are responsible to their customers, offering choices of non-standardized services; that lead by persuasion and incentive rather than commands; that give their employees a sense of meaning and control, even ownership. It demands institutions that *empower* citizens rather than simply *serving* them [15].

Gawthrop adds to Osborne and Gaebler's description by outlining the broad changes in the public sector where both the government and citizens have moved to new roles (14–24).

> But now, at the end of the century, we are faced with a new reality in which the citizen has been reinvented into the customer; interest groups—broadly defined to include private-sector contractors, suppliers, and so on—have been redesignated stakeholders; and, most significantly, public servants have been recast in the mold of entrepreneurs. In the process of reconfiguring public bureaucracies, however, little attention is being given to how this new reality conforms to the ethical moral values and virtues that are deeply embedded in our democratic system [18].

Continuing this argument Gawthrop highlights the necessity of protecting the needs that are core to the values of the public sector. Specifically, this calls for the recognition of the "integral and unique relationship between public-sector management, ethics, and democratic values that desperately needs to be, not re-invented, but emphatically reaffirmed..." (Gawthrop 126). Maintaining these core values places barriers in the path of libraries moving toward entrepreneurial goals.

How Reinvented Government Affects Public Sector Libraries

Public sector libraries have experienced successive budget cuts through the economic downturn that began in 2008. As tax receipts fell, resources available to support public sector organizations including libraries shrank. With reduced budgets the popularity of entrepreneurial librarianship has increased in both interest and in practice. It is important to note that this reaction is not a new trend in libraries. Historically, libraries have been adaptive to new environments. There are many examples from recent history; when telephone service became widespread, libraries incorporated phone reference into their pre-existing in-person and mail reference services. More recently, as instant messaging (IM) became more popular, IM reference service was incorporated into many libraries' reference services. Librarians' ongoing commitment to service improvements drives these types of changes, but the trend toward entrepreneurialism in libraries applies this tradition at a broader level of organizational operations. Beyond simply incorporating a new technology into existing services, entrepreneurialism encourages the development of new services.

Also inherent in the entrepreneurial mindset is generating revenue, which changes the operating or business model employed by the organization. Since most library services and resources generate no revenue, entrepreneurism in this setting introduces new and volatile elements to traditional decision-making models. As addressed above, outputs of the system must be redefined to accommodate the revenue-generating goal of entrepreneurship while respecting the non-revenue generating nature of traditional library outputs. The answer may be found in a hybrid that allows for both.

Obstacles to Entrepreneurship in Public Libraries

Barriers to unrestrained entrepreneurialism and the New Public Administration in general, are formidable. Rules, regulations, and laws created to ensure fair employment practices, equitable use of resources, and other values identified by members of the public and/or the organization create barriers to swift changes. These barriers are significant. For example, restraints on the use of public funds create inefficient barriers to performing work, at least when efficiency is measured solely on the financial inputs needed to produce a set level of outputs. These barriers come in the form of needed approvals, permits, and reviews. At the federal level removing constraints on funds is estimated to allow agencies to accomplish the same level of output or services with a budget reduced by 10 percent (Osborne and Gaebler 9–11).

Constraints that unintentionally hinder efficiency serve an important purpose. For example, restraints on funds are intended to preserve core public sector values and ensure proper use of the funds. These restraints prevent conflict of interest, graft, and misappropriation of funds and resources. The tension between efficiency and core public values is another example of conflicting values held by public organizations and citizens; while efficiency is highly valued, it often conflicts with the value of equity. For instance, measures that exist to ensure equal treatment of applicants create additional steps in the hiring process. When an organization adopts a more entrepreneurial operating model, it is critical to understand why constraints were implemented and the functions they serve before removing them, even if they hinder efficiency.

Customizing public services is an important trend in libraries, as it is in the private sector although most public sector institutions still offer "one-size-fits-all services" (Osborne and Gaebler 168). Citizens are used to many choices and customization options in their private sector experiences. Transitioning from standardized options to customization requires research to identify what customizations are needed. Citizen or customer input is critical in the customization of public services if they are to be successful. Entrepreneurial librarianship aggressively pursues targeted markets as one way to respond to the increasing demand for customized services. This is also likely to improve citizen satisfaction.

Areas of Ethical Risk

To address the risks posed by the tensions between traditional public sector values and those of entrepreneurialism, library leadership must first be aware of them, and then examine various types of relationships within the organization and ask how a proposed initiative would alter them. These types of relationships might include: relationships between employees and administrators; relationships between employees; and relationships between the institution and the public (Rubin *Library Personnel* 3). The existing literature suggests stepping back and looking at each situation from a broader perspective; involving outside colleagues in the process will improve its comprehensiveness and help to identify possible competing tensions.

From a comprehensive perspective, ethical workplace environments require a sustained commitment with regular examination (Buchannan 21). An ethical risk analysis should be included at the planning stage of entrepreneurial projects and revisited throughout the project including at the conclusion of the project if it is discontinued.

There are two broad conceptual areas where entrepreneurial efforts present potential for ethical risks: autonomy and prioritization of specific patrons. Traditional library operations are likely to conflict with entrepreneurial ones. In the public sector, units within the larger institution are often subject to the controls and policies of the larger institution; but in an entrepreneurial environment employees need autonomy to respond quickly to market trends and to meet changing customer demands. Without autonomy, response rates will be stalled by the bureaucratic process. In order for entrepreneurial efforts to be successful, increased autonomy may be essential. However, with this necessary autonomy the entrepreneurial efforts are no longer controlled as traditional functions. This creates a situation where ensuring ethical behavior becomes increasingly difficult.

One area illuminating the tension between values of the public sector and the needs of entrepreneurial efforts is hiring practices. Public sector employment processes focus on equity and practices commonly used to insure that all individuals who are interested in applying are able to apply and fair evaluation of all applications is ensured, and also enact numerous restrictions that protect employees from unfair dismissal. In the public sector, the focus is on hiring the most qualified applicant. In comparison, private sector hiring practices often rely more heavily on personal relationships and networking to create a pool of applicants. The value of a potential employee's personal network may be a potential boon to entrepreneurial initiatives. Networks of friends and family are not evaluated as qualifications.

Additionally, public sector human resources practices and policies are in conflict with the needs of many entrepreneurial efforts. To quickly acquire personnel needed for an entrepreneurial initiative, traditional public sector hiring practices may be too cumbersome and time intensive, which creates tension between traditional practices valuing equity and the needs of a business-focused effort to fill a position quickly. When attempting to implement entrepreneurial hiring practices, Rubin suggests "recognizing the competing forces that shape personnel policies and practices" and finds "it is possible to gain a greater understanding of where ethical tensions arise, and how to deal with them" (15). Another example illustrating the ethical tensions between traditional and entrepreneurial operating models involves prioritizing specific patrons. In general, public sector libraries do not prioritize the needs of specific patrons over the rest. While in academic libraries, teaching faculty may receive additional assistance compared to administrative support staff, overall when there is a line at the reference desk or for any other library service, patrons are served on a first-come-first-serve basis. Entrepreneurialism on the other hand focuses on generating revenue. If three patrons were in line for service, and one was a potential customer for an entrepreneurial service, should the patrons be prioritized? What level of customer service should be provided to traditional library patrons? What level of customer service should be provided to library patrons willing to pay for service? While the answers to these questions depend on the organization and specific programs in question, this situation represents the heart of the ethical tension between embracing an entrepreneurial model and maintaining traditional library values of serving all equally.

Moreover, if three patrons are in line for the entrepreneurial service, typical business models would encourage the entrepreneurial librarian to prioritize the customer who is likely to bring in the most revenue. While the goal of generating revenue is an essential element of entrepreneurialism, numerous traditional library practices restrain the entrepreneurial librarian's flexibility and ability to be successful. The ethical dilemma is centered on "what does the entrepreneurial librarian do?" Again, the answer to this question may be different depending on parent institution, community, and values of each library.

Building on the first broad area of ethical risk, the second area of ethical risk occurs where traditional library policies fail to address critical elements of entrepreneurial initiatives. For example, performance evaluations of entrepreneurial staff would be difficult using traditional performance measures used for "non-entrepreneurial" staff. While performance evaluation processes vary greatly between public organizations, they generally do not provide the type of information needed to evaluate entrepreneurial employees. Traditional evaluations focus on meeting specific goals identified by the employee and include an assessment by the supervisor. This method fails to include the type of information needed about business performance. To effectively manage and evaluate performance, managers may need information about performance as measured in return-on-investment (ROI) and the number of customer contacts and relationships that have been cultivated by the employee. Separate types of performance evaluations may be necessary. It would be unfair to require a reference librarian to demonstrate a set level ROI that may be needed to evaluate an entrepreneurial staff member. Osborne and Gaebler identify incentives as an element needing revision in the move to entrepreneurial models (23). Incentives must be created and structured in ways that encourage entrepreneurial success.

This ethical risk area occurs at many levels beyond simply employee evaluations. From a broader perspective, the same problems exist when evaluating the performance of different departments functioning in dramatically different operating models. Further examining the culture within a hybrid library employing both traditional public sector and entrepreneurial models, evaluations and comparisons across departments may be difficult. Library leadership must also be equipped with the knowledge and skills to effectively manage entrepreneurial programs.

The next area of ethical risk occurs when entrepreneurial initiatives operate outside of traditional institutional structures. Traditional library ethics provide clear guidance on issues like censorship and privacy. A simple example of an area where entrepreneurial efforts are left without guidance from traditional library ethics is pricing structures. Since libraries rarely sell items beyond used and donated books, there is no ethical guideline for the appropriate pricing structure. For an entrepreneurial service, one way to set models for pricing would be to analyze basic supply and demand curves to set a price at which the organization maximizes profits. For entrepreneurs focused exclusively on profit, this model may be the best fit for their needs. However, what should be the profit focus for the entrepreneurial effort in a library? A graduated pricing structure offering discounted rates for those with fewer resources would be one approach to increase access to the service. This pricing model is at odds with the core of entrepreneurialism because it does not maximize profits.

To highlight the areas where ethical risks are heightened with the new entrepreneurial business model, the examples below outline realistic ethical risks. These examples address both tensions between the core values of entrepreneurialism and those of librarianship and/or the public sector and situations in which library ethics fail to provide guidance for entrepreneurial initiatives.

PRIVACY VS. MARKET EXPANSION

The prominent role of advertising and market research in the private sector may be at odds with the value of privacy traditionally held by libraries. Tension occurs between the value of protecting privacy and the desire for detailed information about library users needed in entrepreneurial decision making. Marketing practices commonly employed by the private sector threaten library patron privacy. For example, grocery stores collect detailed information about shopper behavior through membership cards. Libraries could collect a similar level of data by collecting and analyzing patron account information. This situation involves competing values for privacy of patron information and the focus on growing business by expending services and better reaching the public.

Shifts of Power Within Organizations

Revenue generating departments generally tend to hold substantial power within organizations. This situation occurs because the other units within the organization become dependent on the revenue-generating activities to sustain the organization. In an environment with increasingly limited resources introducing an entrepreneurial program, generating revenue could dramatically shift power within the organization. While this is not on face an ethical risk, it may set the stage for on-going ethical risks. Preer argues that the risk of ethical problems increases with increasingly limited resources (53). When implementing entrepreneurial initiatives, it is essential to also implement measures that create a system of checks and balances to preserve core library services and authority. Additionally, when one department becomes increasingly powerful this can cause tension within the organization and workforce.

Mission Drift

Change in organizational priorities is evidence of mission drift. In traditional libraries, revenue is not a significant motivation or goal; instead, funding is provided by the parent institution or tax base. However, with movement toward entrepreneurialism there is an increased demand for revenue. As the organizational values drift toward the expectation of self-supporting services and programs, core library services will become less valued. An increasingly profit-motivated organization will demonstrate significant mission drift as the organizational mission morphs to capture potential revenue and encourage this type of behavior. Simultaneously, services core to the original mission failing to generate revenue along with the larger value of equity will be sacrificed as the organizational mission drifts toward revenues streams. As an example, in an organization realigning to focus on revenue streams it is likely that children's resources and services aimed to assist low income residents would be substantially reduced as they fail to bring in revenue and resources. Organizational resources would instead be directed toward target populations with the financial resources to pay for services.

Conflicts Between Personal and Professional Values

Conflict between personal values and organizational values is a notable area of ethical risk. While this type of risk is not limited to entrepreneurial projects within libraries, this risk area is heightened when adapting traditional ethical guidelines to apply to new types of activities such as entrepreneurial projects. Professionals bring their personal ethics and professional ethics to the decision-making process. Long-time public sector library staff may be ill equipped to meet the challenges posed by the newly adapted business model of entrepreneurialism. Overall, it can be unclear what the base motivating values and core ethics should be for entrepreneurial initiatives in libraries.

Conflict of Interest

Building on the added potential of conflict between personal and professional values entrepreneurial librarianship presents, these efforts increase the potential of conflict of interest between organizational and personal interests. As employees of public organizations, staff are expected to avoid acting in ways that benefit their outside interests. An egregious example of conflict of interest would be for a librarian to hire his or her spouse's construction firm to perform library renovations. In this situation it would be unlikely that the competing firms, if there were any, would be fairly evaluated against the spouse's construction firm. Entrepreneurial librarianship presents a hybrid of public and private operating models. Private sector operations often are informed by on-going personal and professional relationships. Further complicating this issue, entrepreneurial library initiatives often operate outside of traditional guidelines and policies of long-standing library operations. With little guidance for actions or oversight, this presents a significant ethical risk.

EXPANDING GOVERNMENT

Entrepreneurial librarianship changes the essential nature and footprint of traditional libraries. Changing the type of services and expanding their scope effectively broadens the footprint of government. Leaders must decide if this is appropriate for the institution in question. This issue will be especially important if the library's entrepreneurial initiatives directly compete with private firms. For user fees to work the service must be a "private good" that benefits the individuals who use it and when those who do not pay for it can be excluded from the benefits (Osborne and Gaebler 204). One standard answer to this issue will not address all public sector libraries. Instead, this issue will likely need to be negotiated with parent institutions and local governments.

LICENSING CONSIDERATIONS

Focusing on a technical and ethical issue, embracing the entrepreneurial spirit and the associated focus on revenue may require revision of resource agreements and licenses. Many commercial databases offer pricing structures that differentiate between non-profit or academic use and for-profit commercial use. Depending on the scope and nature of the entrepreneurial initiative, library licenses and contracts may need to be renegotiated, which may result in increased fees for resources if the new use is deemed to be commercial. A change in status would impact both current and future licenses. This is especially critical if the entrepreneurial initiative in question will use these commercial information products such as business intelligence databases.

The issues outlined above are not an exhaustive listing of potential areas of ethical risk. Instead the areas of ethical risk outlined above are intended to encourage the reader to evaluate where ethical values and goals may be in conflict in their environment.

ETHICAL PERSPECTIVE TO EMPLOY IN DECISION MAKING

To address the identified ethical risks associated with entrepreneurialism in libraries, an ethical framework or lens is needed to evaluate situations and potential actions. In seeking an ethical framework to guide decision-making, it is helpful to look beyond the traditional library literature to draw from the wealth of scholarship in the area of ethics in public administration. Knowledge gained through the study of librarianship and the broader discipline of public administration provides a solid foundation for the exploration of ethical elements of entrepreneurial librarianship. An advantage of looking to the public administration body of literature is that there is a depth of scholarship addressing tensions arising when private sector elements or characteristics are incorporated into the public sector. Compared to the experiences of the larger sector of public administration, the profession of librarianship is only beginning to grapple with the many challenges posed by the combination of these operating models.

The leading text on ethical decision making and entrepreneurship in the public sector is the 2005 publication by Dean Geuras and Charles Garofalo. In *Practical Ethics in Public Administration* Geuras and Garofalo advocate the use of five frameworks in weighing ethical decisions in the public sector: teleology, deontology, intuitionism, virtue theory, and a unified process (Geuras and Garafalo xxi).

Teleology focuses on the end result of a decision. This approach is associated with Machiavelli. In *The Prince* Machiavelli argued that the decision calculus of analyzing if the ends justify the means should be used for decision making and in making ethical determinations (Bing XX). This utilitarian approach asks actors to evaluate the end result of the action or inaction in exploring ethical elements of the situation. For example, if a library pursues a new entrepreneurial program that offers specialized fee-based searching services for local businesses and law firms, a teleological ethical evaluation of this act would weigh the end benefit to justify the means. For the purposes of this example, the resources used to support the fee-based program would be diverted from collection development funds for children's and teen resources. In this case the end result is likely to include increased revenue and contributions to the local economy by aiding small businesses. On the other hand, the children's collection would suffer. From a teleological perspective if the benefit to the local business community and the library outweighs the cost to the development of children's and teens' collections, then it would be ethical to pursue this venture.

There are difficulties in implementing a teleological framework in a library because it requires evaluating of the benefits of predicted end results compared against the core values of the organization. An extreme example of how a teleological method can lead to drastic and extreme actions is if the library decides that generating revenue is a core value, then defunding and discontinuing all services not generating self-supporting revenue would be justified.

In contrast to teleology, the second ethical perspective, deontology examines the ethical principles of the action. A critical theme in deontological studies is the principle or basis of the action. This framework for ethical decision-making does not include evaluating the end result of the action, only the action itself. Philosopher Immanuel Kant made significant contributions to this area of ethical study. He argued in support of a categorical imperative so that the actions of individuals or organizations could become universal law (Kant 52). Thus, this approach does not allow for exceptions that take the end results into account.

Returning to the earlier example of funding a service for local businesses with funds previously devoted to children's resources, a deontological perspective questions the principle of the action. The question becomes: Is it ethical to reduce support for children's resources? The answer depends on the context within the larger community. If library and community leadership identifies preserving and growing support for children's resources as a core value of the community, this entrepreneurial venture would not be ethical using a deontological framework. It would still not be ethical even if the end result of this program would be to raise library revenue through the fee-based services, which could replace funds previously diverted for the fee-based program. The end result is irrelevant because the principle of the action would violate a core value or guiding principle for the community.

The American Library Association's Code of Ethics (see Appendix) is most closely aligned with the deontological approach to ethics as it promotes general principles including protecting privacy, intellectual freedom, and respecting others. In contrast to teleology, the positive and negative impacts or end results of enacting these principles are not considered. The approaches of intuitionism and virtue theory, described immediate below, are also not taken into consideration by the ALA's Code of Ethics. Instead ALA's Code of Ethics states broad values intended to direct action.

The third approach of intuitionism relies on the inner guiding moral sense of an individual. This is often referred to as a "gut feeling." In the field of ethics, relatively little modern scholarly attention has been devoted to this topic compared to the other approaches addressed. In this approach there are not overarching principles or guidelines for decision making. In regard to a fee-based research service for local businesses, this approach would be ethical as long as library staff felt it was ethical.

Many problems are present with this approach. First, in the public sector intuitionism is difficult to standardize and incorporate into the larger bureaucratic structure. Leadership could not ensure that organizational values are promoted consistency throughout the organization. There are not mechanisms for reviews or standardized actions based on intuition. While all ethical approaches vary in implementation based on the individual, this approach is argued to have the widest range of variance. Additionally, this approach relies on the personal beliefs of employees. This approach doesn't allow a separation between personal beliefs and those held by the public sector organization. An example illustrating one of the many drawbacks of this approach occurs in collection development decisions. If an employee with strong personal beliefs opposing abortion followed his or her intuition and purchased only anti-abortion resources under this perspective the action would be ethical. The teleological ends include creating an unbalanced collection and restriction of access to information among others. Under intuitionism the ethical justification for these actions may be that purchasing pro-choice books didn't feel right. Obviously, this would be very problematic in many other areas of library operations.

The fourth ethical framework is virtue theory. While not widely practiced in public management, it is important to examine this framework as an option because it provides a valuable contrast to the other frameworks. Virtue theory evaluates the ethical status of actions by the characteristic that the action exemplifies. Applying this theory to libraries, a reduction in library hours due to budget cuts, regardless of the cause, evidences the negative character traits of selfishness and a lack of commitment to public service. Similarly, a fee-based research service serves as evidence of a pro-active, creative, and forward-looking approach. This example also demonstrates how one action can evidence contradictory characteristics. While a fee-based research service may be seen as proactive, it could also be argued that an increasingly greedy and money-focused organization is no longer prioritizing library users in an equitable manner.

The shortcomings of this approach are immediately visible. Organizations must balance the needs of multiple groups and are subject to changing levels in available resources. Additionally, this simplistic approach reduces actions to either good or bad. In reality, actions may benefit one group at the expense of another. Additionally, options displaying positive traits are not always possible. In times of fiscal crisis many libraries must reduce services, collections budgets, and staff. It may not be possible to demonstrate positive characteristics when faced with such difficult choices.

The fifth and last framework is a unified ethic, which "combines the different ethical standpoints" (Geuras and Garofalo 60). Recognizing that each individual framework is limited, this last option provides an opportunity for managers to evaluate options using a holistic approach. Managers using this approach would evaluate ethical questions from each of the four viewpoints to inform decisions. Geuras and Garofalo suggest posing questions about an ethical consideration representing each of the four approaches. For example, questions based in teleology would ask about the short-term and long-term impacts of this action. This approach also asks managers to weigh the risk of negative impacts against the benefits of the decision. Moving to deontology, users would look only at the action itself, not the long-term impacts of the implementation. In this line of questioning managers must determine if this potential action is based on a larger or universal principle. Similarly, managers should examine whether or not the basis of this action should become a universal standard for future actions. The intuition approach is perhaps the most simple to apply under the unified ethic. Managers should simply listen to their conscience for guidance. Lastly in respect to virtue theory, the line of questioning for virtue considerations asks about what characteristic the act demonstrates.

The unified ethic often fails to provide one clear answer for ethical matters. However, the strength of this approach is the well-rounded nature of consideration of elements of the situation in question. This approach accounts for the action itself, the implications of the action, and larger considerations such as the adherence to universal principles that is highly relevant to the work of entrepreneurial librarians.

The benefit of embracing a unified ethic extends beyond the ethical evaluation itself. By examining the issue from a range of perspectives or viewpoints librarians will be better able to communicate with library staff, library users, and the larger community. This process reveals many potential objections that may be presented as the decision is implemented and is excellent preparation that can aid public relations efforts when implementing new entrepreneurial initiatives.

Drawing on the discussion above outlining five approaches to evaluating ethical behavior, evaluating ethical questions from multiple perspectives is critical. This comprehensive approach can highlight questions and identify possibly ethically questionable issues. In this evaluation process, the individual needs to step outside of his or her own point of view.

1. To address conflict of interest, consistency is key (Preer 133). Predictable actions are critical to creating a solid foundation for consistent ethical actions. Does the proposed action assist the library in achieving strategic goals? Is it in line with the organizational mission? How does the decision compare to previous actions by the organization?
2. What trade-offs are being made to establish and sustain the new entrepreneurial initiative? What values are represented in this decision?
3. Is the entrepreneurial program self-sustainable? What other resources are needed to continue the program; e.g. staff time to provide the service, building space, managerial time to coordinate the service?
4. How is this initiative related to the core institutional values, mission, and ethics of the organization?

Overall, no singular approach is appropriate for all situations or contexts. A thorough understanding of these five approaches is an aid in ethical decision making. They provide framework in which to view individual situations. Ethical codes and doctrine endorsed by ALA provides the basis for ethical decision-making. Geuras and Garofalo supplement this ethical foundation with a broader lens to view library activities as they expand into previously unexplored areas where new ethical dilemmas will arise. To ensure a strong ethical foundation for decision-making in entrepreneurial efforts, it is necessary for each organization to develop clear organizational values, goals, and an ethic.

Conclusion

Incorporating an entrepreneurial initiative into traditional library structures poses realistic challenges. Libraries and organizations and their bureaucracies are not designed to foster the entrepreneurial business model. To address these potential barriers leadership should be aware of the increased risk for ethical issues to arise. Recognizing areas where tension exists between traditional library and general public sector ethics and entrepreneurial business practice is the first step. Secondly, leadership should analyze where these traditional ethics fail to provide guidance to employees involved in entrepreneurial efforts. By evaluating decisions employing the five ethical perspectives of teleology, deontology, institution, virtue theory, and a unified framework, library leadership and frontline employees will be well equipped to make informed and ethical decisions. Although these barriers exist, there are many benefits to incorporating entrepreneurial business models including improved employee morale. Moving from bureaucratic environments that construct numerous barriers to a more mission and goal driven organization offers a clear vision for the future (Osborne and Gaebler 38). With shrinking resources available to libraries, entrepreneurialism is one method that offers the possibility of growing available resources while better serving library users.

Appendix. American Library Association Code of Ethics

I. We provide the highest level of service to all library users through appropriate and usefully organized resources; equitable service policies; equitable access; and accurate, unbiased, and courteous responses to all requests.

II. We uphold the principles of intellectual freedom and resist all efforts to censor library resources.

III. We protect each library user's right to privacy and confidentiality with respect to information sought or received and resources consulted, borrowed, acquired or transmitted.

IV. We respect intellectual property rights and advocate balance between the interests of information users and rights holders.

V. We treat co-workers and other colleagues with respect, fairness, and good faith, and advocate conditions of employment that safeguard the rights and welfare of all employees of our institutions.

VI. We do not advance private interests at the expense of library users, colleagues, or our employing institutions.

VII. We distinguish between our personal convictions and professional duties and do not allow our personal beliefs to interfere with fair representation of the aims of our institutions or the provision of access to their information resources.

VIII. We strive for excellence in the profession by maintaining and enhancing our own knowledge and skills, by encouraging the professional development of co-workers, and by fostering the aspirations of potential members of the profession.

Adopted June 28, 1997, by the ALA Council; amended January 22, 2008.
Source: <www.ala.org/ala/issuesadvocacy/proethics/codeofethics/codeethics.cfm>

Works Cited

American Library Association. "Code of Ethics." 2008. Web. 18 April 2011. <http://www.ala.org/ala/issuesadvocacy/proethics/codeofethics/codeethics.cfm>.

American Library Association. "Library Bill of Rights." 1996. Web. 27 August 2011. <http://www.ala.org/ala/issuesadvocacy/intfreedom/librarybill/index.cfm>

Bing, Stanley. *What Would Machiavelli Do?: The Ends Justify the Meanness.* New York, NY: Harper Paperbacks, 2002. Print.

Bozeman, Barry, and Gordon Kingsley. "Risk Culture in Public and Private Organizations." *Public Administration Review* 58.2 (1998): 109–18. Print.

Buchanan, Elizabeth A., and Kathrine A. Henderson. *Case Studies in Library and Information Science Ethics.* Jefferson, NC: McFarland, 2009. Print.

"Entrepreneurship." *Encyclopedia of Small Business,* 2 ed. Detroit: Gale, 2002. Print.

Gawthrop, Louis C. *Public Service and Democracy: Ethical Imperatives for the 21st Century.* New York: Chatham House Publishers, 1998. Print.

Geuras, Dean, and Charles Garofalo. *Practical Ethics in Public Administration.* 2nd ed. Vienna, Va.: Management Concepts, 2005. Print.

Heeks, Richard. *Reinventing Government in the Information Age: International Practice in It-Enabled Public Sector Reform.* London: New York Routledge Research in Information Technology and Society, 1999. Print.

Kant, Immanuel Paton H. J. *Groundwork of the Metaphysic of Morals.* Harper Torchbooks. 1st Harper Torchbook ed. New York: Harper & Row, 1964. Print.

Machiavelli, Niccolò Marriott W. K., et al. *The Prince, Uniform Title: Principe. English.* Great Books of the Western World; V. 23; Chicago: Encyclopædia Britannica, 1955. Print.

Osborne, David, and Ted Gaebler. *Reinventing Government: How the Entrepreneurial Spirit Is Transforming the Public Sector.* Reading, Mass.: Addison-Wesley Publishing, 1992. Print.

Preer, Jean L. *Library Ethics.* Westport, Conn.: Libraries Unlimited, 2008. Print.

Rubin, Richard E. "Library Personnel Management." *Journal of Library Administration* 14.4 (1991): 1–86. Web. 15 Apr. 2011.

Rubin, Richard E., ed. *Critical issues in library personnel management.* University of Ill. at Urbana–Champaign. Graduate School of Lib. & Information Science, 1989. *Library Literature & Information Science Full Text.* Web. 23 July 2011.

2 — Running the Library as a Business

Andrea D. Berstler

Introduction

A library director, much like the CEO of a company, needs to have honed certain skills, talents and abilities in order to succeed. While the terms used by libraries differ from those used by their for-profit cousins, the goal is still the same: to be successful. Herein lies the difficulty. What is so easy to define and measure in the for-profit world becomes murky and immeasurable in the non-profit realm.

When asked if their libraries are successful, most library directors will respond that "yes, I have a successful library." However, when asked how they *know* if their libraries are successful, the room becomes surprisingly silent. What is success for a non-profit library? And how does a director know if the library has attained success if it cannot be defined?

There are numerous examples of entrepreneurs who have built successful businesses from the ground up or who have rescued troubled enterprises and turned them into household names. Bill Gates, Milton Hershey, Richard Branson, Coco Chanel and Walt Disney are all examples of individuals who have led their businesses to become worldwide successes. In broad terms, a successful entrepreneur starts or takes over a business, and using creativity, strategic planning, targeted marketing and innovation, the entrepreneur places that business in the best possible position to take advantage of every opportunity to become as successful as possible. Success in business is most often defined by looking at the bottom line: what profit was made, how much is that business worth, how esteemed is the advice and expertise of that owner?

In the non-profit world, those measures are given little weight. What does entrepreneurialism look like in a library? Entrepreneurial librarians use the skills of a successful business entrepreneur: creative thinking, strategic planning and marketing. These skills, combined with the willingness to be creative risk taker, enable the entrepreneurial librarian to place a library in the best possible position to continually meet the needs of that library community, and ensure the library's and the community's success. Success for a library is always defined in terms of the community served. Whether that community is made up of college students, lawyers, local residents, writers or genealogists, a library cannot be successful apart from its community.

The Strategic Plan

Is Your Library a Success?

As a library director, molding the operational structure of a library after the entrepreneurial model means first defining the standards of success for your library. Each library, like the community it serves, is different. Each library's customers have different needs, abilities and interests, different levels of education, and varying access to technology and resources. Success for an urban library in a poor section of the city will look different than success for a rural library serving a middle class community, which will look different than success for an upscale library in a college town. Success for a public library will differ from success for a law library or an academic library or a research library. The first step in applying the entrepreneurial model to any library is to find the answer to the question, "What is success for this library?" Defining success for an individual library is best accomplished by the use of a well-written strategic plan.

The strategic plan is, for the non-profit world, equivalent to a business plan for the startup enterprise. It defines what the organization is going to do, what steps are required to accomplish the organization's goals, how much money will be needed to reach those goals, and what success will look like when those goals are achieved. It also identifies direction and areas for growth. While all types of libraries can benefit from the strategic planning process, the process for public libraries is particularly critical.

Library boards and directors who are weighing the benefits of a strategic plan should review works by those considered leaders in the fields of library management and organization, as well as works on entrepreneurial planning and overall business administration. Entrepreneurial strategic planning is not a new concept, but due to recent dramatic changes in the library field, it is a concept whose time has come. In 1984, Donald Riggs published *Strategic Planning for Library Managers.* In this work, Riggs describes not only the process of strategic planning for libraries, but defines the reasons for implementing a strategic plan and what positive outcomes library directors and boards can anticipate from this type of plan. Though an older title, this work is one of the first to apply the principles of entrepreneurial strategic planning to the library field, addressing the unique and diverse complexities of planning for a non-profit, community focused organization.

While written specifically for a small public library, the principles outlined in *Administration of the Small Public Library* offer a practical overview of library management, with a focus on the need to identify priorities, develop objectives and plan for the library's future in the context of the needs of that library's community. Author Darlene Weingand lays out a systematic process for library administrators that can be applied in even the smallest of libraries.

When considering strategic planning in the library setting, the definitive work is *The New Planning for Results* by Sandra Nelson. This work is written in a concise, step-by-step style, designed to walk a library board through the entire strategic planning process, from identifying the need for a plan through determining information on community needs and setting the future vision for the library to communicating the library's plan, using it to define resource allocation and monitoring its implementation.

To gain an understanding of the difference between strategic planning and traditional library long-range planning, a recommended article would be "Planning for New Library Futures" from the May 15, 2002 issue of *Library Journal.* In this article, author Richard Dougherty compares the traditional library plan to the new and dynamic strategic plan and provides a good framework for library boards and directors to see the benefits to a strategic plan. While Dougherty does not use the term "entrepreneurial" in his article, his description of a process that sets and accomplishes goals, examines the entire system, and is flexible and open to change, could be used to define a entrepreneurial mode of planning.

For a public library, a strategic plan provides a structure for library boards, staff and managers to consider both the inside and outside needs of the organization. *Inside needs* become apparent through the process of outlining the library's service priorities, which would include defining common goals, establishing organizational priorities and assessing which community needs fall within the mission and ability of the library. *Outside needs* are determined by the ability of the library as an organization to define the library's role within its community, to speak definitively about the financial requirements of the library to potential funders, to promote the organization's successes within the community and to recruit potential advocates from within the leaders of the community. Those in the library field tend to speak of their profession in terms of its need to "promote the common good," its ability to "level the playing field of life" and a need to "provide equal access for all." The truth of the matter is that people, especially those successful business leaders and politicians who may be needed to support and fund the library, want to support a success. An entrepreneurial library director must be able to outline for those leaders the successes of the library, as defined by the strategic plan, and how their help will allow the library to achieve greater success. When this is done using terms common to the audience, there is an improved chance of those leaders becoming library champions.

Becoming an entrepreneurial library is hard work, and is not a choice for organizations or individuals who are looking for the easy way. To quote Peter Drucker, a management guru:

> It thus takes special effort for the existing business to become entrepreneurial and innovative. The "normal" reaction is to allocate productive resources to the existing business, to the daily crisis, and to getting a little more out of what we already have. The temptation in the existing business is always to *feed yesterday and to starve tomorrow.* It is, of course, a deadly temptation. The enterprise that does not innovate inevitably ages and declines. And in a period of rapid change, such as the present, an entrepreneurial period, the decline will be fast [emphasis added, Drucker 149].

What benefits will a strategic plan provide for a library director and for the library as an organization? Beyond defining success, a well-written strategic plan:

- Causes the organization's shareholders to think about, discuss and record on paper their goals for the library's future.
- Sets measurable, defined and time specific goals.
- Brings often lofty and theoretical mission and vision statements down to earth.
- Defines the organization's priorities, an essential step when making decisions about what part of a budget to cut.
- Keeps the library "on task," focusing on those great ideas that will make it irreplaceable in the community it serves.
- Allows the board, director, staff, volunteers and customers to know where the organization is going.
- Creates a transparent organization, where there is accountability between the director, the staff and the board.

Libraries are likely to have long range or five year plans. A strategic plan differs from those documents in several ways. A strategic plan sets goals for the coming weeks and months as well as for three to five years. A strategic plan is an organic document, free to be evaluated, altered and changed according to the needs of the community, the situation of the organization, and the talents and abilities of the staff and board members. "One of the attributes of the strategic planning process is that it is future-oriented. It encourages simulation of the future; one can project the future on paper and redo it if the results are not desirable" (Riggs 3). While leaders take a proactive approach to the future, there are things that cannot be foreseen. Through feedback and periodic evaluation, an organization will continually access the effectiveness of its plan and adjust accordingly. In *Strategic Planning for Library Managers* Riggs describes the need for contingencies to be written into a strategic plan. While not every expert includes this as a written step in planning, it is often described as part of the evaluation and monitoring process. In her work *The New Planning for Results* Sandra Nelson recommends "a flexible plan that can be easily adapted to meet new conditions" (Nelson 143). This built-in ability to adjust and refine is one of the strengths of the strategic planning process. Strategic planning does not preclude or prohibit changes in the future. Instead, it provides the structure to include change, a "greenhouse" where innovation is nourished and new ideas are fed.

A strategic plan defines the strategy of the library. A well written plan records the organization's overall mission, the goals the organization considers necessary and the measurable objectives that define how and when those goals will be achieved. In *Strategic Planning for Library Managers*, Riggs outlines library focused definitions for these terms and the place each one plays in an organization's strategic plan.

The entrepreneurial director's position in the planning process is well defined; they are "the linchpin in the development and operations of the strategic planning process" (Riggs 14). Strategy, from the Greek word *strategos*, means "the art of the general." Strategos comes from two words, *stratos*, "multitude, army," and *agos*, "leader." An entrepreneurial librarian is, in many ways, the general of the strategic planning process. "After the library has made the decision to launch into a strategic planning process, it is absolutely essential that the director assume primary responsibility for initiating and overseeing the process.... The success or failure of strategic planning depends, to a large extent, on the attitude of the director" (Riggs 14).

The process of creating a strategic plan provides the insight and understanding necessary to bring success in any endeavor. Employing entrepreneurial thought requires a director be proactive, preparing for future changes by planning now. Entrepreneurs cannot create success, but they can place their businesses in the best possible position to take advantage of circumstances to be successful. Preparation is key to positioning the organization to take advantage of opportunities to be successful. According to John Wooden, basketball coach of ten championships teams at the University of California, Los Angeles (UCLA) "The time to prepare isn't after you have been given the opportunity. It's long before that opportunity arises. Once the opportunity arrives, it's too late to prepare" (Wooden 149).

So what are the steps used to build a strategic plan for a library?

1. Brainstorm and Dream
2. Organize
3. Prioritize
4. Plan
5. Commit
6. Implement

Using this step-by-step approach not only allows organizations to break down the planning process into smaller, attainable goals but also keeps the process moving forward. While it is tempting to combine or skip a step, it is in the best interest of the organization in the long term to complete each step in order.

Brainstorm and Dream

The first step is the one that will take the longest time to complete. As in any project, preparation is crucial to achieve the desired results. The library director, the library board and the staff must do some homework and find out what the community wants from its library. The entrepreneurial director will look for input from all the different populations, or customers, served by the library. In the entrepreneurial model, the library is a customer service organization and those individuals who walk through the door, call on the phone or request assistance via email are customers. They provide the demand for the library's products and services, determine the need for and relevance of the library within the community and determine the priority of the services, materials and resources provided by the library. Setting aside the theory that libraries exist for the "greater good," customers decide if the library will be a success, or even exist at all. In referring to Peter Drucker, author William Cohen states, "as a consultant, Peter first looked at a company's overall objective to see if they matched his basic injunction, which was to determine what business the company was in, who the customer was, what the customer wanted, and what the customer termed 'successful' in fulfilling this want" (Cohen 206).

These groups of library customers must be identified. For a small organization such as a law library, the makeup and needs of the group might be simple to define. In a larger organization, such as a college or university, the population might be more complex, consisting of numerous subgroups with differing needs. Delineations of subgroups can be made according to ethnic differences, family composition, age, life stages, professions, students' majors or various geographic areas within the library's service area. Groups can also be identified according to a customer's pattern of library use. Customers may be defined by their use of the library on a weekly, monthly or yearly basis, or perhaps by identifying the needs of those who never use the library at all. Identification of these groups can be achieved by using oral surveys conducted by the library staff, random selection from the library's customer database or a more formal written or online survey. The principal goals of this initial step are the creation of a list of the primary groups of customers who are served by the library and a roster of individuals who are representative of each of those groups.

The second step in this process will be to recruit members for focus groups, a technique resembling the customer survey and marketing focus groups used by advertising agencies. Invitations to participate in a focus group should be extended by the library board or director and can be sent through email or letters which should include an explanation of what the library board wishes to accomplish, a defined time and date for the meeting, and a statement demonstrating the library's appreciation of the investment of time and energy that focus group participants are giving to aid in the success of the library's planning project. Focus groups can meet at the library or in other convenient places throughout the community. Each group should have a set of questions to answer, a set time to work, and comfortable seating.

Ideally, each sample group should meet together with an objective third party moderator to discuss the answer to the following questions. "What would your ideal library look like? What would it have, what would it do and what would the physical space look like?" While keeping the discussion within the realm of possibility, and while libraries cannot plan as if money were not an issue at all, funding, or the lack thereof, should not keep good, community-based ideas off the table. The point of brainstorming is to focus on identifying the community needs the library should meet. All suggestions from all focus groups should be noted during this first step. The library belongs to the community and this is an opportunity for the community to share what it wants from that library.

The use of an objective third party moderator or facilitator is highly recommended for these discussion/focus groups to allow the discussions to be managed without personal opinions or preferences coming into play from a board member or director who oversees the discussion. The moderator should outline the meeting agenda, keep the discussion on topic, ask questions to encourage participants to share their insights about the library, and record insights on a large tablet or easel. The moderator also needs to wrap up the discussion in a timely fashion, respecting the schedules of those individuals who are donating their time for this process. The library director or a board member should mail personalized thank you notes to each participant when the group meeting is complete. After all sessions are completed and the information is compiled, individual members of each group should receive a copy of the gathered feedback if they so desire.

Several groups that should be included in any list of potential focus meetings are the library board, the library staff, the Friends of the Library and any other group that has a vested interest in the success of the library. Depending on the type of library, members of these other groups may be library trustees, local municipal or other government entities, or college deans, boards, or department chairs.

While this task may seem time and labor intensive, it is necessary for two major reasons as well as numerous minor ones. The first reason is that even the director and the library staff don't know all the services that their customers want from the library. Additionally, staff can have their own ideas that may prejudice them from seeing the potential in something new. Second, by responding to questions and having their responses appreciated and honestly noted, participants begin to "buy-in" or have a personal stake in the success of the plan. The Library needs its staff, board, Friends, funders and customers to assume a vested interest in the plan and its success. This is the time to help them see that their success and the library's success are tied together.

Reactionary statements such as "we tried that and it doesn't work," and "there's no money for that" are not fruitful in forwarding discussion. Moderators must refrain from judging the comments provided in these sessions but overly negative perspectives should be discouraged in these discussions. While conducting these groups, facilitators or moderators should remember that there are no wrong answers. Everything gets written down. There will be time later to modify and compile elements from the plan, but for now, everything is put on the table.

ORGANIZE

Once all the focus groups have met and all the responses have been gathered, these need to be organized. Depending on the amount of information collected, this task can be completed by two or three individuals or it may require the input and discussion of the entire board. The library director should not complete this task individually. Many responses can be interpreted in various ways and the input of more than one person will bring various perspectives to the organization of these insights.

Each idea, concept, dream, want or need should be assigned to a major category or service response. Some possible categories might include:

• Buildings & Facilities
• Staff (training, reviews and competencies)

- Non-print Resources
- Information Literacy
- Outreach, community involvement, promotion
- Technology
- Programming/Instruction

It is important to note that the committee or board reviewing the input should not remove anything from the list, but only organize the items. This organization gives some structure to the information and is a first step in seeing the new plan take shape. Additionally, structuring the information in this fashion will reveal any areas that may have been neglected as well as areas which have the most need for change.

PRIORITIZE

Before work can begin on step three, a Strategic Planning Committee needs to be created. This committee will be a small group of representatives from some of the largest customer groups served by the library. Selection of this committee is the responsibility of the library's director along with the board president, department chair or other governing official. An entrepreneurial director should not hesitate to be involved in the selection process. The input of the staff and director is vital in assuring that each major community group has a voice in this process. Should a director lack a counterpart to participate in creating this committee, the director should seek advice on individuals who would be active participants. Advice can come from long term staff members, respected leaders in the community, or peers or mentors who have first-hand knowledge of the library.

In order to accomplish the task of building a sound, constructive committee, the director will need to assume the role of an entrepreneurial leader. The focus of a leader is on the "big picture." A leader sees the library's place in the overall community structure. Entrepreneurial leaders understand the need for satisfied customers in the here and now; however, they also want to position the library to have satisfied customers for the next ten years. A library director operating as a leader will view the library as an organization among organizations and will see the contributions that the library can make to the community it serves and the support that the community should give back to the library. Entrepreneurial leaders speak in terms of team building, partnerships and shared resources and understand that in today's economic and global community, no organization is an island.

This committee should include the library director, a board member, a member of the Friends, a staff member, and at least three other individuals who represent different groups served by the library on a regular basis. These individuals need to be able to understand the library's mission to serve a complete community as well as to be able to articulate their needs the library from their own perspectives. This Strategic Planning Committee will be a working committee through the rest of the strategic planning process.

After the committee is formed, the task of this group will be to review the list created by the focus groups which has been organized by categories, and then to prioritize those. For example, the technology column may have the following goals listed:

- increase number of public computers to 25
- purchase software for print management
- purchase a new projector for meeting use

- institute use of handheld checkout devices
- obtain headsets for roving reference

In this example, after considering the needs of the library's community, the Strategic Planning Committee decides that the most important of these would be the print management software, the projector and the headsets, with the handheld checkout devices coming in last. These items should be prioritized according to the needs/wants/desires of the library's community and not according to which ones the committee believes will be the easiest to finance. Nothing is removed from the list. The committee is only placing them in order of importance.

PLAN

The creation of the library's strategic plan will be the next step for the Committee. This document will include not only the organization's goals and objectives but also descriptions of the actions which will be taken by the library to achieve those goals; the group, committee or department which will be overseeing the implementation of the goals; estimates of the costs; and the length of time expected for the completion of each goal. Each goal should also have at least one objective, which defines how the Planning Committee will determine if that goal is successful. Objectives can be simple or complex but each goal should have at least one. Goals determine where the finish line is located; objectives map out how the organization plans on reaching that finish line. As an example, a goal would be to have dinner completed by 6:00 P.M. The objectives might include shopping for ingredients, preparation of those ingredients, time needed to cook that meal, and the presentation of the food as well as a timeline showing when each of these steps will be completed.

The creation of this document is most often at the center of any conversation about long range or five-year plans. It should be noted that the initial three steps are crucial and no plan should be written without these steps having been completed.

Reviewing each of the categories, the Strategic Planning Committee should select no more than two or three goals for each category. One goal is fine, especially if the plan is for a small library. For each goal, a timeline needs to be developed and the steps by which the organization can reach the goal should be described. If there is a cost associated with the goal, the plan should include how the library is going to pay the bill. At least one objective should be written for each goal, showing the standard or milestone the committee will use to decide if that goal was successfully reached.

How is this "wish list" converted into a well written strategic goal? To make this transition, the committee will need to answer several questions regarding the chosen goal. These questions include: What steps are needed to reach this goal? What is a realistic timeline for this goal? What expenses will be needed to achieve this goal? Who will oversee the work of this goal?

Using the technology example, the committee decides to put the purchase of a new projector into the plan. An outside consultant may have to be hired to survey the library's facility and determine the best projector for the library's meeting or program room. The next steps might be to find financing for this projector, purchase it, and have it installed in the library. The library's computers may require a software upgrade in order to function properly with this new item. Finally, the library staff will require training on how to use the projector. The Planning Committee would consider this list of steps and may determine that eighteen months will be necessary to complete this goal.

The timeline should be as detailed as possible and should include the length of time anticipated for the completion of each step. The timeline for this example may include two months for creating the request for proposal and receiving bids, two weeks for the selection of a unit, ten months to find and secure funding, and six months to buy, install and train staff in proper use of the new equipment.

Included in this goal is the anticipated cost to the organization of $5,000. Plans to secure funding may reflect the intention to request monies from support organizations such as the Friends group or local business groups and grants for which the library plans to apply, or should indicate that the projector purchase will be funded within the library's operating budget. This goal is simple and easy to measure. The objective for this goal would state that a new projector will be installed and ready for use within 18 months and that all staff will attend at least one training session and will demonstrate a basic ability to set up and use the new projector.

Lastly, the Planning Committee should make a recommendation as to what department or group will be responsible to oversee this project or goal. In this example, the individual or team responsible for computers and technology in the library may be assigned to oversee this project and submit regular progress reports to the director at each major point on the timeline.

The formal statement of this goal may look like this:

The Main Street University Library will demonstrate its commitment to stay current in all areas of technology by purchasing and installing a new projector which will be available for use for library classes and programs. This projector will be selected and installed, and staff will be trained in its use within 18 months. The technology department of the library will oversee the selection and installation of this new projector and will arrange for a training schedule for library staff. Estimated cost of this goal is $5000.

The accompanying objective would state

The success of this goal will be determined by the installation of a new projector, ready for use within 18 months. All staff will attend at least one training session and will demonstrate to the head of the technology department a basic ability to set up and use the new projector." During the process, the committee should be prepared to define the changes needed to implement the goal. If a new class or workshop which the library plans to offer requires use of this new project, the timeline established for the new class will need to take into consideration the 18 months required for the new projector.

Another example might be a goal to increase awareness of the programs and resources available for young adults. In this case, assume that funding is not available to purchase advertising space in the local newspapers. So how does one reach that group? The Planning Committee could decide to try an organized, systematic marketing drive, using social networking tools such as Facebook, MySpace, Twitter or LinkedIn. Access to social networking is free; however, if the plan calls for posting to these networks multiple times per day, the library could include the need to invest in one of the online social network management tools as part of the goal. Online tools such as Hootsuite, Tweetdeck, or CoTweet allow organizations to manage multiple social media accounts and post to those accounts simultaneously. In this process, the Committee would discuss the goal, the timeline and expenses. It then writes a formal statement of this goal. A well-defined goal for this project needs to be measurable and time-defined, as in the example below:

The XYZ Public Library will increase its presence to individuals within the library's community between 18 — 25 years old through a marketing campaign utilizing online social networks. The success of this goal will be measured by use of online surveys, in-house sampling and attendance at programs geared directly for this age group. This campaign will be carried out over a period of four years. Estimated cost for this goal is $100 to purchase social media management software. Two staff members selected by the director will be responsible to oversee this goal.

The objectives which will define the success of this goal may be similar to any of the following:

- A 25% increase in the number of young adults (defined as those between 18–25 years of age) who say they know about the library's programs and resources designed for their age group within one year
- A 15% increase in the number of young adults who visit the library within two years
- A 25% increase in the attendance at programs designed for young adults within one year
- Within the next four years, the library will implement at least five new programs designed for and presented to library customers who are in the young adult age group.

This goal will be achieved by a systematic set of posts through various online social networking tools. Costs for this goal are estimated to be $100 not including staff time and will fall within the scope of the library's current marketing budget. Approximately six months will be needed for staff to be trained in the use of this software and become comfortable in its use.

Each goal will require several parts:

- The goal. (The XYZ Library will...)
- Implementation plans for achieving that goal. (Through a marketing plan...)
- The tools needed to reach the goal. (Through online networks, via yearly mailings, by the use of staff training...)
- The objective(s) used to demonstrate the success of that goal. (A 25% increase in attendance, a 15% decrease in cost...)
- A list of tools being used to measure the success of that goal. (The success of this goal will be measured by...)
- The deadline for that goal. (Within one year, by September 1, 2014...)
- Estimated costs for this goal. (The estimated costs for this project are $100; projected costs are between $1500 and $2000...)
- Potential sources for acquiring the funds. (The operating budget, a grant, funds from book sale.)

It becomes evident why the number of goals needs to be limited to one or two items per category. With each additional goal and objective(s) selected, the plan becomes more complex and difficult to implement. If a plan is developed for a large, academic library, where staff and student workers can be utilized to help implement, measure and adjust the plan, then two or three goals are workable. A plan for a small public library with a staff of three or four needs to be significantly smaller and simpler. This smaller library should have no more than five categories and no more than 10 goals in total. A lengthy list will overwhelm the staff and board and become useless. Better to have five well written, well executed goals than 10 half-baked, half-heartedly carried out goals.

COMMIT

All of those involved in the process of implementation must buy in to the plan. Each group should have had input and now is the time for the group's members to take ownership of the plan and invest personally in the plan's success. Gaining support for the plan requires taking the time for discussion, including the reasons for the plan and the why's and how's of implementation. The director or other member of the Strategic Planning Committee should present the plan to staff and other stakeholders and allow time for them to consider all the implications of implementing this plan. A second session should be scheduled to provide a time for staff to ask questions and gain clarification as to the plan and their part in it.

The plan's presenters should be prepared for lots of questions. These questions are not personal attacks on the director or on any member of the Committee. Staff will be attempting to incorporate the information which is being shared with what they already know, and patience with them is critical. Committee members should answer the questions to the best of their ability and should take notes about areas where information gaps may occur in the initial draft of the plan. The staff needs time to consider their investment. As the meeting comes to an end, the presenters should ask staff for their commitment to make this plan a success. The individuals presenting the plan to library staff need to instill in the staff the understanding that the success of the organization is dependent on them, and their success as a library staff is tied to the success of the organization.

IMPLEMENTING THE PLAN

A planning committee should not waste the time or energy of the library board, staff or other shareholders by creating a plan that the library board, director or staff has no intention of putting into practice. Plans are sometimes written to satisfy a state's or other governing body's requirement, because one board member has a desire to have a plan in place, or as an exercise in a workshop or seminar. Authors of such plans are often well meaning; however, without utilizing the process of surveying the library's community and then prioritizing and selecting goals and objectives, the plan becomes a weak document, based on a limited perspective of the library. A plan sitting on the shelf is nothing more than shelf paper.

Change is hard and sometimes messy and while writing the plan is an exercise that produces benefits, those benefits are not the ultimate goal. There are several steps a library board or library director can take to insure implementation of a plan. During the planning process, keep library stakeholders informed. These individuals have a vested interest in the library's success and probably have participated in the planning process at some point. Create an accountability to them by keeping them "in the loop" as to the status and results of the plan.

Keep the staff informed. These individuals are essential to the success of the plan. They should see their input as vital, their assistance as crucial and their participation as mandatory to the plan's success. This is a second level of accountability for the director and board. Strategic planning requires more than lip service. The ivory tower theorist will never have a successful strategic planning program. The success of strategic planning is not measured by the publication of an impressive, neatly typed "Five-Year Plan." An aspiring plan will not happen merely because it is neatly documented; the library manager must still make it happen. Strategic planning has gained currency as a way to give libraries greater leverage for progress or survival in a changing and unstable world. This, in a nutshell, is the reward for using strategic planning (Riggs 122).

Implementing the strategic plan will require the entrepreneurial director to be an effective manager. Being a good manager will mean seeing the library as a living entity, serving the community, and meeting the needs of the people who live, work, and go to school in this "neighborhood," whether that neighborhood is a geographic area, a school, a place of business or a community created by shared needs. A disciplined, organized, hands-on manager is focused on the day-to-day operations of the library: managing the schedule, ordering supplies, working at the desk, and seeing that the customers are satisfied every day. In a small organization, the library director will need to take a hands-on approach to managing the plan. In larger organizations, the director may delegate this task; however, the responsibility still lies with the director to see that it is accomplished.

To manage the implementation of the plan, the library director will keep the plan's deadlines in front of the staff and board. While the Strategic Planning Committee should set up the deadlines for each goal, the library director or the department or staff overseeing the implementation of that goal can assign milestones. Deadlines should be put on a calendar, either printed or online, where they can be referred to by staff and board members. Goals with a longer time frame may need to be broken down into steps with milestones for each step, so that the process does not become overwhelming. The use of milestones also allows the library staff and board to experience a sense of achievement as each milestone is reached on the way to the larger goal.

For example, a scenario in which the library's strategic plan has a goal of five business programs within the next two years might evolve as follows. The library director needs to work back from the two year deadline and consider possible dates for these programs, factor in the amount of lead time needed to recruit or hire speakers, and decide on what groundwork should be laid with local business groups to promote these workshops. Timelines have advantages as they show where the project should be and what has been accomplished at a glance. Each milestone should also be on the calendar. Calendars can take many forms, according to what works best for the management style of the library director and the library staff. Calendars that display a full year are useful, giving a complete overview of the project. A monthly calendar allows the staff and director to focus on the current parts of the project without being overwhelmed with upcoming deadlines. Select the one that displays the information needed in a format most useful to the staff and use it. Post it where it can be viewed by all staff involved with or affected by the goal. Use it to keep the project moving forward and to keep the director and staff focused on the new plan. This is the "Master Plan." The library as an organization has committed to this, now the director must make it happen. The beginning of this section includes a list of several positive results that are the outcome of a well written and executed strategic plan. Here is one more; it allows the director and staff to share the library's success. This chapter opens with the statement that most librarians believe their library is a success, but cannot describe what defines their success. When librarians get together and talk about the successes of their library, they tend to tell individual stories: the child who is learning the alphabet, the student who discovers a field of study, an unemployed dad who can apply for work online, a single mom with little money who can find information and entertainment at the library, or the individual learning to speak and read English for the first time. These are heartwarming stories describing successes. They are not, however, always the best way to define success to those outside the library field, which requires the ability to communicate in a style which appeals to that particular audience.

If we, as librarian entrepreneurs, wish to have our message understood, we need to speak the language of those individuals we want to persuade to become stakeholders in our organization. For example, in presenting the library to a group of local government officials, we, as the presenters, need to talk to them about how the library can add to tax revenues or can decrease the cost of schools for taxpayers by providing free supplemental materials that parents, teachers and students would have to otherwise pay to access and improve the quality of life.

Librarians should share facts on how having a library in the community raises the value of housing. Studies on these issues are available and should be used to bolster the library's position as an asset to the community. The Free Library of Philadelphia completed a report in 2010, performed by Fels Research & Consultation, that shows that, "Homes within ¼ mile of a Library are worth, on average, $9,630 more than homes more than ¼ mile from a Library. For homes between ¼ and ½ mile of a Library, the additional value is $650" (Fels Research & Consulting 13). Why use this statistic? Is it relevant because tax revenues drive the "business" of running a municipality or township? Librarians should demonstrate to local government officials that having a well-funded, prosperous library could increase the value of the homes in that area, and they will connect the dots to see that added value means a more secure tax base. The Fels' study demonstrates how this impacts the city of Philadelphia as whole. "Libraries are responsible for $698 million in home values in Philadelphia. That's an increase in home values that homeowners can borrow against to finance education, home improvements and other types of spending. The additional home values generated by proximity to a Library produce an additional $18.5 million in property taxes to the City and School District each year. Under a scenario of accurate and timely assessments, this is how much property tax revenue could be lost per year if all libraries were closed" (Fels Research & Consulting 6). These are facts that address what is important to government officials. Librarians must talk about issues of central importance to them, use the terms and measurements they know, and demonstrate the success and importance of the community library.

Here is another possible message to share. In 2007 Pennsylvania commissioned a study on the return on investment of public libraries in Pennsylvania. This study included the costs that would be incurred if there were no public libraries, broken down by certain professions. The findings, published by the School of Information and Library Science at the University of North Carolina, stated that if public school teachers could not access resources of a public library, "Teachers would save $72 million in their time and money in not visiting in-person or remotely. However, it would cost teachers $168 million to obtain needed information from alternative sources. Teachers would lose $8 million in information that saved them time (e.g., to finish a publication faster) or money (e.g., saving on travel to a conference) when they don't know where to obtain the needed information" (University of North Carolina, School of Information and Library Science 35). In using such a report, ask a local government official where that additional eight million would come from? Make it obvious that having a successful public library saves the taxpayers money.

Perhaps you, as a library director, need to address local business officials. Speak to them about return on investment, including how much traffic a library creates for the town center, how many parents and children attend your programs in the late morning and will be looking for some place to eat lunch. Referred to as the "Halo Effect," the study done by the University of North Carolina estimated that should there be no libraries to visit, Pennsylvania businesses could see $80 million dollars in lost revenues. Look at the commercial benefits of your library and then help those business owners see the benefits too. Another tool to help individuals see the value of the library in dollars is the Library Value Calculator, provided by the New York Library Association <www.nclaonline.org/issues-advocacy/library-value-calculator>. This online tool allows customers to fill in a short form online and see in dollars and sense what they are saving by using their library. Using this calculator, the customer who visits the library every other week and borrows 2 hardback books and reads 2 magazines would see a bi-weekly benefit of $43.14.

Libraries are chameleons; they can become many things to many people. Find out what is important to the group you need to address and then help them see how the library is their ally in obtaining those important goals. This is where the library's plan comes in to play. Use the plan to demonstrate expertise and ability to deliver needed services. Use the library's survey and programming statistics to show that library programs and services are bringing more young adults to the town center. Help local businesses to see that the library's success means their success.

Promoting the Library's Plan?

This chapter has outlined the reasons that a library needs a well written strategic plan and the benefits derived from the process of creating that plan. Assuming that the library has gone through the steps to write that plan, there are now measurable goals, an established and reasonable timeline, and a budget to back up the priorities established by the Strategic Planning Committee. Changes will have been instituted as needed and the library staff will have begun the task of putting this plan to work. After the plan is complete and changes are underway, it is time to share with the library's customers that changes are in the works and that this library has an eye toward the future and is continually working hard to be a better library. There are changes in store for the library and the library director will want to make sure customers know about these changes and how these changes will improve the library's services. The question is, "How is that done?" The library has a plan, but can the director and the staff sell it?

Librarians are well-known for bragging about their services to other librarians but often need to work on reaching out to customers and potential customers. Librarians know their libraries have much to offer, but are often at a loss for how to reach those future customers. Here are a few questions designed to focus an organization's marketing strategy.

WHO IS THE LIBRARY TRYING TO REACH?

During the initial stages of developing the strategic plan, was there any particular group that came to the forefront as an underserved population? What set of individuals do not visit the library, but may benefit from the library's resources or workshops? Define the group which will be targeted so everyone involved will know exactly who they are. Is it new moms, young teens, 30-somethings, college freshman, seniors, non-traditional students? What individuals are to be the focus of the library's new resource, class, outreach or program?

What Is the Library Offering to the Target Group?

What program, resource or workshop in the new strategic plan focuses on this group? Is it an up-to-date collection of resources on finding money for college, an online database of parenting tips, employment assistance? What service, resource or other item is the library developing or purchasing for this group that they may not yet know about?

Where Will the Library Locate Members of the Target Group?

Consider the group of individuals the strategic plan has identified as underserved. How and where do these potential library users get their information? Online? Newspapers? Grocery stores? Coffee shops? Where do they congregate? Local bars? Restaurants? Find where they are and take the information to them.

Why Should They Come?

Once this group is defined and their preferred means of collecting information identified, be sure make the sale. Sell the benefit, not the product. This is a time-honored mantra of many sales professionals. The product is obvious, but what you need to sell is the benefit. "Using Product A will moisturize your skin" is selling the product. "Using Product A will make your skin appear younger and will give you a youthful confidence" is selling the benefit.

For example, the library's goals may include a goal of reaching more new and young parents, including those who have not previously been library users. In order to meet this goal, the library sets an objective to start a new storytime for babies and invites a local lactation specialist to hold a support group in the library immediately following each baby storytime. Library staff will, of course, market to those already using the library. As director, you may use your newsletter, or social network page or website to talk about this new program. These initiatives are all good marketing strategies, but part of the plan was to reach new parents who were not library customers, and you need to develop strategies to reach this audience. Using this example, walk through the questions:

- **Who is the library trying to reach?** New and young moms, especially those who are not already library customers.
- **What is the program offering them?** A baby storytime and access to a trained lactation specialist each week.
- **Where does the marketing need to be placed in order to reach them?** How can the library make those who aren't library users aware of the program? Publicizing programs to new users is an area in which the library staff can be challenged to think outside the box. Using in-house and traditional marketing venues (newsletters, website, social networks) is a basic strategy, but what other methods can be used? In developing a publicity plan, ask: Where do young parents get their information? One strategy would be to partner with local pediatricians and distribute flyers and information through their offices. Local fast food restaurants can be contacted about holding storytimes in their locations in exchange for promoting the library's programs. If the community is small enough, library staff could send information to those whose birth announcements are posted in the

local paper, inviting new parents to the new baby group. Posting information in maternity stores, baby supply stores and ob-gyn offices might even attract interest before the baby arrives.

• **Why should these new parents attend? What benefit will the library sell them?** Certainly everyone knows that children exposed to reading at an early age have an advantage. Reading is an essential skill in our society, so parents should take every opportunity to expose children to the written word. That's the product. What's the benefit, especially to these new moms? Moms will have the opportunity to ask questions of trained professionals (both the librarian and the lactation specialist), a free morning out of the house, a chance to socialize their children, and the opportunity for some grown up conversation, a definite plus. Sell the benefit, not the product. A good entrepreneur will help the customer focus on the benefits of the product, not just the product itself.

The strategic planning process is a necessity for any library looking to succeed and thrive in the coming years. Whether it is a public, private, academic, legal or special library, the process of creating and implementing a plan will help that organization to focus on its primary targets.

In summary, the successful entrepreneurial librarian uses creativity, strategic planning, targeted marketing and innovation to build a successful library. The entrepreneurial director continually looks for ways to place the library in the best possible position to take advantage of opportunities to meet the needs of their community, both present and future, and thereby be foundational in the success of the community the library serves. Directors are proactive in addressing needs, they prioritize training for themselves and their staff, and they use a strategic plan to develop new opportunities and to establish their libraries as successful enterprises. Working with the library staff, board and the strategic planning committee, the entrepreneurial director builds a community-based, organic organization which meets the needs of its customers, both present and future.

Works Cited

Blanchard, Ken, Spencer Johnson and Constance Johnson. *One Minute Manager.* New York: Morrow, 1982. Print

Buckingham, Marcus and Curt Coffman. *First Break all the Rules.* New York: Simon and Schuster, 1999. Print.

Cohen, William A. *A Class with Drucker.* New York: Amacom, 2007. Print.

Doughtery, Richard M. "Planning for New Library Futures." *Library Journal* 15 (May 2002): 38–41. Print.

Drucker, Peter. *Innovation and Entrepreneurship.* New York: Harper & Row, 1985. Print.

Fels Research & Consulting. *The Economic Value of the Free Library in Philadelphia.* Independent Research. Philadelphia: Fels Institute of Government, Pennsylvania University, 2010. Web. 1 June 2011. <http://www.freelibrary.org/about/Fels_Report.pdf>

Gross, Valerie. "Transforming our Image through Words that Work: Perception is Everything." *Public Libraries* 48.5 (2009): 24–32. Print.

Nelson, Sandra. *Strategic Planning for Results.* Chicago: American Library Association, 2008. Print.

Nelson, Sandra. *The New Strategic Planning for Results.* Chicago: American Library Association, 2001. Print.

New York Library Association. *Library Value Calculator.* Web. 2 August 2011. <http://www.nclaonline.org/issues-advocacy/library-value-calculator>

Riggs, Donald E. *Strategic Planning for Library Managers.* Phoenix: Oryx, 1984. Print.

Stephenson, James. *25 Common Characteristics of Successful Entrepreneurs.* Web. 1 June 2011. <http://www. entrepreneur.com/homebasedbiz/article200730.html>

University of North Carolina, School of Information and Library Science. *Taxpayer Return-on-Investment in Pennsylvania Public Libraries.* Independent Study. Harrisburg: Commonwealth of Pennsylvania, Office of Commonwealth Libraries, 2007. Web. 15 May 2011. <http://www.palibraries.org/associations/9291/files/FullReport.pdf>

Weingand, Darlene E. *Administration of the Small Public Library.* Chicago: American Library Association, 2001. Print.

Wooden, John. *Wooden on Leadership.* New York: McGraw-Hill, 2005. Print.

Section II
Intrapreneurs

3 — Creating an Open-Access, Peer-Reviewed Journal

The Journal of Learning Spaces

JOE M. WILLIAMS *and* STEPHEN H. DEW

Introduction

This chapter describes an open access publishing initiative currently underway at the University Libraries, The University of North Carolina at Greensboro. Through this initiative, the Libraries have begun to provide open access (OA) journal hosting, archiving, and support services at no cost to The University of North Carolina at Greensboro's (UNCG) academic community. In order to provide working examples of this new publishing enterprise, this chapter will also look specifically at the creation and development of one new OA journal that is being led by University Libraries faculty: the *Journal of Learning Spaces*. Details of both the *Journal of Learning Spaces* and the Libraries' broader publishing project are discussed, including the entrepreneurial aspects of these undertakings, how each began, where each project stands as of this writing, and what will come next. The authors also share their personal perspectives on how these projects have fared so far, summarize their lessons learned, and suggest how others might follow in this path.

Starting or hosting an open access publication can be a fairly simple project or a large and time-consuming undertaking, depending on the goals and scope of the intended venture. Regardless of the scope, there is a good deal of background work involved in developing an open access publication. One of the first decisions in the process of starting a new open access journal concerns the choice of a business model to use in financing the publication; another early decision concerns whether open access will be provided to articles immediately upon publication (gold open access) or after an embargo period of a specific number of months (green open access). Many open access publications rely heavily on the voluntary time and efforts of editors, peer-reviewers, contributors, and others involved with the journal, allowing the journal to avoid what would otherwise be significant expenses; however, most open access journals must also raise some level of funds in order to cover a range of expenses, especially marketing.

Some gold open access journals use an author-pays business model, in which the author pays a fee to the journal for the open-access publication of his/her article, and such fees vary widely, from around $100 for some social science and humanities journals to $1,000 and more for some science journals. Some gold open access journals raise funds by selling advertising space on the journal's website or by soliciting contributions from readers, authors, and other supporters. Many green open access journals are financed by membership dues or subscription fees, with the result that only members or subscribers have access to articles until the end of a specified embargo period, when open access is provided. For state-funded academic institutions, these fee-based questions can be particularly difficult to consider and manage. For scholarly publications, questions related to the peer review process must also be addressed.

First and foremost, however, there should be a perceived need for a proposed publication in some intended market. Once the need is established, one has next to consider technical questions: What system will be used to publish this work? Who will host and archive the publication? Who has the technical expertise and long-term commitment to uphold those services for the life of the project? What is the project's scope and focus? What should the underlying structure of the publication look like? Who are the stakeholders? How and when should the stakeholders be contacted? What roles are needed to see the project through publication, and who will fill those roles? These questions will require thoughtful attention by any library contemplating launching an open access publication, just as numerous librarians and other academics have weighed, documented, and described over the past several years.

Literature Review

For general background information on the many issues involved in launching and publishing an open-access journal, researchers will find that there are several useful book-length resources available. John Willinsky, widely recognized as the founding father of the Open Journal Systems, published *The Access Principle* in 2006, and it still provides a superb summary of why open access journal publishing is important for academic research and scholarship worldwide. Possibly the best resource for information on best practices for open-access publishing is the *Online Guide to Open Access Journals Publishing*, which is available freely over the Web through the Directory of Open Access Journals (DOAJ). In addition, two other excellent resources are available freely over the Web through the Public Knowledge Project — Lorna Shapiro's *Establishing and Publishing an Online Peer-Reviewed Journal* and Kevin Stranack's *Getting Found, Staying Found, Increasing Impact*. In 2008, David Solomon published a very useful book with background information and recommendations for those new to open access publishing, *Developing Open Access Journals: A Practical Guide*, and in addition to his book, Solomon used a Creative Commons license to provide free Web access to a condensed seventeen-page outline of the book's key highlights.

For information on the development and the use of OJS software, by far the best resource is *Open Journal Systems: A Complete Guide to Online Publishing* by Willinsky, Stranack, Smecher, and MacGregor which is freely available from the OJS Website. In addition, although it was published in 2005 and is a bit dated now, Willinsky's journal article, "Open Journal Systems," provides a good summary of the early development and use of OJS. In a 2010 article in the *Chronicle of Higher Education* about the widespread use of OJS by faculty publishing open access scholarly journals, Willinsky was described as follows: "He seems genial, but John Willinsky is a dangerous man ... (who is) equipping scholars around the world with a tool to foment revolution" (Schmidt A-1). The article noted the radical nature of OJS, free software that allows faculty to forego the information restrictions of commercial publishing in order to provide free and immediate access to research articles. While this access opens scholarly dialogue and discovery worldwide, the article nevertheless also provided a dire warning about one possible result of OJS use, "By making it much cheaper and easier to produce academic journals and allowing scholars to place research that has not been peer-reviewed in universally accessible online repositories, open-access publishing can also make it easier to establish questionable publications and disseminate shoddy scholarship" (Schmidt A-1). The radical nature of OJS publishing was also a central point of Terry Anderson and Brigette McConkey's 2009 article, "Development of Disruptive Open Access Journals."

A few articles highlight particular technical aspects of the OJS software. A brief technical summary on how to download and use the OJS software can be found in Bakht, Hovey, and McLeran's online report, "Open Journal Systems." In three articles (two with Chia-Ning Chiang), Rick Kopak noted the importance of OJS developing a set of reading tools, such as annotation and linking modules, which would enhance the online reading experience and improve the quality of critical engagement. Although Anderson and McConkey, like Kopak, emphasized the usefulness of the reading tools, they also noted that the tools are only available when readers access articles in HTML; the reading tools are not available when editors or readers choose PDF (83).

A number of published works focus on libraries that have acquired OJS software in order to support faculty publishing electronic journals. In an article about the University of Idaho Library's use of OJS to help a faculty member publish an environmental journal, Ben Hunter noted how OJS allows the library to join faculty in publishing scholarly open access journals at a relatively low cost. In two articles concerning the University Library at the University of Illinois at Chicago, Mary Case and Nancy John emphasized how library goals supported the use of OJS and how the acquisition and use of OJS allowed the library to become a key campus role player, supporting faculty research and scholarly communication in a new and profound way. Case and John noted how OJS allowed the library to take on a "leadership role" (Publishing 15), and they concluded that, through OJS, libraries worldwide could greatly influence scholarly communication:

> The Library knows that this is only a beginning. We are convinced that as more libraries join us in taking a proactive role, the library profession, in partnership with faculty, will change the way scholarly information is vetted and distributed, making it more widely available and cost-effective [Opening Up, n.p.].

With two Canadian universities (The University of British Columbia and Simon Fraser University) being involved in the creation of OJS, other Canadian universities naturally became early supporters and users of the software, both as individual institutions and as consortia, such as Synergies (Devakos and Turko; Felczak, Lorimer, and Smith; Lorimer and Maxwell; Kosavic). Like Case and John, Kosavic emphasized how OJS empowers the library to increase its importance as a role player on campus. As Kosavic phrased it, "Providing such a service (OJS) ... can be equally rewarding, as it positions the library as both partner and colleague in the publishing process" (310). In addition, Felczak, Lorimer, and Smith emphasized the need for continuous and ever-changing marketing efforts, especially by the editors and publishers of new OJS journals.

Other libraries worldwide also have been involved in acquiring and using OJS to support publication of online open access journals. Bobby Graham highlighted the use of OJS by the National Library of Australia, and Anja Kersting and Karlheinz Pappenberger reported on OJS use at the Library of the University of Konstanz, Germany. In their report on OJS use at the Library & Information Centre of the University of Patras, Greece, Panos

Georgiou and Giannis Tsakonas emphasized increased campus respect for the library after the introduction of OJS; they stated: "This programme (OJS) is an opportunity for the library to claim a leading role inside the institution." Several articles have emphasized the many benefits that OJS provides for scholarly publishing and communication in the developing world (Abraham and Minj; Willis, Baron, Lee, Gozza-Cohen, and Currie; Saghaei).

In at least one case, librarians have used OJS to launch a new journal entirely on their own. Seeing a clear need for a scholarly journal devoted entirely to information literacy, Stewart Brower and Christopher Hollister, who were librarians at the University of Buffalo at the time, decided that they would create and launch a new online journal—*Communications in Information Literacy*. With no financial or technical support from their library or any other institution or organization, Brower and Hollister downloaded OJS onto private computers and launched their journal, clearly demonstrating that, if with knowledge of the process and the server capacity, potential editors and publishers can use OJS to publish a journal from home. As independent publishers, they had to deal with a number of expenses; nevertheless, they were able to declare that they needed just $150 per year to publish. To help cover some of their expenses, they were able to offer print copies of each issue for sale on lulu.com, making about $15 with each sale. Of course, production costs will vary among journals depending on a number of different factors, especially how much is spent on management and marketing; however, OJS, as free open-source software, allows publishers and editors to greatly reduce the budget necessary to finance an online journal. Most articles that discuss the production costs of OJS journals emphasize the ability to produce a peer-reviewed scholarly journal at very low or minimal costs (Anderson and McConkey; Hunter; Schmidt; Willinsky and Mendis; Willis, Baron, Lee, Gozza-Cohen, and Currie).

Academics with an entrepreneurial idea and a willingness to take on the risks involved in creating and launching an electronic journal are a growing phenomenon in the publishing industry, and commercial publishers are witnessing a steady rise in the number of competitive journals being published by universities and other non-profit organizations. As an open source software enabling academic faculty and librarians to publish open access journals at a minimal cost, OJS has significantly opened the doors for entrepreneurial publishing projects on university campuses worldwide. With access to OJS, academics with an entrepreneurial spirit are empowered to create, launch, and develop peer-reviewed open access journals that contribute to the scholarly discourse of their professions. Journal publishing is no longer cost prohibitive, and a risk-taker with a good idea and access to OJS can take advantage of that.

Open Access Publishing on UNCG Campus

In 2006, key staff in the Libraries began a conversation with a faculty member in UNCG's Department of History offering to provide technical support for his publication of an online journal. The Libraries' administrators decided to support this project in-house and not acquire any special software. In concert with the faculty member, Professor Robert Calhoon, the Libraries created an online journal, the *Journal of Back Country Studies*, by developing a basic Web site supported by individual Web pages for each issue, with links to articles in PDF. By the spring of 2010, several other faculty members had contacted the Libraries, and they also expressed an interest in obtaining our help to publish electronic journals, which led the Libraries to investigate the availability of special software that could support such an effort. In March 2010, the Libraries acquired the Open Journal Systems (OJS) software and key project members began the process of learning how the system operated and how it might be used to support our faculty's needs.

During the summer of 2010, the *Journal of Back Country Studies* was migrated to OJS, and the Libraries began discussions with a number of other faculty members about their possible use of OJS. By August, when the Libraries' OJS Website was launched (libjournal. uncg.edu/ojs), four additional journals were in the initial stages of development: *The International Journal of Critical Pedagogy, Women & Girls in Sport, The Richard Hogarth Society Newsletter,* and *The Journal of Black Masculinity.*

In their institutional goals, several libraries have found ample justification to support OJS publishing as a new venture (Case and John; Graham), and even though the effort to help faculty publish electronic journals was new for the Libraries, we found ample support for the effort voiced in the Libraries' "Goals" and its "Customer Service Values" <library. uncg.edu/info/mission_statement.aspx>. One goal commits the Libraries to "Build and preserve print, electronic resources, and other unique collections that support the University's mission and programs," and given that statement, OJS definitely empowered the Libraries to support faculty research and publication needs by building and preserving electronic journals. Another goal commits the Libraries to "Seek out and take advantage of appropriate entrepreneurial opportunities," and the support that the Libraries provide to faculty wishing to publish electronic journals certainly opens entrepreneurial possibilities for them and for us. In addition, the Libraries' "Customer Service Values" also supported our entrance into the field of electronic journal publishing. The following two statements were especially supportive — "We must provide an environment that encourages creativity and innovation in the delivery of our services," and "We will create systems, services, and procedures with our customers' needs foremost in mind." Through the use of OJS to support faculty publication of electronic journals, the Libraries clearly had the needs of faculty foremost in mind, and support for electronic journal publication was a creative innovation in library services. UNCG Libraries will always perform its traditional role on campus of being the primary information provider, but with OJS, the University Libraries suddenly became a publisher and information creator as well. We are now part of the worldwide publishing industry.

This foray into the publishing trade represents an entrepreneurial move for the University Libraries, a non-traditional entrant to the field. Like many entrepreneurial ventures, the Libraries' publishing initiative began as a small, internal enterprise within the Libraries, but is now purposefully transforming into a much broader venture that includes many new partners and stakeholders, such as faculty from across both the UNCG campus and other institutions throughout the country.

While entrepreneurial ventures often seek to earn profits, the University Libraries do not intend to gain financially from their publishing efforts through subscription fees, publishing fees, or advertising costs. Still, there are some potential rewards associated with each successful publication, such as furthering library collaborations across disciplines and institutions (Richard 39; Furlough 191), advancing local scholarly communications efforts, and contributing to the literature across various subject disciplines.

This publishing venture also represents significant risks, particularly in terms of time commitment, funding for advertising and marketing, and effort in creating a not-for-profit project that intends to grow and self-sustain. Participants must commit their resources to this open access project idea, instead of one or more other competing scholarly or creative projects. For example, journals wishing to publish their content in portable document format must have the particular skills and available time needed to invest in that kind of content production. Dedicated proofreaders and other pre-production editing staff may be desired if a new journal anticipates a high volume of submissions, which may depend on the breadth and appeal of the journal's topic. The *Journal of Learning Spaces*, for instance, addresses a topic that the editors feel has very broad appeal.

Identifying a Need for a Journal

Several factors contributed to the conception of the *Journal of Learning Spaces* project. First, the topic of learning spaces was an area of personal interest and experience for several faculty in the University Libraries. In the past few years, the Libraries had made and evaluated several changes to their spaces that accommodated group study and research. Library use was increasing and further renovations were already underway. In addition to this, in May 2009 UNC Greensboro's Chancellor identified the creation of learning communities as a strategic goal for her administration and the University in the coming years (University of North Carolina at Greensboro). The University would build upon its rich history of educational leadership and learning community development—from the institution's early, social ground-breaking days as a residential women's college in the 1890's, focused on pedagogy, business, and domestic science, to becoming a state leader in teacher education today, and hosting the acclaimed Lilly Conference on Teaching and Learning.

The University is home to several programs with deep interest in learning spaces and research, such as the College of Education, the Department of Library and Information Science, and the College of Interior Design and Architecture. In addition, the school maintains a strong and active Teaching and Learning Center and a Residence Life program that has remained deeply engaged in learning communities for decades, beginning with the establishment of Ashby Residential College in 1970, one of the first living-learning communities in the nation (*Residence Life*).

When the University Libraries' Electronic Resources & Information Technology department began supporting the Open Journal Systems publishing platform in 2010, the above-mentioned pieces began to come together to form the idea of an open access publication that focused on learning spaces in higher education. Since learning spaces often involve and affect a wide range of individuals, including teaching faculty, instructional technologists, architects and interior designers, librarians, and residence life staff, a publication on this topic could easily be envisioned as a multidisciplinary resource.

An initial scan of the current literature revealed that research on learning spaces and the connections between space and learning was currently being published, and had been consistently for the past five years. There were a number of journals in each subject area that reliably published learning spaces research, such as *Active Learning in Higher Education, Architectural Record, British Journal of Educational Technology, Educause Quarterly, Innovations in Education and Teaching International, Learning, Media, and Technology*, and *New Review of Academic Librarianship*. However, key investigators found that none of those journals focused solely on the topic. Further investigation indicated that very few of the journals publishing frequently on the topic of learning spaces were doing so as open access publications. The perception developed that a void existed across the literature in several subject areas that could be filled by a journal dedicated to learning spaces. In effect, this journal would serve as an online learning space about learning spaces.

Having decided upon the journal concept and its general focus, the principal investigators consulted the Startup Guide on open access publishing from the Directory of Open Access Journals, <doaj.org>, to determine our next steps. Following the guide, identification and contacting potential partners in this publication venture began. To begin, a one-page project vision document was drafted (see Appendix 1) that outlined the general concept and rationale behind the proposed publication. The letter described the target audience for the journal, identified possible competitors, and explained the advantages that were perceived for the journal over those competitors. In short, the two Educause publications, the *Educause Review* and the *Educause Quarterly*, were the closest competitors since they were open access publications targeting a higher education audience, often dedicating entire issues specifically to the subject of learning spaces.

While these Educause publications appealed primarily to information and instructional technologists, librarians, and administrators, the proposed new journal would appeal to that group as well as a wider readership that included teaching faculty in multiple disciplines. The journal would also publish research and case studies that involved more pedagogy than typically appears in the Educause publications. To further illustrate the type of works that were intended for this publication, and to underscore the currency and relevance of the proposed focus, the vision document also included a number of current citations to learning spaces research from the literature in several different subject disciplines.

The vision document was first circulated to the University Libraries administrators for comment, and for their consideration for personal involvement and/or institutional support. The Associate Dean for Public Services and the Assistant Dean for Administrative Services were both interested in participating, as was the University Libraries as an organization. With their expressed support and interest, the vision document was then distributed more widely to other colleagues across campus who had an expressed or likely interest in the topic of learning spaces, for their reactions and consideration.

In a matter of weeks, a small group of faculty and staff on campus had expressed interest in helping the project take shape. Some of these early stakeholders also provided lists of other colleagues in the area who would likely be interested in seeing the journal succeed. Most of these communications thus far had taken place by phone or email. At this point, a face-to-face meeting of all interested parties was scheduled to take place in the Libraries to discuss the project in more detail, to finalize the scope and focus of the journal, to confirm the degree of commitment from all interested parties, and to begin developing a timeline and organizational structure for the journal.

During the course of this 90-minute meeting, the group refined the scope and focus for the *Journal of Learning Spaces* as follows:

> A peer-reviewed, open-access journal published biannually, *the Journal of Learning Spaces* provides a scholarly, multidisciplinary forum for research articles, case studies, book reviews, and position pieces related to all aspects of learning space design, operation, pedagogy, and assessment.
>
> We define *learning* as the process of acquiring knowledge, skill, or understanding as a result of study, experience, or teaching.
>
> *Learning spaces* are designed to support, facilitate, stimulate, or enhance learning and teaching. *Learning spaces* encompass formal, informal, and virtual environments:
>
> - formal: lecture halls, laboratories, traditional classrooms
> - informal: learning commons, multimedia sandbox, residential study areas, huddle rooms
> - virtual: learning management systems, social media websites, online virtual environments

We invite submissions of practical and theoretical works from practitioners and academics across a wide range of subject disciplines and organizational backgrounds, including Architecture, Interior and Product Design, Education, Information and Library Science, Instructional Technology, Sociology, and Student and Residential Life. Submissions should focus primarily on learning spaces and their impact on or relationship to teaching and learning ["Focus and Scope"].

For the publication, the idea of a "learning space" was broken into 3 categories: formal, informal, and virtual. This division would only be conceptual, at first: a way to help the editors identify and route submissions to the appropriate staff quickly. Editors and peer reviewers would be appointed under each section. We sought these staff members from the various subject backgrounds we were trying to attract in the journal's readership.

Journal editors then reviewed our scope and goals and discussed the types of works that would best meet those needs. To aid this discussion, we reviewed numerous peer publications for their approach to submissions. This process helped us determine the submission categories and lengths for our publication. Finally, we agreed that the following four types of submissions would be accepted for consideration from any subject discipline, provided the submission fit with our Scope and Focus:

Research manuscripts (3,000–5,000 words) present and describe original, primary research (broadly defined) on topics of current importance that may impact learning space research and practice in higher education.

Position pieces (1,500–2,500 words) are essays intended to inform readers of, or to stimulate discussion about, significant issues in current learning space research and practices in higher education. These pieces may be primary or secondary research and will provide complete references.

Case studies (1,500–2,500 words) describe mature projects and programs that provide or demonstrate innovative or instructive learning space designs, programs, or practices in higher education. Case studies dealing with pedagogy, assessment, or unique partnerships and collaborations will receive greatest preference.

Book reviews (1,000–1,500 words) provide concise summaries and evaluations of current books related to learning space research or practices in higher education. Book review authors select and procure books to review, based on their professional perception of the book's real or potential impact or relevance to current research and practice.

All of the attendees at this face-to-face meeting confirmed their willingness to participate in either an editorial or advisory capacity for the first two years of the journal's biannual publication cycle. To ensure the highest quality of output, the group agreed that the journal would publish as a double-blind peer reviewed publication. As one final agenda item for this meeting, Stephen Dew, the University Libraries' Collections & Scholarly Resources Coordinator and one of the authors of this chapter, provided attendees with a preview of the OJS software that would be used to publish the journal.

Selecting and Implementing OJS at UNCG

At UNCG, the University Libraries' experience in choosing OJS software was very similar to that of the University Library at the University of Illinois at Chicago (UIC), where bepress and ScholarOne were considered, but were determined to be too expensive (Case and John, Publishing, 12). Like at UIC, there were three prime factors for UNCG in choosing OJS — (1) it supports the entire process of publishing an online journal, from submission to final publication; (2) it is free open-source software; and (3) it is based on a platform (PHP, MySQL, etc.) that matched the expertise of the library's technology staff. The fact that OJS is free was probably the major factor, however, especially given the fact that, with the downturn in the economy beginning in 2008, UNCG faced a very difficult budget situation in 2010, and the University Libraries were in no position to be able to purchase a commercial product. Deciding to use OJS was relatively easy — it had the entire package for publishing an online journal; it was free; and the library's technology staff was proficient with the software.

OJS is a journal management and publishing system that was developed by the Public Knowledge Project (PKP) <pkp.sfu.ca>, a partnership of faculty members, librarians, and graduate students from Simon Fraser University, the University of British Columbia, and Stanford University. PKP is dedicated to "exploring whether and how new technologies can be used to improve the professional and public value of scholarly research." Supported by a number of grants, PKP designed OJS specifically to assist faculty and researchers in publishing peer-reviewed open-access journals, and they developed OJS as an open-source solution, making it freely available on the Web <pkp.sfu.ca/?q=ojs>. PKP's intent is to improve the scholarly quality of publishing processes worldwide, and the purpose of OJS is to make "open access publishing a viable option for more journals, as open access can increase a journal's readership as well as its contribution to the public good on a global scale" <pkp.sfu.ca/?q=ojs>.

OJS Supports the Entire Publishing Process

When a publisher decides to publish a journal, online or otherwise, determining a methodology for sustaining the workflow is critical. Setting up a review board, determining a scope of work, deciding on methods for allowing author submissions, tracking copyright, and adhering to publication dates are critical to successful implementation, and OJS was created support the entire journal publishing process. OJS is a journal management and publishing system that was designed specifically to assist faculty and researchers in publishing peer-reviewed, open-access journals at every stage of the process, from submission to final publication.

Any review of the online features for journals using the OJS software reveals that the homepages of most OJS journals have a very similar look. Information and tabs usually appear across top and right side of the homepage for OJS journals in a very similar, if not identical, arrangement. In addition, the homepage for every OJS journal has a link to the OJS homepage. Although the look for almost all OJS journals will be very similar, knowledgeable individuals, such as information technology staff, can adjust the look to a limited extent, and they can add photographs, prints, or other images to the masthead to give each journal a special look or brand.

OJS is set up to support a wide variety of roles for individuals who are involved with the journal, and it has special features and functions for each role. Although all roles can be utilized, OJS is very flexible, and it allows for some roles to be utilized, while others are not. The particular roles used depend on what the journal needs. For a peer-reviewed journal, the primary roles are performed by authors, readers, managers, editors, and peer reviewers. Additional roles also facilitate use and division of tasks and make the editorial process easier.

Authors can submit articles online through links provided on the journal's homepage, and any time after submission, the author can log onto the journal and check on the status for any submission (whether the manuscript is still under review, in editing, in copyediting, in proofreading, etc.) If the editors allow it, authors can also automatically be involved in the final proofreading of articles prior to publication.

OJS is specifically designed to support open-access journals, with readers gaining easy, seamless access to all articles, without needing to register or provide any identification; however, some OJS journals request that readers register with the journal, so that announcements can be sent to the entire registered readership, which can be done automatically with the OJS software. Although most OJS journals are open access, the software does support subscription-based journals as well, and in such cases, readers must be registered with the journal and have an assigned username and password (usually supplied by the subscription manager).

The manager has the primary authority for setting the policies and parameters for the journal within the OJS software, and the manager's powers include the following:

- Creates and edits the information provided in all policies that are displayed on the journal's Web pages
- Creates and edits the information about submission procedures, publishing options, and publishing schedules
- Creates all of the sections for the journal (articles, book reviews, letters, case reports, etc.)
- Creates and edits templates for peer-review forms and automatically generated emails
- Creates and edits announcements that are posted on the journal's Web site
- Determines which roles will be utilized by the journal and assigns individuals to each role

Editors also play a key role in OJS journal publishing and the system provides the editor with total control over the editorial process, including decisions on the appropriateness of submissions, the assignment of peer reviewers, editorial decisions on manuscripts, and the final assembly and publication of all issues. The OJS software is quite flexible and frequently provides the manager and editor with several options for the journal's operation. For any peer-reviewed journal, a great deal of correspondence will be generated between editors, authors, and peer reviewers. To assist editors in the cumbersome task of corresponding with authors and peer reviewers, the OJS software includes an automatic peer-review process, in which the software handles all submissions of manuscripts, generates automatic emails, distributes manuscripts to peer reviewers, and manages all communication, tracking each article through the review and publication process. If the editor decides not to use the automatic peer-review process, then the editor must handle all correspondence with authors and peer reviewers individually, through whatever email system is available; and in addition, the editor would have the burdensome responsibility for saving all necessary correspondence. With its automatic peer-review process, OJS provides the editor with all of the tools necessary to initiate, complete, and record the communication and decision making process for each manuscript submitted.

Peer Reviewers

For peer-reviewed journals, the only remaining essential OJS role is that of the peer reviewers. Readers who are registered with each OJS journal may volunteer to be peer reviewers, and the editor has the freedom to select or reject such volunteers. As individuals are selected to be peer reviewers, OJS creates a working list of peer reviewers, and whenever a manuscript is received, the editor can use this list to assign the work to particular reviewers. As peer reviewers are selected for each manuscript, automatic emails that include a list of peer-review guidelines are generated and are sent to the selected individuals, who may choose to review or not to review the manuscript by clicking on a link supplied in the email. The OJS system saves all correspondence between the peer reviewers and the editor and tracks the progress of the reviews, which is a feature of the system that significantly eases the complicated nature of the work between the editor and peer reviewer.

Journal of Learning Spaces

To launch the *Journal of Learning Spaces* project, the initial group of editors decided to announce calls for editor and peer reviewer applications to regional and national groups in their various areas of expertise. This call went out on January 25, 2011. Applications were submitted and reviewed through the journal's OJS installation, which gave all editors an opportunity to route and review documents with the software prior to reviewing submissions for our inaugural publication.

A first call for authors was announced on March 7th, with submissions due by June 30, 2011. Meanwhile, editors and advisers discussed potential column and feature content ideas, sought peer reviewers and advisers in under-represented subject areas, and discussed possible future projects to tie in with the journal project; namely, the idea of hosting a regional conference on learning spaces, to continue the journal's virtual conversation in a face-to-face forum. The journal could potentially publish the proceedings from this conference as a supplement. This concept was included in the vision document outlining the original journal project, and the idea was met with enthusiasm from several editors and advisers. While the project was deemed to have merit, staff agreed that time constraints made this project unfeasible for the journal's inaugural year of publication.

As of June 1, 2011, the journal had all core staff in place: editors and peer reviewers in all of the initial target subject areas, with backgrounds working in formal, informal, and virtual learning spaces. Technical support was being provided by the Libraries' technology support staff, and journal design and layout issues were handled by our staff layout editor. Submissions would be published initially in both HTML and PDF formats by the layout editor.

With a month remaining before the first call for authors closed, the journal had only received a handful of submissions. These were routed to section editors and reviewed. The decision was made that if the journal did not receive enough submissions to warrant a first issue, a second call for authors would be announced for a revised publication date. The editors also began discussing revising the journal's publication schedule altogether, to become less constrained by publishing conventions of print journals (e.g., biannual publication) and possibly embrace the benefits of open access more deeply: quick turnaround on submission reviews and faster publication of current research through the web. These discussions will continue among the editors and advisers, regardless of the success of the journal's first issue.

By the spring of 2011, two journals, *The International Journal of Critical Pedagogy* and the *Journal of Backcountry Studies*, had published several issues and were both freely available from the Libraries' OJS Website, "UNCG Hosted Online Journals" <libjournal.uncg.edu/ ojs>. Although the *Journal of Learning Spaces* was still in development, its homepage and information for potential authors and readers were also freely accessible from the site. In addition, the Libraries were providing support for five more journals in different stages of development, with plans for all of the journals to be published and available from the Libraries' Website before the end of 2011:

- *International Journal of Nurse Practitioner Educators*
- *Women & Girls in Sport*
- *Journal of Applied Peace & Conflict Studies*
- *Richard Hogarth Society Newsletter*
- *UNCG Technical Reports*.

Lessons Learned

Looking back on the first year of OJS at UNCG, there were a few lessons learned. Two lessons concerned how much teaching and assistance faculty would need. First, some of the OJS software is not intuitive, so there was a learning curve and the need for some library assistance to faculty; and second most faculty members were not familiar with how to get journals indexed, so assistance from liaisons and reference librarians was necessary.

Other lessons concerned an appreciation for the flexibility of the system. OJS is a journal management and publishing system that was designed specifically to assist faculty and researchers in publishing peer-reviewed, open-access journals at every stage of the process, from submission to final publication. Journal editors and staff also discovered, however, that there is a good deal of flexibility with OJS — it can also be used to support subscription-based publications, as well as non-peer-reviewed publications, especially professional newsletters and technical reports. In addition, the flexibility of OJS allows for a wide range and number of individuals to be involved in a variety of roles, depending on each journal's needs. A journal has the option of utilizing up to ten roles, and a large number of individuals could be involved in the journal's editorial and publishing processes, especially for peer-reviewed journals. On the other hand, an OJS journal or other serial could utilize a very limited number of roles, and a small number of individuals could be involved in the editorial and publishing processes. For instance, a newsletter or technical report series might have only one or two people involved in production and publishing.

One of the most satisfying lessons learned was that, by supporting faculty research and scholarly communication in a new and profound way, the creation of open source electronic journals would lead to an increased leadership role for the library on campus. Our experience in this matter was undoubtedly similar to the libraries at the University of Illinois at Chicago (Case and John), York University (Kosavic), and the University of Patras (Georgiou and Tsakonas), which all noted an increased leadership role on campus following implementation of an electronic journal publishing program. When UNCG Libraries decided to use OJS to support faculty interested in publishing online journals, we hoped to get a very positive response from our faculty. Although only a limited number of faculty have accepted the challenge of using OJS to start a new journal, those who have done so find OJS to be a great service. In addition, a significant number of faculty and administrators who have not been directly involved with OJS have expressed the opinion that this service is a positive and important development, and they see the University Libraries playing an increasingly important and expanding role on campus.

With OJS at UNCG Libraries, we have joined the worldwide publishing industry. Libraries faculty and staff have embraced the entrepreneurial idea of venturing into this new market, willing to accept both the potential benefits and risks of such an undertaking. Through volunteer efforts, enthusiasm, and cooperation, the Libraries will be using the new open access publishing platform and service to develop and strengthen partnerships and collaborations across campus and beyond. We are no longer only information providers; we are now information creators as well. The *Journal of Learning Spaces* is just the beginning. Wiley and Elsevier, Beware!

Appendix 1. Proposal Letter to Potential Advisers, Editors, Reviewers, Stakeholders

NEW OPEN ACCESS JOURNAL PROPOSAL:
JOURNAL OF LEARNING SPACES

University Libraries, University of North Carolina at Greensboro— 05/24/10

CONCEPT

The *Journal of Learning Spaces* will be a peer-reviewed, open-access journal published biannually and hosted by the University Libraries, UNC Greensboro.

The journal will provide a scholarly, multidisciplinary forum for research articles, case studies, book reviews, and position pieces related to all aspects of learning space design, operation, pedagogy, and assessment.

The journal will define learning space as encompassing formal, informal, and virtual spaces (learning management systems, social media websites, online virtual environments, etc.).

Like a virtual learning space itself, the journal will be a collaborative, multidisciplinary, faculty development effort that combines both practical and theoretical content. Journal content will be solicited from several disciplines, marketing primarily to the fields of education (including distance education and instructional design), architecture, library and information science, and sociology.

The journal editorial board will include UNCG Faculty from the primarily-targeted disciplines.

The University Libraries will host a small, regional conference on learning space issues to help advertise the journal. The proceedings of the conference will be published as an annual journal supplement.

MARKET

Over the past several years, the subject of learning spaces has received considerable and growing attention in higher education. Many colleges and universities have begun implementing and experimenting with physical learning spaces in their libraries, classrooms, computer labs, residence halls, etc., and virtual spaces, such as Learning Management Systems, e-portfolio software, Second Life, etc.

Successful learning spaces in academia are often the result of collaborations between two or more departments or units. As a result, research on learning spaces takes place in several disciplines. However, there are few journals that focus consistently on learning space issues and those that do typically cater to audiences within a single discipline.

Two primary examples of multidisciplinary journals that do publish on this topic consistently are EDUCAUSE Quarterly Magazine and EDUCAUSE Review. These two periodicals cater primarily to librarians, instructional technologists, and academic IT professionals and they focus little on the physical design or pedagogical aspects of learning spaces.

The proposed *Journal of Learning Spaces* will be marketed to readers in multiple fields, with the goal of promoting information sharing as well as future collaborations and innovation across disciplines. This journal will capture a large and loyal base of readers by:

- Offering practical and current information to colleagues across disciplines— information that individuals may not come across through their usual information sources.
- Providing content in an online, peer-reviewed, open access format.
- Enhancing the online journal community with a small, regional meeting to give further momentum to the topics covered in print during the year.

Works Cited

Abraham, Thomas, and Suvarsha Minj. "Scientific Journal Publishing in India: Promoting Electronic Publishing of Scholarly Journals in India." *First Monday: Peer-Reviewed Journal on the Internet* 12.10 (2007): *n.pag.* Web. 14 April 2011.

Anderson, Terry, and Brigette McConkey. "Development of Disruptive Open Access Journals." Canadian *Journal* of Higher Education 39.3 (2009): 71–87. Web. 14 April 2011.

Bakht, Salman, Pehr Hovey, and Aaron McLeran. "Open Journal Systems." *Transliteracies Project* (2009). Web. 21 April 2011.

Brower, Stewart M., and Christopher V. Hollister. "Communications in Information Literacy: An Example of Librarians as Publishers." *Journal of Electronic Resources in Medical Libraries* 7.4 (2010): 320– 325. Web. 14 April 2011.

Case, Mary M., and Nancy R. John. "Opening Up Scholarly Information at the University of Illinois at Chicago." *First Monday: Peer-Reviewed Journal on the Internet* 12.10 (2007). Web. 14 April 2011.

_____, and _____. "Publishing Journals@UIUC." *ARL Bimonthly Report*, 252/253 (2007): 12–15. Web. 14 April 2011.

Devakos, Rea and Karen Turko. (2007). "Synergies: Building National Infrastructure for Canadian Scholarly Publishing." *ARL Bimonthly Report*, 252/253 (2007): 16–19. Web. 14 April 2011.

Felczak, Michael, Rowland Lorimer, and Richard Smith. "From Production to Publishing at CJC Online: Experiences, Insights, and Considerations for Adoption." *First Monday* 12.10 (2007). Web. 14 April 2011.

"Focus and Scope." *Journal of Learning Spaces*. Web. <http://libjournal.uncg.edu/ojs/index.php/jls/ about/editorialPolicies>

Furlough, Michael J. "The Publisher in the Library." *The Expert Library: Staffing, Sustaining, and Advancing The Academic Library in The 21st Century.* Ed. Scott Walter and Karen Williams. Chicago: Association of College and Research Libraries, 2010: 190–233. Web. 30 May 2011.

Georgiou, Panos, & Giannis Tsakonas. "Digital Scholarly Publishing and Archiving Services by Academic Libraries: Case Study of the University of Patras." *Liber Quarterly: The Journal of European Research Libraries* 20.2 (2010). Web. 14 April 2011.

Graham, Bobby. (2007). "Open Publish 2006: Open Access Journals." *National Library of Australia Staff Papers* (2006): *n. pag.* Web. 28 April 2011.

Graham, Slobodanka (Bobby). "Open Access to Open Publish: National Library of Australia." *First Monday: Peer-Reviewed Journal on the Internet* 12.10 (2007); *n. pag.* Web. 14 April 2011.

Hunter, Ben. "Moving Open Access to Open Source: Transitioning an Open-Access Journal into the

Open Journal Systems Journal Management System." *Technical Services Quarterly* 28.1 (2011): 31–40. Web. 14 April 2011.

Kersting, Anja, & Karlheinz Pappenberger. "Promoting Open Access in Germany as Illustrated by a Recent Project at the Library of the University of Konstanz." *OCLC Systems & Services: International Digital Library Perspectives* 25.2 (2009): 105–113. Web. 14 April 2011.

Kopak, Rick. "Open Access and the Open Journal Systems: Making Sense All Over." *School Libraries Worldwide* 14.2 (2008): 45–54. Web. 14 April 2011.

_____, and Chia-Ning Chiang. "Annotating and Linking in the Open Journal Systems." *First Monday: Peer-Reviewed Journal on the Internet* 12.10 (2007). Web. 14 April 2011.

_____, and _____. "An Interactive Reading Environment for Online Scholarly Journals." *OCLC Systems & Services: International Digital Library Perspectives* 25.2 (2009): 114–124.

Kosavic, Andrea. "The York Digital Journals Project: Strategies for Institutional Open Journal Systems Implementations." *College & Research Libraries* 71.4 (2010): 310–321. Web. 14 April 2011.

Lilly Conferences on College & University Teaching. Web. 28 April 2011. <http://www.uncg.edu/tlc/lilly conference/>.

Lorimer, Rowland, and John Maxwell. "Canadian Social Science and Humanities Online Journal Publishing, the Synergies Project, and the Creation and Representation of Knowledge." *Publishing Research Quarterly* 23.3 (2007): 175–193. Web. 14 April 2011.

Lorimer, Rowland, Johanne Provençal, Brian Owen, Rea Devakos, David Phipps, and Richard Smith. *Digital Technology Innovation in Scholarly Communication and University Engagement.* Vancouver: CCSP Press, 2011. Web. 28 April 2011.

Lulu Enterprises. Web. 5 May 2011. <http://www.lulu.com>.

Online Guide to Open Access Journals Publishing. Directory of Open Access Journals, 2011. Web. 20 April 2011.

Residence Life, University of North Carolina at Greensboro. Web. 24 May 2011. <http://www.uncg.edu/res/>.

Saghaei, Mahmoud. "Establishing an Online Editorial and Publishing System: One-year Experience with the *Journal of Research in Medical Sciences.*" *First Monday* 12.10 (2007): *n. pag.* Web. 14 April 2011.

Schmidt, Peter. "New Journals, Free Online, Let Scholars Speak Out." *Chronicle of Higher Education* 56.23 (2010): *n. pag.* Web. 14 April 2011.

Shapiro, Lorna. *Establishing and Publishing an Online Peer-Reviewed Journal: Action Plan, Resourcing, and Costs.* Public Knowledge Project, 2005. Web. 20 April 2011.

Solomon, David J. *Developing Open Access Journals: A Practical Guide.* Oxford, England: Chandos Publishing, 2008. Print.

_____. *Developing Open Access Journals: A Practical Guide.* Web. 14 April 2011. <http://www.developing-oa-journals.org>.

Stranack, Kevin. *Getting Found, Staying Found, Increasing Impact: Enhancing Readership and Preserving Content for OJS Journals.* Public Knowledge Project, 2006. Web. 20 April 2011.

Willinsky, John. *The Access Principle: The Case for Open Access to Research and Scholarship.* Cambridge, MA: MIT Press, 2006. Print.

_____. "Open Journal Systems: An Example of Open Source Software for Journal Management and Publishing." *Library Hi Tech* 23.4 (2005): 504–519. Web. 14 April 2011.

_____, and Ranjini Mendis. "Open Access on a Zero Budget: A Case Study of Postcolonial Text." *Information Research* 12.3 (2007): *n.pag.* Web. 28 April 2011.

Willinsky, John, Kevin Stranack, Alec Smecher, and James MacGregor. *Open Journal Systems: A Complete Guide to Online Publishing.* Burnaby, British Columbia: Simon Fraser University Libraries, 2010. Web. 20 April 2011.

Willis, Jerry, Josh Baron, Reba-Anna Lee, Mary Gozza-Cohen, and Amity Currie. "Scholarly Knowledge Development and Dissemination in an International Context: Approaches and Tools for Higher Education." *Computers in the Schools* 27.3/4 (2010): 155–199. Web. 14 April 2011.

4 — INSIDE Idaho

Intrapreneurship Through the Collaborative Sharing of Geospatial Data

BRUCE GODFREY *and* GAIL Z. ECKWRIGHT

Introduction

Digital spatial data collections have existed at state and federal institutions for decades, and by the early 1990s a few notable libraries, including the University Library at the University of California — Santa Barbara and the Homer Babbidge Library at the University of Connecticut, were making strides toward developing GIS collections (Boissé and Larsgaard 288–289; McGlamery 116). The situation with GIS access in libraries took on new urgency when the federal government issued its 1990 decennial Census of Population as a data file. A few far-sighted librarians took this as a "call to arms" for libraries to address the burgeoning GIS data needs of their users. Boissé and Larsgaard summed up the question of providing GIS services very compellingly:

> Libraries have very little choice in the matter: either they find a way to provide information in this fashion or scholars, students, and others will obtain the information they need from sources outside the library. If this were to happen, the library would be marginalized for the significant part of the academic community which has increasingly worked with geospatial data in recent years. Libraries that do not respond to user needs are unlikely to prosper or even to survive [288].

While there seemed to be a clear mandate for libraries to provide access to digital spatial data, the exact manner and content of such services was necessarily left for librarians to determine.

The Association of Research Libraries (ARL) launched its GIS Literacy Project in 1992, with the goals to "...introduce, educate, and equip librarians with skills needed to provide access to spatially referenced data in all formats and to provide effective access to selected electronic information resources in library collections" (Adler 234).

While the ARL initiative could inform and educate librarians on "who" (libraries) and "what" (GIS services), ARL could not inform librarians and institutions on "how" to go about developing GIS services at their individual libraries. It was essential for each institution to determine which services to provide and which entities to enlist as collaborators. Determining services and collaborators, however, presented a vast undertaking, particularly as GIS services in some academic institutions were already being provided by various units in a fragmented manner. The ultimate challenge was to unify these services and their providers in a manner agreeable to all, with the library playing a principal role in the overall program. Additionally, libraries were uniquely well-qualified to address attendant concerns, such as resource sharing, continuing collaboration, data accessibility and the provision of metadata. Such challenges lend themselves to an entrepreneurial problem-solving approach, using a proactive and innovative program to establish the library's role in providing GIS services.

Literature Review

Library concerns relating to digital spatial data and GIS have been documented at conferences and in the professional literature for twenty years. Among the earliest discussions was the keynote "The Challenges and Opportunities of GIS for Libraries" given by Allan B. Cox at the Map and Geography Roundtable Session of the American Library Association Annual Meeting in June 1992. Cox later published a GIS overview article in a special issue of the *Journal of Academic Librarianship (JAL)* devoted to GIS in academic libraries. Cox laid out the issues inherent in libraries incorporating GIS into their services. He identified a variety of challenges, including: data accessibility; proper data documentation, or metadata; and adequate funding (Cox 245–246).

An additional thirteen articles were published in a special issue of *JAL*. Prudence Adler contributed a thoughtful introduction in which she effectively explained why libraries need to offer GIS services. Adler identified traditional library functions and convincingly argued the appropriateness of including GIS services as a part of those traditional functions (Adler 234). Boissé and Larsgaar (288) emphatically supported Adler's assertions regarding the need for libraries to offer GIS services. They also offered suggestions and recommendations for setting up various levels of GIS services, as well as tips for locating funding.

Over the next ten years, librarians made significant strides in providing GIS services to users. As more libraries began to address their users' GIS needs, articles about GIS in libraries proliferated. Some articles focused on digital preservation issues; others described how to build library GIS services "from scratch"; still others continued the discussion of the importance of including geospatial data resources as part of library services. All contributed to the continuing conversation of how to provide GIS services at academic libraries (Bethune, Lazorchak and Nagy; Cady et al.; Florance; Houser; Sweetkind-Singer, Larsgaard and Erwin).

The North Carolina Geospatial Data Archiving Project (NCGDAP) investigated data preservation constructs among state and local governments, through an agreement with the Library of Congress as part of the National Digital Information Infrastructure and Preservation Program (NDIIPP) (Morris 26). Among other important findings, the NCGDAP project revealed "A key component of spatial data infrastructure is the development and support of standards ... for data creation, data discovery and access, and metadata development" (Morris 36).

Another project funded through the Library of Congress's NDIIPP is the National Geospatial Data Archive (NGDA). This archive was established in 2004 as a joint project between the University of California at Santa Barbara and Stanford University. A goal of the partnership was to "provide long-term access to at-risk geospatial data" (Erwin and Sweetkind-Singer 6). High on the list of technical lessons learned from this project was the need to have "high quality, usable metadata" (20).

By the mid–2000s the concept of Enterprise Geographic Information Systems (EGIS) had emerged as a viable approach to offering GIS services (Witkowski, Rich, and Keating

78–79). An EGIS offers "common infrastructure to share geospatial data and associated services: and among other attributes, allows participants to share the added costs of providing these services" (Witkowski, Rich, and Keating 59) Witkowski, *et al.*, also found metadata to be a troublesome problem when sharing data across organizations.

History of INSIDE Idaho

In the mid–1990s, the University of Idaho Library was regularly receiving digital geospatial data on CD-ROMs as part of the Federal Depository Library Program. The data was housed on the first floor of the library, on shelves set aside for compact discs, inside the Government Documents Reading Room near the circulation desk. The room was often utilized for government documents research; most patrons, however, were unaware of the vast amount of digital geospatial data available on these CD-ROMS. These data included Topologically Integrated Geographic Encoding and Referencing (TIGER) data (census blocks, tracks, groups and other layers), aerial imagery, scanned topographic maps, and digital elevation models—all containing valuable information that was virtually inaccessible to library patrons. In other words, "[w]ithout a GIS ... a user could not manipulate these [TIGER] data files, thus there was no access to them..." (Adler 233). These data were cumbersome and very difficult to access when patrons did, on rare occasion, seek them out; the head of University of Idaho Library Government Documents at that time, Professor Lily Wai, was frustrated by the disconnect between the vast wealth of data available and the fact that she was not able to make these geospatial data available to patrons in an efficient manner. Wai's frustration, along with a strong desire to be involved in the ever-changing ways of disseminating government information, drove her to apply for funding opportunities to create what would become INSIDE Idaho <insideidaho.org>. Her vision for a resource at the UI Library—one that would support Internet GIS and bring together academic, governmental, tribal, public, and private-sector expertise on digital geospatial data — began to take shape. She knew early on that her idea for the clearinghouse would fill a void in the current services, because "[w]e were told many times that the site was extremely useful, even before [it was] officially available" (Wai).

Wai's vision, called Interactive Numeric and Spatial Information Data Engine for Idaho (INSIDE Idaho), became reality in the late 1990s out of combined funding from the Idaho State Board of Education, the University of Idaho Research Office, and a grant from the Institute of Museums and Libraries Services Leadership. Wai admits:

> I thought big, I knew the idea was good, so I dragged along and tried to write grants ... [eventually] the grant was approved in 1998. We got a big jump start, and that's how I began to look big and then have a bigger picture, a bigger vision ... that's how it got started; we had ... three quarter of a million dollars to start with for three years ... [but then] all [UI Colleges] wanted a piece of the pie. I wrote directly to [the University president] justifying how I would deserve this and explaining why the library would be the best place: we were neutral, we were non-confrontational, we provide service, and we're inclusive.

Wai's "big thinking" mirrored the thoughts of leading GIS librarians in the 1990s, who recognized the economic benefits of resource sharing within academic institutions:

> To the academe of the library within that enterprise, it may be helpful to rethink this concept as a circular process—how does the use of GIS influence the academic library, impact

the enterprise benefits, and finally broader social and research and development issues, given research and education's investments? All of these interactions redirect and influence the nature and types of services that academic libraries provide [Adler 234].

Wai was driven by a desire to help, improve and transform the way an academic library thought about and managed geospatial data generated through research: she identified an opportunity, secured financial support, and created a valuable resource. For this venture to be successful Wai knew she needed to take some risks (risk-taking lying at the heart of entrepreneurship) in order to seize the opportunity to initiate change in the way academic libraries provided services for geospatial data.

Assembling a Team

As work on the data clearinghouse began, Wai assembled a team that procured hardware and designed the software architecture. This team also launched a web site and began the process of migrating data from offline media to online servers. Data included digital elevation models, digital line graphs, digital orthophotography, and digital raster graphics published by the U.S. Geological Survey as well as TIGER products published by the U.S. Census Bureau.

As the initiative began to take shape in her mind, Wai contacted and secured the services of Fred Gifford, who was one of the early founders of NRIS (Natural Resource Information System), a digital geospatial clearinghouse hosted by the Montana State Library. NRIS was one of the earliest examples of the digital geospatial data clearinghouse concept and is quite well known throughout the geospatial community (both regionally and nationally) for its efficient and accessible format for the online data sharing. It is also one example of a clearinghouse that is located within a library environment, and thus provided an example of what the University of Idaho could accomplish along similar lines. Gifford brought with him a great deal of experience in making geospatial data available via the Internet.

Wai hired two additional team members: Bruce Godfrey, recent graduate of the University of Idaho Master's Program in Environmental Science and one of the authors of this chapter, as the GIS Specialist; and Professor Jeff Matthews of Lewis-Clark State College as a hardware consultant to build the physical system for the clearinghouse.

From its inception, the concept that would become INSIDE Idaho was interdisciplinary and multi-institutional; in this, it crossed numerous boundaries that had not previously been breached. Hal Anderson, a former administrator for the Idaho Department of Water Resources, describes this creative collaboration among multiple and disparate entities when he says "INSIDE Idaho is the realization of a long-held vision by the GIS user community to establish a geospatial data clearinghouse within the library environment. Increasing data access and providing a repository for GIS products leverages significant additional value from the investment made by Idaho government agencies in geographic data." INSIDE Idaho serves as an interesting crossroads of multiple users both within and outside of the university and makes available data from a number of university, state, and local agencies.

Overcoming Objections

There were, however, skeptics about the ambition and scope of this University of Idaho initiative from the beginning. There was, as Wai puts it, initial resistance from various sectors:

But I went ahead and got the startup money for INSIDE Idaho, and it dedicated three quarters of a million to the library to be the administrator. That was a big huge step to get started. [And] at first the acceptance from the state agencies was very lukewarm. We were viewed as one of those university short-lived projects that would go away in a couple years when funds run out. We had to show a lot of demonstrations.

The interconnectedness of the clearinghouse concept created some anxieties about where the data should be housed and who should house it. Wai notes that "[p]ersonal networking was critical to get faculty and students to buy into this project." For example, one particularly difficult misunderstanding about the initiative was the perception it was a "data grab" on the part of the University, an attempt to gather, house, and thus "own" a large amount of digital geospatial data associated with the State of Idaho. While this is an unfortunate misconception, it is not unusual, as Enterprise Geographic Information Systems architects have discovered: "Stakeholders [of such undertakings often] voiced concerns about potential problems with data access, ownership..." (Witkowski, Rich, and Keating 65).

Yet the distinction must be made between data and the documentation of those data. While the University of Idaho enjoys large bandwidth capacity, thus making sense to store some large datasets on INSIDE Idaho, the intent was never to house physical copies of all publishers' data, a costly and resource intensive feat, but instead to provide access to data through the retrieval of standardized documentation from partners' servers. This standardized documentation is a collection of reference questions consisting of the who, what, where, when, and why for a particular resource. These data might be housed in Boise, or Pocatello, or Coeur d'Alene, but INSIDE Idaho's servers in Moscow on the University of Idaho Campus would simply provide metadata — the documentation for the actual data, equivalent to the concept of an entry in a Works Cited Page of a research paper — and would allow patrons to link to those data directly. Team members viewed the initiative as a real-time interlibrary loan for digital geospatial data. At the same time, we were keenly aware that content used to populate the INSIDE Idaho catalog would be provided by professionals trained in GIS and not those trained as catalog librarians or those having backgrounds as information specialists. To this day poorly populated documentation continues to be a problem and one for which some potential solutions have been proposed but not yet implemented.

The concerns about "data grabbing," then, were never central ones for Wai or other project team members, simply because these distracted from what they saw as the heart of this project: to *open up* access to data for a wider range of users, not to co-opt data, steal it or take credit for it. INSIDE Idaho adds value to data by enabling access to it while requiring strict documentation, documentation that clearly contains provenance and credit for each data set. These high standards for data documentation serve as another example of the innovative, forward-thinking nature of the project.

The faculty, students, and administration of the University slowly began to see the great value and utility of this clearinghouse, as did the various state agencies in Idaho and INSIDE Idaho was officially designated as the state clearinghouse in May 2002 by the Idaho Geospatial Committee (IGC). This designation was the realization of a long-held vision by the GIS user community to establish a geospatial data clearinghouse within the library environment. The University of Idaho Library was recognized as an important collaborator in acquisition, integration, storage, discovery, dissemination, use, archiving and curation of Idaho's digital geospatial data.

The Importance of Metadata

The importance of uniform, accurate documentation is in some ways no different for digital geospatial data than any other library resources. Prior to INSIDE Idaho these data were difficult to find, and, if they were found, many times there was no metadata. "That's another thing I insisted we have for the clearinghouse," Wai argues: "Metadata from the first." Missing metadata makes quality research all but impossible, and "meaningful sharing of data is difficult when metadata are lacking or incomplete, when data are not well-organized..." (Witkowski, Rich, and Keating 74). Students and faculty interested in producing strong research need to know who the author(s) of a data set are, what type of data they are, and where, when, why and how those data were produced.

Geospatial metadata, however, do present some specific challenges for the library community. First and foremost, populating some elements of digital geospatial metadata needs to begin at the commencement of data creation; it should not wait until a research "product" is deposited into a data management system. Elements such as "Process Steps" (information about events that take place on a data set) are ones that need to be populated as they take place or important details will be lost. Due to such difficulties, it therefore becomes essential that librarians be involved with research projects as proposals are developed This requires that librarians establish and cultivate relationships with researchers to recognize the importance of creating authoritative documentation on their data. Librarians, as Co-Principal Investigators on data intensive research grants being pursued by faculty, can provide expertise in developing data management plans because they are committed to helping researchers manage, organize, describe, store, and share their research at all stages of the data lifecycle.

Wai and her team members knew the hurdles they faced when they decided that data would not be made accessible through INSIDE if it lacked metadata. To support these efforts, INSIDE was awarded geospatial metadata training grants through the National Spatial Data Infrastructure Cooperative Agreements Program (NSDI CAP) in 1999, 2002, 2004, and 2005. The grants funded INSIDE Idaho staff to conduct metadata workshops for academic educators, students, and GIS professionals across Idaho and surrounding states. These workshops focused on familiarizing participants with the FGDC-STD-001-1998 standard, on integrating metadata creation and maintenance into the work they did each day, and on teaching them methods for making their metadata records available to state and local data clearinghouses. Such strict metadata requirements have advanced the understanding of geospatial data documentation and helped promote its importance within the academic and professional GIS communities. Complete, detailed and accurate metadata also make the data more widely discoverable and more valuable since the methods used to create them are repeatable.

Metadata Cataloger

For years, Wai lobbied for a geospatial metadata cataloger for INSIDE Idaho, realizing that if her initiative depended on complete and accurate metadata, a professional metadata cataloger would be critical to the program's success. Wai also recognized early on that information professionals (i.e. catalog librarians) needed to be responsible for much of the geospatial metadata content. It takes the time, knowledge, and interest of an individual familiar with documentation standards to create a well-populated metadata record that will facilitate discovery and use. It is unrealistic to ask faculty, students, or GIS professionals to complete all the required elements of a geospatial metadata record on their own; an information professional should be available to provide some context and assistance. Library professionals regularly document the difficulty of missing metadata, and as Steven Morris put it:

> Metadata are frequently absent when data are acquired from local agencies, and to the extent that any metadata are received, it often needs to be enhanced in the following ways:
> - Synchronization to improve concurrence of the data with the metadata
> - Normalization to adhere to a standard structure to support further metadata processing, including metadata element extraction as part of repository processing
> - Remediation to fix major errors and to enhance the suitability of key access fields for use in catalog and discovery environments
>
> In practice, the inconsistent nature of structure and content in received metadata makes this added value work very expensive [36].

One reason behind the difficulties with metadata that Morris cites is that those creating data are often not the best ones to be creating standardized documentation on those data. INSIDE Idaho staff and Professor Wai recognized this, and eventually Professor Wai's original vision for uniform metadata and for a permanent geospatial metadata cataloger became reality. The University of Idaho Library, at the time of this writing, is preparing a position announcement for a geospatial metadata catalog librarian.

Contributions to Data Literacy

Promoting information literacy is a core mission of academic libraries and INSIDE Idaho contributes to a sub-segment of this mission: it promotes data literacy. The data provided through INSIDE are regularly used in the classroom for teaching, as well as outside the classroom for projects and research; the clearinghouse has made it easier for students and faculty to find and use geospatial data. The GIS Specialist for the University of Idaho Library regularly conducts classroom presentations about INSIDE Idaho, and these lectures have helped educate students and faculty alike; they become more knowledgeable consumers of geospatial data. In these class lectures and discussions, students and faculty also begin to realize that documentation is an important part of the data creation process and that time needs to be allocated to this effort. While discovery of data is important, INSIDE Idaho is also providing applications within which to use data and publishing web services which can be accessed in desktop and web-based user programs.

Funding Entrepreneurship Through Engagement

There have been a number of instances in which INSIDE Idaho's intrapreneurial, collaborative efforts have led to entrepreneurship in the form of searches for funding. As one example of the way data connects users throughout the rural northern Idaho community, a graduate student in the UI College of Natural Resources was conducting grizzly bear research and he needed accurate, up-to-date information on the location, type and age of roads for a large area in northern Idaho. At the time, acquiring the data entailed contacting local entities (primarily county governments) in the area of interest, acquiring their data either online or offline, and then merging it into a single data layer. The process was cumbersome and time-consuming. Frustration with the process led to a resourceful data integration effort. Through a cooperative agreement with the U.S. Geological Survey (USGS), a small amount of money was secured to develop a data integration method that could potentially be a model for populating *The National Map*. In the summer of 2006 a small group of GIS professionals gathered at the offices of the GIS Department of the Coeur d'Alene Tribe in Plummer, Idaho to simplify this effort which became known as the Idaho Collaborative Roads Project. The Coeur d'Alene Tribe began contacting local data producers across northern Idaho, and INSIDE Idaho began enhancing an existing application to retrieve and geoprocess data provided by the data stewards. An automated application, running each weekend, began retrieving and normalizing road data into a useable, regional layer. Through this cooperative effort it became apparent that, in some cases, the same features were being collected and maintained by multiple entities. This pilot project quickly demonstrated the need for this type of coordinated effort. Research and government business processes that require roads information in North Idaho became much easier as a result of these efforts ("Coeur d'Alene Tribe" 2007), and the effort has now been taken state-wide for multiple data sets. While this entrepreneurial effort has been funded by government entities, it has elevated the discussion about whether it could be beneficial to form public-private partnerships to further facilitate data integration across jurisdictions.

Further funding of entrepreneurship has occurred with INSIDE Idaho, as well. In 2004, the State of Idaho facilitated the collaborative procurement of 1-meter natural color orthoimagery for the State. INSIDE was the primary point of distribution for these data. At that time, most users wanted a physical copy of either a portion or all of the 850 GB of data, even though INSIDE was able to make the data available as a web service. Web services provide users the ability to directly link to data from desktop GIS applications and allow developers to develop web browser-based and mobile applications against INSIDE Idaho web services, allowing them to create their own maps and web pages to advance information and knowledge discovery. Web services were then just beginning to be used within desktop GIS, and for many users, accessing the data across networks was too slow. Five years later in 2009, the State of Idaho received 1-meter natural color + IR orthoimagery for Idaho and web services has become the preferred method of access to these large datasets. Recognizing the need and promoting it to agencies to acquire funding allowed this entrepreneurial project to continue to enhance services. For three years, funding to make these web services available was secured through the Idaho Imagery Consortium — a consortium made up of sovereign nations, federal government agencies, state agencies, regional planning organizations, county government agencies, city government agencies, higher education institutions and private companies. For over a year, the web services associated with these data have been the most heavily accessed services available through INSIDE Idaho.

Community Outreach

The ability to connect all types of users both within and outside of the university setting is one of the most rewarding aspects of working with INSIDE Idaho. Every day we help connect people to data that has significant impact on their lives and their work. INSIDE Idaho receives many requests for information from Idaho citizens who are not connected to the university's academic community. In some cases these people are unaware or unable to easily access needed information. Over the years INSIDE Idaho has received calls from farmers who were just beginning to use GIS and wanting to acquire satellite imagery and other climate data in order to outline their fields and track the crops they plant. Project members received a call from a gentleman living in an extremely rural, remote community in north-central Idaho who was being sued over a water right; he asked for help locating historic imagery of his land to see if there was an indication that the spring had existed there for many years. This man relied on the data INSIDE could provide him to help make his case. When INSIDE Idaho indexed aerial photos of rural Benewah County from the 1930's and 1940's, team members were surprised and delighted that they could provide these photographs to a local author who was researching a book on the history of logging in that area. These are just some of the ways that the work at the University of Idaho Library helps the INSIDE project reach out and connect with citizens of rural Idaho.

The resources available through INSIDE Idaho, then, are valuable for the faculty, students and staff of the University as well as the far-flung farmers, ranchers, poets, and essayists who live in the woods and mountains far away from the university campuses. Many academic libraries are associated with metropolitan areas, but the University of Idaho is in the heart of a wheat farming, rural area — serving mostly other rural areas of the state. Because of the University of Idaho's remote location and its land-grant status, it has strong ties to its rural roots, and embraces its role as information provider to those who have less access to information. With these constituents in mind we seek ways to make more information and data available through the Internet. It is frequently impractical for rural families to drive 30, 40, 50 or more miles to an academic library for information. However, through databases like INSIDE Idaho, as well as other digital collections, we are able to bring some of the best library resources to rural Idaho residents in their homes. INSIDE Idaho helps connect its rural users in more ways than one: it connects patrons to credible and in-depth digital geospatial data; and also connects them with a community of library faculty and staff who are engaged in the curious, sometimes frustrating, but always rewarding pursuit of knowledge.

INSIDE has also aided the discovery of data by enabling documentation to be indexed by web crawlers, making it discoverable through popular search engines and opening up avenues of access for a wider number of site users. Additionally, INSIDE has participated in National Spatial Data Infrastructure (NSDI) activities exposing data to Geospatial One-Stop <www.geodata.gov>. Participation in Geospatial One-Stop increases accessibility because many geospatial data consumers use this web site to discover data holdings in states across the U.S.

The past several years have seen INSIDE Idaho become an integral part of the geospatial data management capabilities of the University of Idaho and the State of Idaho. In 2007, for example, the National Science Foundation (NSF) Cyberinfrastructure Council published "Cyberinfrastructure Vision for 21st Century Discovery." The document lays out a vision to guide NSF's future investment in cyberinfrastructure. Cyberinfrastructure is composed of complementary areas of computing systems, data, information resources, networking, digitally enabled-sensors, instruments, virtual organizations, and observatories, along with an interoperable suite of software services and tools. This technology is complemented by the interdisciplinary teams of professionals that are responsible for its development, deployment and its use in transformative approaches to scientific and engineering discovery and learning. The vision also includes attention to the educational and workforce initiatives necessary for both the creation and effective use of cyberinfrastructure (National Science

Foundation). INSIDE Idaho has evolved into an important component of Idaho's geospatial cyberinfrastructure ecosystem. The relationships developed over the years with faculty resulted in funding for INSIDE Idaho being included in several large geospatial data-intensive grant proposals. In one important example of this collaboration, in early 2011 new NSF requirements for Data Management Plans went into effect, and the NSF now requires all proposals to include plans for data management and sharing of the products of research. The Data Management Plan is reviewed as part of the intellectual merit or broader impacts of the proposal. The University of Idaho recognizes the need for an institutional commitment to long-term data management to be competitive for grant funding. The University is addressing the Data Management Plan requirement by establishing relationships that will lead toward the creation of The Northwest Knowledge Network (NKN); INSIDE Idaho will likely become the geospatial arm of the Northwest Knowledge Network, carrying out the important work of providing access to and a context within which to use geospatial data generated by researchers at the University of Idaho.

In many ways, though, INSIDE Idaho anticipated formal Data Management Plans such as these by a number of years. INSIDE established a framework for managing geospatial data generated though research; the mechanisms it provides to facilitate data transfer, documentation, discovery, visualization and use of geospatial data have greatly benefited faculty and students. Professor Wai points out:

> [Our project has made it] easier to access geodata for ... research projects, and for undergraduate and graduate students, [it has provided] proper background training for their future professional careers because they already know how to use these online resources to find GIS data. [The only] drawback [for students] could be finding that not every state provides a site like we do for this kind of data. Faculty members have a much easier way of teaching their students because they have a readily available data to use to do demonstrations.

Moscow Community "Green Map"

Online, interactive mapping helps build consensus in addition to communicating information. Another INSIDE project called "Green Map," an online map funded through a sustainability grant that identifies "green features" of the campus and Moscow community, such as bicycle parking areas, community gardens, and recreation areas, serves as a good example of this. Moscow, Idaho, location of the University of Idaho, is a community well-known for its support of sustainable practices. The town has a regionally popular local farmer's market, an extensive network of bike paths and recycling bins, and a much-loved local food co-op. The University of Idaho is a land-grant university with close ties to the town of Moscow, and in keeping with the community's values, the university's faculty, staff, and students are always looking for new ways to promote sustainability on campus. The term "sustainability" applies to many aspects of campus life: waste management, transportation, consumer behavior, climate change, and the management of resources such as water and energy. Lack of information, however, is one of the obstacles in promoting sustainability practices. Many university students and new Moscow residents would not know where to find a recycling bin or a bicycle rack. They don't know the history of a grove of trees on campus. Green features located in the city or on campus were not shown on any consolidated map or entered in any GIS database (Godfrey).

The University of Idaho Sustainability Center was created in 2006 as part of a campus and statewide initiative to move toward better sustainability practices and increase campus awareness of the importance of sustainability initiatives. In the fall of 2007, the University of Idaho Sustainability Center made a request for proposals that would advance campus sustainability. Not only has the Sustainability Center funded student-led projects to increase sustainable behaviors and awareness, but the center also supports faculty and staff research endeavors that work toward these green goals (Godfrey).

The University of Idaho's INSIDE Idaho Green Map project received one of these highly sought-after sustainability grants. INSIDE Idaho staff pooled their local knowledge and expertise to create an online Green Map of the University of Idaho Moscow campus and surrounding community. The Green Map, located online at <greenmap.uidaho.edu>, highlights 157 "green" features of the campus and community such as parks (both dog and human), arboreta, bus routes, recycling venues, bicycle parking, and environmentally friendly buildings such as the University of Idaho power plant.

After registering with <greenmap.org>, INSIDE project staff members created the green points geodatabase feature class using GIS information from University of Idaho Facilities Services and the City of Moscow. Initial green features were limited to public places primarily on the university campus, and data was organized by already-established greenmap.org categories. To begin creating the actual green points that would show up on the Green Map, INSIDE Idaho staff began with a simple and commonly recognized type of green site on campus: walkway recycling bins (Godfrey). We continued to build the map — with the help of university facilities service personnel — by adding campus and city features for bicycle parking racks, special trees, public forest and natural areas, composting areas, solar energy sites, cleaned-up/rebuilt sites, water recycling, and eco club/organizations. All features were digitized on-screen using 2006 orthoimagery of the University of Idaho campus and the City of Moscow.

Simplicity was the major consideration in designing the geodatabase and Web application. As INSIDE Idaho staff moved through the planning and implementation phase of the Green Map, they kept the intended user in mind. They envisioned Green Map users as average members of the public: students and citizens who were interested in the green features of the community and campus but were not necessarily familiar with GIS. Consequently, INSIDE Idaho staff kept the Web interface as clean, colorful, and uncomplicated as possible while still providing detailed historical information about sustainable sites in the area (Godfrey). Project staff implemented map tips to allow Green Map users to display information when hovering over a green icon, and map users can access short descriptions of each green feature or more detailed information about green sites. For example, a short description might tell what kind of recycling options are available at a site. For a local park, such as Moscow, Idaho's East City Park, the map provides information about the Renaissance Fair that takes place there each May.

As another innovative example of community outreach, INSIDE Idaho staff created a map option on "Green Map" that allows any user to mark a point on the map and submit a comment about an existing or new green feature of the town or the university campus. With this map option, members of the community who have a green roof or an organic vegetable garden from which they sell produce can submit their green practice or green site to project staff at any time. This functionality creates an interactive and collaborative picture of Moscow and the University of Idaho's sustainability practices. This is a powerful way to communicate, and one that fosters community mapping. Users can shape the content of the map. This type of mapping has recently become popular and is generally referred to as "community mapping" or "crowdsource-mapping."

With the creation of the Green Map, university students and citizens of Moscow have an organized way to learn about the sustainability practices of their campus and their community. But in addition to making this information quickly available, the Green Map lets long-time citizens, university staff, faculty, and students see their surroundings in a new way. The campus contains many hidden green stories that Green Map brings to light. For example, in 1911 United States President Theodore Roosevelt planted the first tree in the university's Presidential Grove. The grove includes trees planted by former President William Howard Taft and Eleanor Roosevelt and has been visited by numerous dignitaries. The Liberty Grove, planted on Memorial Day in 1919, commemorates the 32 University of Idaho students who lost their lives in World War I. With the creation of the Green Map, the community now has a repository for these and other important pieces of local green history that will be accessible for years to come. "With today's focus on environmental efficiency, the green map project allows us to identify and recognize local contributors to that goal," said Ed Flathers, INSIDE Idaho's lead developer at the time (qtd. in Godfrey). In keeping with the collaborative nature of the project, Green Map's creators envision that undergraduate and/or graduate students will have a role in maintaining the point feature class and expanding the functionality of the Green Map Web application. Long-term maintenance of the site will also hinge on the relationship between INSIDE Idaho and the University of Idaho Facilities Services because Green Map staff will need to be notified when campus green sites are changed.

INSIDE Idaho's Role in Census 2000 Redistricting

INSIDE Idaho frequently demonstrates flexibility and innovation in the services it provides, these being two key attributes of a truly entrepreneurial venture. For example, the clearinghouse often provides support to state government, and was called upon in the fall of 1999 to enlarge the scope of its services to better meet the needs of Idaho citizens in a particularly interesting way. Lily Wai was approached by the Senior Budget and Policy Analyst at the Idaho State Legislative Office, Ross Bordon, who wanted to integrate libraries more directly in the 2001 Census redistricting (Wai, Watson, and Woods). The idea was "to provide ten Idaho libraries around Idaho with computer workstations, GIS redistricting software, and data to allow citizens to draw their own legislative and/or congressional districts. Patrons could then submit their plans to the Idaho Redistricting Commission for consideration" (Wai, Watson, and Woods). The Idaho Legislature approved $400,000 for hardware, software, and training for library representatives who would assist patrons. The final plan included having INSIDE Idaho host the geospatial data and associated Census PL 94-171 redistricting data which patrons could use to draw districts. Team members created a web site on INSIDE Idaho was created which contained resources to support the State of Idaho Redistricting 2001 process, and when the process concluded, citizens submitted a total of 66 legislative plans and 15 congressional plans.

Ten years later, Ross Borden's vision of having "interactive, ubiquitous, Internet-based redistricting capability for the next go-round" is becoming a reality (qtd. in Wai, Watson, and Woods). The 2011 Idaho Redistricting Commission will be using Maptitude for Redistricting software from Caliper Corporation, allowing any interested Idaho citizen to draw legislative and congressional districts from their own computer (Idaho State Legislature). Libraries around Idaho, and INSIDE Idaho, played a pivotal role for the State of Idaho to migrate from a paper process to a digital process (Wai, Watson, and Woods).

Benefits

With the proliferation of spatially-aware applications on mobile and desktop computing devices, it is evident that geographic information is increasingly being recognized as a vital component of the information technology a modern society requires to operate efficiently. INSIDE Idaho plays a critical role in facilitating the discovery and use of such geospatial data, data that may be used to analyze and solve critical issues surrounding economic development, the demands of growth, emergency and natural resource management to name a few. INSIDE also provides a platform for geospatial data and metadata management as is evident from the emerging requirement of data management plans by the National Science Foundation and other funding agencies. INSIDE Idaho will continue to explore intrapreneurial and entrepreneurial opportunities as the boundaries of geospatial data and metadata management within academia and beyond continue to be pushed.

Lessons Learned

In an environment such as ours, where INSIDE Idaho has carved out a niche for itself to provide services that our library patrons needed, it seems like we can never spend enough time on marketing and promotion. In many cases, we have had to battle for funding and part of those battles amount to consistently promoting ourselves and the valuable services we provide. Now that the effort has evolved from a project to a program and been well-established for over 10 years, our need for the "marketing and promotion" of our value has subsided somewhat, but funding stability continues to pose challenges.

From the outset, those involved with INSIDE Idaho sought to be inclusive in its planning and implementation. Cultivating relationships within academia and with the constituents we serve is critical and will continue to be so. To effectively manage and curate digital geospatial data takes the expertise of people with diverse skill-sets and interests. It draws on the disciplines of library science, computer science, information management and others. It is important, therefore, that INSIDE Idaho staff continue our transdisciplinary collaborations and that we pursue professional development opportunities as they become available in order to stay relevant and well-informed.

Metadata is a critical component of geospatial data and arguably too little effort and too few resources are allocated to its creation and maintenance. Metadata isn't a form to fill out, but rather a collection of answered questions that adds authority to the data. The documentation produced by the geospatial community has to improve and libraries can play an important role in making this happen. As the program has advanced and the years have passed we have come to realize the great value of our push for quality metadata.

Finally, the line between providing services as a resource of land-grant research library and being entrepreneurial is not always clear. It's more of a transition zone riddled with funding opportunities and challenges that can result in losing sight of our mission and vision if we are not careful. Without question being creative — entrepreneurial — with funding sources for this effort has been necessary from the start. The bigger trick, however, has been maintaining the consistency and certainty that funding opportunities are pursued which are in line with the mission and vision of the program. There have been times when funding opportunities have arisen that fall outside the scope of what INSIDE Idaho does. The temptation to pursue those funding opportunities and then trying to bend the deliverables to fit the original vision of INSIDE can be problematic. Fortunately INSIDE Idaho has avoided "scope creep" and remains true to its vision and mission.

Into the Future

INSIDE has evolved into a cornerstone for the University of Idaho and the State of Idaho as it figures prominently in academic and state government data management plans. Once data and metadata began to flow regularly to INSIDE Idaho, library patrons from both within and outside the university community began to rely on the services provided by this digital geospatial data clearinghouse. By 2002 the Idaho Geospatial Committee had recognized INSIDE Idaho as the Geospatial Data Clearinghouse for Idaho, and a formal agreement was signed with the State of Idaho honoring this recognition. In 2002 INSIDE Idaho received a Special Achievements in GIS Award from ESRI ("Special Achievement in GIS"). Recently, INSIDE Idaho has undergone extensive hardware and software upgrades as numerous geospatial data are made discoverable and accessible through this vital resource. The web site alone sees approximately 50,000 hits per day, proving the central role it has secured in the university, state, and broader geospatial community.

INSIDE Idaho's intrapreneurial and entrepreneurial efforts have resulted in a resource that is not only valuable to students and faculty of the University of Idaho, but to geospatial data users world-wide. This innovative resource, developed because of the industrious effort and unwavering determination of Professor Wai, has evolved into a cornerstone of the geospatial data management efforts of the University of Idaho and the State of Idaho. It has created opportunities for new research activities and enhanced existing ones by forging relationships across the institution and state where they did not previously exist.

Works Cited

Adler, Prudence S. "Special Issue of Geographic Information Systems (GIS) and Academic Libraries: An Introduction." *The Journal of Academic Librarianship* 21.4 (1995): 233–235. Print.

Bethune, Alec, Butch Lazorchak and Zsolt Nagy. "GeoMAPP: A Geospatial Multistate Archive and Preservation Partnership." *Journal of Map & Geography Libraries* 6.1 (2010): 45–56. Print.

Boissé, Joseph A. and Mary Larsgaard. "GIS in Academic Libraries: A Managerial Perspective." *The Journal of Academic Librarianship* 21.4 (1995): 288–291. Print.

Cady, Carol, William H. Walters, William Olsen, Eric Williams-Bergen and Bart Harloe. "Geographic Information Services in the Undergraduate College: Organizational Models and Alternatives." *Cartographica* 43.4 (2008): 239–255. Print.

"Coeur d'Alene Tribe Works with county Governments on the Idaho Collaborative Roads Project." *Federal GIS.Connections*. ESRI. Summer 2007. Web. 6 April 2011. <www.esri.com/federal>.

Cox, Allan B. "An Overview to Geographic Information Systems." *The Journal of Academic Librarianship* 21.4 (1995): 237–249. Print.

Erwin, Tracey and Julie Sweetkind-Singer. "The National Geospatial Digital Archive: A Collaborative Project to Archive Geospatial Data." *Journal of Map & Geography Libraries* 6.1 (2010): 6–25. Print.

Florance, Patrick. "GIS Collection Development within an Academic Library." *Library Trends* 55.2 (2006): 222–235. Print.

Geospatial One Stop. n.p., n.d. Web. 6 April 2011. <http://gox2.geodata.gov/wps/portal/gos>

Godfrey, Bruce. "Showcasing Sustainability." *ArcUser.* ESRI. Summer 2008. Web. 6 April 2011. <http://www.esri.com/news/arcuser/1008/greenmap.html>

Houser, Rhonda. "Building a Library GIS Service from the Ground Up." *Library Trends,* 55.2 (2006): 315–326. Print.

Idaho State Legislature Redistricting Commission. n.pag., n.d. Web. 6 April 2011. <http://www.legisla ture.idaho.gov/redistricting/redistricting.htm>

McGlamery, Patrick. "Identifying Issues and Concerns: The University of Connecticuts's MAGIC — A Case Study." *Information Technology and Libraries* 14.2 (1995): 116–121. Print.

Morris, Steven P. "The North Carolina Geospatial Data Archiving Project; Challenges and Initial Out-comes." *Journal of Map & Geography Libraries* 6.1 (2010): 26–44. Print.

National Science Foundation Cyberinfrastructure Council. "NSF 07–28, Cyberinfrastructure Vision for 21st Century Discovery." National Science Foundation. 10 July 2008. Web. 6 April 2011. <http://www. nsf.gov/pubs/2007/nsf0728/index/jsp>

"Special Achievement in GIS." User Conference 2002. *ESRI.* Web. 6 April 2011. <http://events.esri. com/uc/2002/sag/list/detail.cfm?SID=47>

Sweetkind-Singer, Julie, Mary Lynette Larsgaard and Tracey Erwin. "Digital Preservation of Geospatial Data." *Library Trends* 55.2 (2006): 304–314. Print.

Wai, Lily, Elaine Watson, and Stephen Woods. "Idaho Librarians' Role in Census Redistricting." *The Idaho Librarian.* Idaho Library Association, August 2003. Web. 6 April 2011. <http://www.idaholibra ries.org/newidaholibrarian/200308/REDISTRICTING.htm>

Wai, Lily. Personal interview. 18 Jan. 2011.

Witkowski, Marc S., Paul M. Rich and Gordon N. Keating. "Metrics of Success for Enterprise Geographic Information Systems (EGIS)." *Journal of Map & Geography Libraries* 4.1 (2007): 59–82. Print.

5 — The Library as Partner

Sustaining Relevance in a Collaborative, Student-Focused Technology Center

CHRISTY GROVES *and* HEATHER LAMBERT

Introduction

The Digital Media Studio at Middle Tennessee State University's Walker Library is an innovative new service that connects students to technology and library services and offers them the opportunity to work with one another in a media-rich environment. Debbie Schachter notes that innovation is a hallmark of information professionals.

> Innovation is a key feature of today's information professional and of our information center and libraries. The ability to provide new and innovate services to our customers, when and where they want or need them is one of the most significant contributions to our organization. Much of this innovation and change is being driven by technology [32].

Creating new spaces that integrate technology with a high level of service and connecting students to media-rich resources is innovative. Innovation is a characteristic of an entrepreneur, as the entrepreneur is defined as a "creative innovator" (Scott). The Digital Media Studio was envisioned to not only meet student demand for a collaborative media-rich center, but also to serve as a place to experiment with service models that can be applied to the Library as a whole. The Studio was designed to firmly establish the Library as a partner with students who may no longer possess a traditional view of library services. The focus on innovation, risk taking, and user-focused management decisions make the Digital Media Studio an entrepreneurial venture. Additionally, the Studio was created and implemented with limited staffing and resources, which serve as further examples of entrepreneurship. Economists define entrepreneurship as "making judgmental decisions about the use and coordination of scare resources" (Scott). The new work flows, user-focused management styles, and synchronization of human and capital resources solidify the Digital Media Studio as an entrepreneurial project.

The Digital Media Studio fits neatly into the six characteristics of an entrepreneur as outlined by Stephen Fadel (23):

1. Idea or opportunity: The Digital Media Studio was created to meet an expressed need of Middle Tennessee State University students.
2. Innovation: The Digital Media Studio management structure empowers student workers to develop policies and procedures. Library faculty and students work as equals and teach each other technology skills. Student patrons provide constant feedback that directs everything the Studio implements and how it provides service.

3. Plan: Through extensive project planning and early development of comprehensive procedures, the Digital Media Studio was created with limited resources. Institutionalized benchmarks, with a focus on relevancy, help ensure that the Studio remains current in the long term.

4. Research: The Digital Media Studio focuses on gathering entrepreneurial information versus organizational information. In other words, what is gathered in the Studio applies to the operation and improvement of the services offered. Traditional institutional benchmarks are secondary.

5. Creativity: Several features of the Digital Media Studio showcase creativity, from the way it is supervised to the collaborative atmosphere and options for student involvement with one another and with Studio staff.

6. Funding: The Digital Media Studio was made a reality with a small budget. It was designed with purposeful funding opportunities to ensure future growth. Grant development is a part of the annual Studio to-do list, and many new partnerships are under development.

The Studio's sustainability is dependent upon ongoing entrepreneurial planning. Entrepreneurial characteristics are found in Walker Library's Studio personnel, who are firmly committed to connecting to users in need of help, technology, and multi-media *at* their point of need.

Literature Review

In the early 1990s, the widespread availability of the Internet challenged libraries to rethink their role in information access, research, and learning. However, the library was not doomed by technology (MacWhinnie 242). Libraries quickly recognized the importance of creating integrated centers for research, teaching, and learning with a strong digital focus (Bailey 277). Successful, vital libraries continued to redefine their roles in fulfilling the many goals of both users and higher education and understood the increasing importance of how electronic resources continue to affect collections, services, and staffing (Cowgill 433). In fact, the library literature is replete with success stories heralding libraries with outstanding Information Commons implementations. Typically, Information Commons on academic campuses combine computers and technology from Information Technology units (IT) and research support from the Library. For nearly twenty years, libraries have been partnering with campus constituents covering campus networking, information technology, computer support, etc. to effectively plan and successfully launch Information Commons learning spaces in their buildings, and the results have ensured libraries' continued relevance to universities' educational mission. Cowgill states that successful libraries' commitment to an Information Commons and the resulting high level of student use significantly raises the profile of a library on campus (437).

Financial conditions are normally the impetus for campus IT and libraries to come together for an Information Commons. Each unit brings its skills to the table, and sometimes, little cross training of personnel is required. If cross training is needed, however, this may stretch personnel outside their skill base and/or comfort zones. The provision of necessary training, as well as patience and understanding of personnel, must come from both party's leadership. Thus, the true key to success for these partnerships is each party's "shared commitment to effective management" (McKinzie 340). If executed with sound leadership, each unit can effectively work through librarian and IT professional differences to ensure the Commons' success. Further, it is important that these partnerships be part of an overall organizational environment that encourages, shepherds, and nurtures evolutionary change (Bailey 277). Massis notes that these mergers can be spearheaded from either IT or the library, a clear indication that both parties are often willing to overcome differences and work together (88). Sullivan reiterates that successful collaborations get beyond the subtle barriers created by their professional roles (134). To help ensure this success, there must be a clear intent on the part of the library administration and IT to not only create, but also to support and maintain these services (Bailey 277).

However, other authors maintain that while these mergers can be successful, social and cultural differences between the two professions (IT and librarianship) pose obstacles (Oden 19). Crocket et al. point out that the library culture tends to emphasize services and are focused on quality customer service, whereas, IT personnel are typically less concerned about the end user (182). Thus, it is critical that the "gap between the library and computing cultures ... must be bridged for the sake of the staff" in both IT and the library (Crockett 182). While these obstacles can certainly be overcome, Stahl suggests that "it is a terrible mistake to make a library into an IT operation or vice versa" (A39).

McKinzie states that local campus conditions truly drive the creation of successful IT and library mergers (342). At some institutions, administrative support on either side may be lacking. At others, funding may be lacking. At still others, there may be cultural circumstances preventing the merger. Again, the library literature showcases both successes and failures of IT/library mergers. It provides tips and suggestions for fostering successful partnerships and describes the great benefits of IT and libraries working closely together. Everyone agrees, certainly, that the ultimate goal of institutions is to provide users with the technology, tools, research, and learning spaces necessary to succeed academically. After all, these services are part of an institution's efforts to cater to millennial students' learning styles. Most of these students come to the library to use the computers (Gardner 415). Gardner and Eng state that libraries should capitalize on this need and provide services that maintain their relevance (415).

It is clear from the literature that Information Commons have been created for users to work with one another toward their mutual academic success. In many instances, librarians' traditional role has been to provide research support and high quality customer service. IT professionals' traditional role has been to provide sound technology assistance. Rarely does a Commons staff person reverse these roles, due to obvious professional and training differences.

The Library at Middle Tennessee State University (MTSU) chose to forge ahead independently on the Digital Media Studio project, due to local conditions on campus including budget cuts and staff shortages. The Digital Media Studio staff provide both research *and* in-depth technological assistance independent of campus IT. Further, the Digital Media Studio offers specialized software and hardware not found anywhere else on campus, making it a unique service point for MTSU students, faculty, and staff. The following paragraphs will describe the Studio's implementation and marketing; its success due to high quality customer service and ongoing collaboration with students; and tips for maintaining necessary relevance. Lastly, the authors will showcase how the process solidified the Library's good position on campus and created stronger internal staff relationships and workflow.

Background

Middle Tennessee State University has grown in recent years to become the premier undergraduate institution in middle Tennessee. Most recently the campus has focused on creating new and growing existing graduate programs in an effort to elevate the University's Carnegie status. The President of MTSU continues to demonstrate financial commitment and support of both undergraduate and graduate research and is supportive of the James E. Walker Library.

Walker Library is the main university library and is centrally located on campus. The building is only ten years old. The benefits of the newer building include over sixty group study rooms, space for collection growth, and a central atrium. Service points are located around the atrium on the ground floor. There are five large multipurpose rooms which are open to future development. There are, however, design limitations. When the building was planned over fifteen years ago there was no emphasis on mobile computing, collaborative study, and flexible work spaces. Walker Library has a traditional feel with staff work spaces isolated from the general population. Service points, while located on the same floor, are built for specific functions like security or circulation, and adapting them to other tasks is difficult. The book stacks are located in the back of the building, and the services and staff are located in the front of the building. Closed doors separate study areas and service desks. Carrels and heavy wood furniture fill the floors. Signage is very formal and uses library jargon. The result is a beautiful, centrally located building with a formal feel and institutionally focused workflows.

Despite the building's physical limitations, staff work hard to create a culture of user help through intense outreach, roaming, online help, library instruction, and social media. As a result, Walker Library enjoys an average monthly gate count of 520,000 persons. Most students commute to campus, and they seek out the Library for quiet study, computing, and research assistance. Although the Library has experienced the typical reduction in circulation of physical materials, there is still a high occurrence of research questions from students. Over 17,000 questions are answered annually. So, while the Library is still quite busy, it is clear that change in the physical space is needed to better serve millennial students and improve staff access to users at their point of need.

In 2008, the Library began high level planning for an Information Commons, and the Information Commons committee was formed. The Commons project addressed the importance of flexible, collaborative learning spaces as well as technology and services to enrich student learning. In 2009, Walker Library made the short list of projects eligible for capital funds. However, the project was tabled indefinitely because that academic year's un-invested capital project money was used to fill budget gaps.

The Library's Information Commons committee decided to break the project into segments to help secure funding. The piecemeal approach allowed the Library to look at smaller fundraising and grant options. The most discrete phase of the project was the creation of a multimedia lab which was to be called the Digital Media Studio. The Studio was envisioned as a location where students could work with high end, media rich computers and receive personalized service and training.

Challenge and Opportunity

An opportunity to fund the Digital Media Studio came in spring 2010. The Library had unexpected year-end money. The outgoing and interim deans agreed to apply the funds to the Studio phase of the larger Information Commons project. They felt it would have an immediate impact and show campus administration that the Library's large open spaces were not available for use by groups outside the Library. There was also the possibility that the University would receive Tennessee Recovery Act money, and the Library wanted to show that it had a project in the pipeline and could use the money quickly and wisely if it became available.

The money earmarked for this project ($45,000) had to be encumbered or put on a purchase order or contract by the end of Fiscal Year 2009/2010. Additional campus funding opportunities were available to the Library for the Studio phase of the project, and Library administration decided to apply for this financial support as well.

Funding for student-focused campus technology is derived from the Middle Tennessee State University technology access fee (TAF) which is assessed to each student, and the Library is able to annually apply via detailed project proposals for money from these revenues. A campus wide technology committee reviews the project proposals and assigns dollar amounts to projects deemed beneficial to student technology on campus. This MTSU TAF committee also controls the placement, staffing, and operation of all campus computer labs. The Library learned its proposal to fund the Studio's computers and printers was accepted in spring of 2010. Since the Library's TAF allocation ($45,000) had to be spent by the end of the FY 2009/10, the Library had a tight implementation timeline. However, the Library administration and personnel were firmly committed to this project, and it was given the green light with the following parameters: sixteen weeks to encumber the funds, a change of Library leadership to an interim dean, a small budget, a fixed physical space, and no new staff. In house support consisted of three Systems staff responsible for the maintenance of an existing three hundred forty computers, fifty laptops, and printing (MTSU offers free printing to all students). The interim dean created a Digital Media Studio planning committee consisting of two original Information Commons committee members, three additional User Services employees, the head of the Microtext Department, and one Systems staff member. The Emerging Technologies Librarian headed the committee.

Against the Grain: Saying No to Institutional Partnerships

The Studio planning committee first had to decide if they could undertake the scope of the project. Similar to many universities nationwide, local conditions at MTSU were significantly impacted by state budget issues in FY 2009/10. Because Walker Library has fewer faculty and staff than libraries at peer institutions, the MTSU climate would seem ripe for an institutional partnership. In fact, the limited budget, tight restrictions on the Systems' staff time, and general apprehension regarding the nature of the project made partnering with campus IT appealing. Initial partnership discussions with campus IT revealed that the Library would be at a disadvantage for the Digital Media Studio project. IT would control Library space needs in areas outside the Studio space, student staffing rates and ratios, and the implementation time line. When the Studio planning committee spoke with them, campus IT expressed their interest in taking over the Library's computers as a large generic computer lab. However, the above mentioned restrictions along with twenty four hour Library access, limited late night staffing control, and diminished personal service were considered unfavorable by the Library. The Digital Media Studio planning committee was unwilling to compromise on these issues of service and training because the Studio space was intended to be a collaborative, studio environment rather than a passive lab.

Instead of adhering to the parameters identified by the potential IT partnership, a conscious choice was made to implement the Digital Media Studio project internally without assistance from IT. The Library would be able to control the parameters of the Studio (who uses it, who runs it, etc.) and take overall ownership of its success. Additionally, MTSU's IT department continues to be extremely busy with other equally important campus projects, such as the implementation of more master classrooms to accommodate the technological needs of a growing student body. There was also some resistance from the Library, particularly from the internal Systems staff. As noted, the Library Systems department is understaffed. A media-rich Studio naturally would mean an increased technical component and a larger demand on their limited time. Additionally, the Library and the majority of campus are PC based. The Studio planned to introduce a dozen Macs. Systems staff had limited experience with Macs. Addressing Systems' concerns was a major part of the planning process.

Digital Media Studio Mission: What We Are and Who We Serve

In order for any technology-driven service to be successful, it must be meet the needs of its clientele; in the Library's case, the Middle Tennessee State University student body. What begins as a cutting-edge facility can quickly become obsolete, full of outdated software, untrained staff, restrictive hours, and old hardware. The graveyard of Microtext, designed a decade earlier, was a physical reminder to Walker Library personnel that a plan for continual change was needed.

Relevant, as defined by the Oxford Dictionary of English, is to be "closely connected or appropriate to the matter at hand" (Matthews). In order for the Digital Media Studio services, technology, and equipment to be related to student needs long term, it was of primary importance to construct mechanisms that regularly update Studio offerings based on expressed student needs. The Digital Media Studio was purposely built to absorb and respond to the changing needs of users. The challenge was making sure that Digital Media Studio staff could easily identify these needs for technology, services, and equipment and reactively make changes to the Studio offerings in response.

Flexibility was built into the Studio purchasing timelines, feedback schedules, training and staff models, and evaluation procedures. For students and faculty this means that the Digital Media Studio will always have the best and most current equipment, with trained staff and resources available to help them when and how they want it. Since Walker Library is the main library for the MTSU community, it was important to everyone that this space, despite being media-rich, be open to all students.

From the inception of the Digital Media Studio design, the planning committee identified high quality service as a key component and built it into the Studio mission. It was also agreed that the Studio would be relevant and would serve all students regardless of experience or major. To reach to the next step, the planning committee created a formal planning document, starting with a mission statement.

Creating a mission statement can be a challenging exercise, but it was critical that the Library do so for a number of reasons. First, the mission statement helped the Library achieve consensus across departments as the Digital Media Studio was developed. Second, the statement served as an accounting tool throughout the development process to ensure the Library was not backing away from services offered when they seemed too overwhelming to implement. Third, it helped in guiding the design of the space, the ordering of materials (hardware, software, etc.), and the creation of Digital Media Studio policies and procedures. In sum, the mission statement helped to craft a vibrant service point that could reach across barriers (technology, customer service, and research) so that students could learn how to create a presentation or media-rich project that reflects today's world. The goal was for the Digital Media Studio to provide users with the tools and applications that will benefit them as they embark on their careers, i.e., something beyond traditional PowerPoint.

Digital Media Studio's Mission Statement

The Digital Media Studio provides knowledgeable staff that offer direction to appropriate resources, train users on the use of media applications, and collaborate on projects. We offer the latest digital tools and unique facilities to enable the exploration of rich digital media for learning experiences, collaboration, and creative expression. The Digital Media Studio is a welcoming, collaborate space for users of all abilities, disciplines, levels, and interests ["Mission Statement"].

To fulfill the Library's mission of launching the Digital Media Studio, it was critical to have knowledgeable staff in the planning phase. The Library capitalized on the expertise of the Emerging Technologies Librarian and heavy input from student workers to guide choices. Because some of the librarians were concerned that they would have to learn a lot of unfamiliar software applications in a short time, the Library's challenge was to stay true to the mission statement but not overwhelm vital human resources. It was also critical that the Digital Media Studio offer the latest digital tools and unique facilities. Doing so required a major commitment by the Library to stay current on software and hardware. Thanks to support from Library administration as well as the MTSU technology access fee funding, the Library will be able to maintain necessary Digital Media Studio updates. Lastly, the Studio's physical layout was planned with the user in mind, so seating was purposefully designed for student collaboration.

Always Have a Plan

The Library's ability to launch the Digital Media Studio by the established deadline was due to effective project management. Because the Library had few staff resources and a small budget, it was critical that good project management strategies were utilized to balance the Studio's integration into the Library. The planning committee's manager ensured that things proceeded according to the timeline, and a team-oriented approach was utilized to execute tasks.

There were serious challenges to making the Digital Media Studio a reality. Staff had to be retrained, job descriptions had to be changed and/or created, new technologies had to be introduced, and an existing space had to be modified. Members of the planning committee actively participated in committee activities in addition to their primary responsibilities in the Library. Because it would be run with limited staff and little work could be done on the fly, it was imperative to create a tight, comprehensive framework for the Digital Media Studio.

Project management was critical, but even more important was building in flexibility. This cannot be overemphasized. The project management phase was like building a spine. Solid components like training, policies, and service guidelines were created to frame the entire project, but each section was independent. This meant a lot of pre-planning but resulted in a framework that moves and adapts over time. Breaking the project into manageable chunks kept the planning committee from getting overwhelmed or bogged down in details. During the planning phase, judgments were made based on the best information available at the time, but the Studio planning committee also built in reflection and periods of self-evaluation so that adjustments could be made. Now it is easy to make targeted adjustments to the Studio's daily operations.

The Digital Media Studio project was managed with as little paper as possible. The planning committee used Google Docs to store agendas, timelines, sketches, procedures, and other planning documents. This meant that whenever a committee member had the time, he/she could access and work on his/her sections. It also meant that everyone in the group could see what had and had not been done; this promoted accountability. Every committee member was assigned to one or two project portions depending on their specialty. Each section had a modified Gantt chart, task list, and timeline provided by the committee head. Examples of the sections include marketing, staff training, equipment, policies, and infrastructure. Weekly planning committee meetings were broken into two parts. The first part was a progress report by each committee member on his/her section; the second part was an open time to make group decisions or approve completed projects. The agenda was sent out two days prior, so meetings moved quickly and were highly productive. The project manager kept all the tasks organized by following a master Gantt chart and modifying the timeline as needed. A summary of the weekly Studio planning committee meeting minutes was published for the entire Library to read.

The Studio planning committee developed several tactics to help non-committee Library staff feel included in the project and become excited about it. To communicate with staff, Library-wide updates on the project's progress were provided weekly via emails and flyers in staff elevators, and feedback was actively solicited. To encourage the Studio staff to be vested in the project, they were given robust training on hardware and software applications as well as the Studio's policies and procedures. During the planning phase, staff training was carefully organized, and a two pronged approach was developed. First was a comprehensive overview of the Studio. Digital Media Studio employees were not expected to be experts at the beginning, but it was important that staff be familiar with the equipment and aware of the procedures. To this end, the Studio planning committee scheduled a two day boot camp open to all staff in the Library. At the boot camp (which was kept to three hours a day), staff worked with a partner to complete three projects: edit a picture, create a webpage, and create a short movie. They could use open source or commercial software on the Mac or PC. Staff responded well to the training. If they wanted to work in the Digital Media Studio, they also had to take a refresher course on Microtext and a Lynda.com introduction to Macs. Student workers, or Studio Assistants, had a checklist of trainings that was self-directed and included meeting with select Digital Media Studio staff for policy and procedure training as well as self-guided Lynda.com tutorials on software.

For reference, two documents were created; for long-term training, a quick consultation notebook on policies and procedures was created and kept at the Digital Media Studio help desk; for more in-depth questions, an electronic training manual, which student workers have the ability to edit, was created. In addition, a separate drive on Digital Media Studio staff computers with common Digital Media Studio documents was established. These documents were updated regularly with pertinent policies, procedures, and additions.

The Digital Media Studio manager communicated with Studio personnel regularly, sending weekly email messages and sharing documents. These included training tips and tricks for using the software more effectively, most of which the staff learned while assisting users. Some librarians expressed anxiety about working in the Digital Media Studio because of all the new hardware and software. Setting realistic expectations for staff and student assistants regarding the amount of technical knowledge necessary helped alleviate a lot of this anxiety. Further, no one was required to work at the Digital Media Studio and several opted out. Those who did so expressed their lack of comfort, even after training, with the complex technical questions asked by Digital Media Studio users. The Studio planning committee recognized at the implementation stage that the Library's personnel possess a wide range of technical expertise and incorporated this into planning some flexibility to accommodate varying levels of participation. Regardless, the Digital Media Studio definitely created new opportunities for staff to become part of the service model.

Another example of flexibility centered on feedback. The planning committee established three review periods at two, four, and six months. An agenda for these reviews was also created. Recommendations for feedback and frequency were made as well as what type of institutional and service based statistics to collect.

Going Green: Repurposing Outdated Space

Prior to the Digital Media Studio, this service point's footprint was the Microtext unit. Both Library administration and the MTSU TAF committee observed that the Microtext area had lost relevance and value. A great deal of the unit's physical space was occupied by outdated, unused, and, frequently, out-of-order equipment, resulting in significant wasted space. Further, there were very few interactions with patrons in this space, other than to quickly demonstrate how to use the microfilm equipment. Because of general patron aversion to microfilm and equipment that was typically out of order, this service point was not a customer service, customer friendly area. It is important to note that in the process of transforming the Microtext space, the Library did not remove the collection. Rather, the broken and unnecessary equipment was recycled or sold and replaced with three state-of-the-art digital microform machines which fulfilled the needs of Microtext users. Additionally, the qualified Microtext staff for the Digital Media Studio were retained, repurposed, and trained in the new technologies offered at the Studio. Rather than eliminating an existing, albeit under-utilized service, the Library added value to Microtext by integrating it into the renovated service point.

To create a more informal feeling in the space, LED task lighting was added, and a casual logo for the Studio was created. The logo, made into a window cling, was put on the glass of the existing Microtext area and is viewable from the Library's atrium. Because the sign is removable, it will be easy to modify if the look or role of the Studio changes.

One Stop Shop: A Snapshot of the Digital Media Studio

The Digital Media Studio was created to provide service to students. The Studio planning committee conducted environmental scans of services offered (and not offered) elsewhere on campus to determine what features would be prudent to include in the Studio. Microtext and research help were included from the beginning, expanding the services already offered in the space. Hardware and software assistance for the multimedia applications offered in the Digital Media Studio were added, including one-on-one technical coach appointments, small group training, and classroom collaborations. Also added was the circulation of hardware: headphones, pen tablets, card readers, and other relevant multimedia peripherals. Students appreciate the color printer and laminating machine added, along with a project finishing station, which includes equipment and office supplies for finalizing hard copy multimedia printouts. Here, students can mount pictures to posters, cut, bind, hole punch, and otherwise put the finishing touches on their projects. This is an inexpensive feature that adds a lot of value for students. Assistance in the Digital Media Studio is available from a visible stationary service point and via roving student assistants.

The computers in the Digital Media Studio are high-end Dell PCs and Macs. The Digital Media Studio offers half proprietary and half open source software. As noted, Systems staff were unfamiliar with Macs, so the interim dean sent one Systems staff member to get Mac certification. Student workers with Mac experience from Systems and the Studio worked together to give advice on, update, and manage the Macs. This was a large compromise for Systems but has yielded good results. Studio Assistants now dump drives and install screen savers, saving the Systems team time.

Open source applications provide more flexibility in Studio offerings, but have a trade-off regarding upkeep and the known commodity factor. Open source applications require frequent updates, sometimes weekly, so a considerable amount of staff time and attention are required to support them. In order to work within Systems' staffing limitations, the Studio sends an annual schedule of programs, and the software is loaded monthly. Students are invited to give feedback on the new software, and this combined with usage statistics determines if the program stays in the Studio. Programs are only removed twice a year, again to accommodate Systems.

Proprietary software does not normally require a significant commitment to maintenance and updates, but such applications can be expensive, particularly for academic libraries. Because Studio software is ordered annually and the rest of the Library's software is updated every four years, the interim dean compromised and software costs are not funded solely from Systems' budget. Ultimately, the Library wanted to provide users with as many options as possible, but due to funding limitations, a mix was provided.

The Digital Media Studio consists of twenty four computer stations with scanners. The scanners have film negative attachments. There are five open source PC's and five open source Macs. Ten Macs have CS5 with iLife and iWork. Five PC's have CS4. Displayed on each row of computers is a QR code which lists the software available on that range. This information is also available via the Digital Media Studio website.

There are also four Microtext machines with internet access and recording software. The Studio help desk has three computers: one Mac and two PC's, each facing a different part of the Studio.

Students are allowed to bring in external equipment like video cameras, laptops, external drives, and keyboards. There is currently no tape to digital conversion equipment in the Digital Media Studio because that service is offered (and rarely used) in a lab near the Library.

The software offerings in the Digital Media Studio include movie making, DVD creation, picture editing, presentation, art/drawing, web design, file conversion, screen capture, and audio manipulation. To help with the training on these complex applications, all computers have access to Lynda.com training tutorials and an extensive list of webinars, online tutorials, and the Library's e-book collection.

Faculty have a variety of options when working with the Studio. They can arrange class training on a particular piece of software for an assignment or on copyright information with links to royalty free and copyright friendly resources. Faculty also send over class assignments ahead of time and encourage their students come in to the Studio on their own. Professors have begun assigning two-part projects which require students to attend both traditional library instruction and seek assistance from Digital Media Studio staff on creating a multimedia presentation. Additionally, professors send students to the Studio to conduct Microtext research on a variety of topics from headlines on their birthday, and old advertisements and art covers, to civil rights, and historical media coverage of important events.

Students may come to the Studio to do simple word processing or color printing. They may come in to edit a movie or create a more robust PowerPoint presentation. They can get assistance by asking at the desk, speaking with a roaming student, using books or online training resources, or scheduling a forty five minute technical coach appointment. Studio Assistants are trained to be as inclusive and responsive as possible. The Assistants help with research, training on software, and answering basic technical questions on saving, printing, exporting projects, and editing photos. When a Studio Assistant hears a question repeatedly from multiple users, they do a Studio blog post about it for future reference. Studio Assistants will not complete the assignment for students, nor will they allow students to violate copyright with images or music. Rather, they direct the students to the Studio's copyright friendly media resource list. Students are encouraged to work in groups, and the Studio stations are large enough for two chairs. Extra chairs are placed around the Studio for easy access. There are also several round tables for students to work together in larger groups.

Studio Assistants' number one priority in the Digital Media Studio is to interact and engage with students. At first, staff were concerned that constant roaming in the Studio would be viewed by users as an annoyance, but peer to peer interactions have proven very popular, as evidenced by gathered feedback. Studio Assistants walk the entire Studio area every thirty minutes. They make eye contact or talk to as many students as possible. The area is not designated a quiet zone, so quiet conversation is not a distraction. The rapport that Studio Assistants have built with students has been a remarkable benefit. When students are asked to move computers to allow another to access specialized software, there is rarely a complaint. Students will often ask questions of the Studio Assistants after he/she has walked around a few times, and when surveys or questionnaires are handed out, students fill them out without hesitation.

Don't Hide a Great Thing!

The Digital Media Studio is an outstanding example of the Library integrating technology assistance with research assistance, resulting in a full service multimedia experience.

It was important to effectively market this service to users, and a marketing plan plays a large role in communicating with users about the breadth of services provided. One major event was planned for each demographic: library personnel, campus faculty, and students. Traditional shotgun marketing, press releases, blog posts, signage, and direct mailing, were also employed. A communications plan was created for each demographic. For example, social media, email, and campus signage were used to reach students while faculty received hand mailed updates.

Communicating with Patrons

The Walker Library Emerging Technologies Librarian collaborated with the Library's Marketing Specialist to ensure advertisement of the Digital Media Studio was organized, timely, and relevant for library users and the MTSU community. Marketing was executed from a number of important and innovative angles to ensure the Library reached users where *they* are. It was important to demonstrate from the outset that the Digital Media Studio provides technology to support a wide array of users and abilities, so a marketing and promotion campaign was designed that was not too tech heavy.

Together, the Emerging Technologies Librarian and Marketing Specialist implemented a campaign using a variety of media to promote Studio services; these included blogs, word of mouth, the campus newspaper, news flyers in the Library restrooms, handouts, library instruction, etc. In addition, social media was employed to reach students who were active on those sites. The Emerging Technologies Librarian and Marketing Specialist continue to promote the Digital Media Studio on Facebook™, foursquare™, the Library blog, and the Library's Twitter™ account.

In addition, QR codes and fork signs were created and distributed at strategic locations throughout the campus; these QR codes connected to the Digital Media Studio website. A Library-wide student worker flyer was distributed to over two hundred student employees announcing the Studio. Flyers called the *Studio Notes* were hung on each work station in the Digital Media Studio; they showcased new software and hardware in the Studio as they were introduced. In addition, Digital Media Studio student workers designed screen savers for the Digital Media Studio computer stations which contain up-to-date information. The campus newspaper wrote a feature article about the Digital Media Studio, and the Library teamed up with the MTSU Mass Communications department to produce press releases and TV interviews.

The Digital Media Studio marketing strategy culminated in a campus-wide Library Amazing Race that students could enter to win a Kindle. The Amazing Race included a "stop" at the Digital Media Studio to ensure users would become well acquainted with this new service point. All of these marketing tactics were crafted during the Studio's inception and planning phase to ensure inclusion of both internal staff and as well as external users.

Generating Staff Buzz (and the Unanticipated Benefits)

Communicating with Library Staff

When undertaking any major library project, especially as a solo effort, it is critical to create institutional support and staff buy-in by keeping staff informed of important changes at every phase of the project. Houghton-Jan states that without early involvement of the people affected by change "we set ourselves up for failure" (27). Houghton-Jan reiterates that nothing destroys a project more quickly than gossip and rumors spurred by lack of information (28). To avoid this, a communication plan for Library staff was designed. Weekly updates were published in the Library's well established staff newsletter. Staff enthusiasm was also generated through the fall 2010 Staff Kickoff. Fall Kickoff was a day of staff play and recognition. Tours of the Studio and other Library areas were intermixed with bingo, book truck races, food, and paper airplane launches. Fall Kickoff created positive feelings and allowed employees up close access to the new service point in a relaxed environment.

The communication plan resulted in unsolicited requests from personnel outside the Digital Media Studio's department seeking regular involvement in staffing the Studio help desk. Staff from Collection Management, Circulation, Systems, and Periodicals have worked in the Studio. This was somewhat unexpected, but has resulted in even more cross-departmental partnerships throughout the Library. Another benefit was that staff had the opportunity to learn new skills as they used the Digital Media Studio both for professional and personal projects. It was apparent that they felt comfortable with this Library-generated initiative and even had a sense of ownership of the Digital Media Studio. Library staff continue to use the Studio to transfer home movies, scan photos, do school projects, and some have even used Microtext for their research.

COMMUNICATING WITH FACULTY AND BUILDING AWARENESS

The Faculty is typically viewed as the most important constituent of academic libraries: faculty members create assignments that require students to utilize library resources and assist in helping select materials. In short, it is critical to ensure that all faculty are aware of new services, features, and events in the Library. Sometimes, however, librarians have heard faculty members say that there isn't anything for them in the library anymore, though this tends to vary by subject discipline and institution. Schonfeld and Housewright authored ITHAKA S+R's faculty survey 2009 report, which shows some troublesome findings about university faculty and library use. The report findings show that "basic scholarly information use practices have shifted rapidly in recent years, and as a result, the academic library is increasingly being dis-intermediated from the discovery process" (Schonfeld 4). The report goes on to state that, sadly, faculty no longer consult directly with the library as the first stop in their research process and that their perceived importance of the library as a starting point for research has declined (Schonfeld 6). The survey further reveals that faculty seek teaching and research support and suggests unique opportunities for libraries to develop campus relationships with them (Schonfeld 16). Thus, the Digital Media Studio planning committee recognized the importance of helping to educate faculty about what was offered and encourage them to utilize the Digital Media Studio. Showcasing and marketing the new Studio was a way to achieve three important things:

1. Reintroduce faculty to the Library. What better way to create interest than by highlighting a new and exciting service/feature?
2. Reach faculty who have discounted the Library as irrelevant and give them a new reason to come in. Some of these disciplines include theatre, documentary history, electronic communication, interior design, aviation, etc.
3. Solidify the image of the Library as a "doer"—not just a partner.

To generate excitement, the Library's Emerging Technologies Librarian and Marketing Specialist developed and heavily advertised a Digital Media Studio Open House. The open house actually took place a few months after the Digital Media Studio opened, so modifications could be made before it was showcased widely. Because MTSU faculty do not widely adopt social media, "Save the Date" cards were hand mailed to them, followed by invitations. These invitations were followed by a campus wide email reminder. The campus and student newspapers and television stations also covered the open house, which generated a lot of interest from faculty after the event. To highlight services offered and pinpoint exactly how the Digital Media Studio could collaborate with faculty, a restaurant style menu was created. Faculty could read a summary of services and then check the boxes that interested them. These menus could be turned in at the event or submitted at a later date. Some of the traditional, standard services that the Library has always offered, like library instruction, were looked at with renewed interest when framed in the a la carte menu. Over twenty service requests from faculty came from the menu. Menus were also sent to department heads to distribute to faculty and staff. A sharp spike in Studio attendance, over fifteen percent in one month, followed the open house as faculty started sending students to the Library. Many students stated that they didn't know the Studio existed having missed the earlier marketing efforts. This further solidifies the importance of faculty in reaching students.

After the open house, some campus departmental labs asked to partner with the Digital Media Studio to host their specialized software. These departments offered to pay for the programs, but wanted the Digital Media Studio's dedicated staff assistance as well as broader availability due to extended Library hours. Faculty groups and departments also contacted the Digital Media Studio to work with or speak to department faculty en mass about service and collaboration opportunities. Subsequently, the Emerging Technologies Librarian developed better resources on copyright and a procedure for sending class groups to work on projects or homework at the Digital Media Studio.

Don't Forget About the Students

Student empowerment is as important as faculty engagement. Because so many student workers are employed at the Library and in the Digital Media Studio, it was obvious immediately that these student workers could play an important role in generating excitement on campus. Satisfied, empowered, and well trained student employees can contribute to the sustained success and relevance of a new enterprise on campus. Thus, the Studio Assistants were empowered as partners in the Library's evolution as a student centered technology, research, and multimedia service point. Some examples of this innovative empowerment of the Digital Media Studio student employees include:

1. Students created their own blog posts on tips and tricks they learned. They train each other.
2. Students updated the Digital Media Studio training procedures based on what they learned.
3. One outstanding student was promoted to team leader; this student now provides weekly online updates to the other Digital Media Studio students.
4. Because of the students' expertise, librarians and student assistants were peers in the Digital Media Studio. They had their own roles and they worked well

together. Not only did the students train each other, they often trained the librarians!

5. All Library student workers were asked friend the Library on Facebook and follow Library blogs. The Library gained two hundred friends in two weeks.

6. Feedback from student workers was used to revise their training program. Initially, a self-guided checklist was used for training; students found this too intense and not very helpful. With their help the training program was redesigned into smaller modules. Not everyone completed every module. Since three staff were at the Studio desk, the training requirements were divided among them. Following the redesign, a student may take four hours of tutorials on Illustrator only, while another will do iMovie. When working together at the desk they observe and train each other when helping students.

7. Staffing the Digital Media Studio desk was a contentious issue as well. Unlike many libraries the Walker Library Reference Desk had never used student workers before, so librarians had no experience working with students behind the desk; in contrast, in Microtext there had never been a librarian before, so students there had no experience reporting to a librarian. Each group felt the other one was in the way. The Studio Assistants' and librarians' feedback clearly showed the need to modify the Digital Media Studio staffing model. A team approach was instituted which included a Library staff member, Digital Media Studio grad student, or reference librarian as the team leader on any given shift. All team members were equal, and everyone had clear responsibilities. Librarians were educated about what the students could and could not do, and the students were empowered to see the value of the librarians and staff members. This team approach forced students, staff, and librarians to talk to each other and work together. The Studio model could also be implemented throughout the Library. The Studio model was not a hierarchical management structure. Instead it was based solely on what provided the best service for users. The Digital Media Studio help desk teams were composed of peers with different specialties. This led to some remarkable collaborative experiences and helped to improve service to users.

8. Student workers were encouraged to email suggestions for new resources, policies, and workflows, and they were publicly recognized for contributing.

Remaining Connected: The Circle of Life

Active and ongoing feedback is critical for sustained relevance. Part of the Digital Media Studio planning and implementation incorporated mechanisms to gather user feedback. Staff time was limited, so extensive qualitative studies could not be conducted. Instead, questions were divided into two categories: what the planning committee had to know, and what they would like to know. The following were required:

1. User satisfaction level
2. Users' wish lists
3. Staff observation of Digital Media Studio staffing model success
4. User and staff observed problems
5. What was being used and when

The following were not required, but helpful for further planning:

1. How do users interact with the Library?
2. How can Digital Media Studio staffing and service models be applied to other areas of the Library?
3. Are students utilizing the Digital Media Studio space effectively?
4. How can the Library be even more collaborative with users?

Feedback gathering tools were created that could be utilized regardless of staffing issues. For concerns, problems, and wish list items, verbal feedback (solicited and unsolicited) was recorded in staff notes at the Digital Media Studio desk. Feedback forms were provided for users to fill out both online and in person.

A sixty-second survey was utilized each semester for one week that asked the planning committee's "have to know" questions. The survey ran for a week or until ten percent of the door count was received. Both times the survey was done, over three hundred results were received in three days. Quick polls were created with PollDaddy.com regarding new software, and students were encouraged to share their comments regarding software they wanted but which wasn't offered. A link to this survey was on every desk top. Students were very receptive and often requested software and books. Quick turnaround ensured that students felt their requests were taken seriously, and the Studio has received over two hundred requests to date. A "No Log" was created to track what types of inquiries from users resulted in a "No" answer from staff. The "No Log" highlighted services and features students were asking for that weren't provided at the Studio. On the flip side, the "No Log" was used as a training tool to determine when/if staff were telling users "no" regarding Digital Media Studio services provided and features offered. To have an idea what applications students were using and how often, the LabStats software tracking program was utilized. The data from the logs, the software tracking, and the surveys were entered into a monthly chronicle that was shared with Library administration as well as with Digital Media Studio personnel. Also, a librarian and student worker survey was constructed and utilized to identify issues with training and staffing models, as well as furniture configuration.

The tactics described above were step one of an ongoing process. Survey results were tallied and top problems identified. A follow up survey with a list of possible solutions to each problem was created and distributed. The results of this survey were also tallied, and the Digital Media Studio implemented the most popular solution. Generally, solutions were implemented within one month of the survey to showcase commitment to listening to user feedback. Responding to suggestions is another way to instill trust and a sense of partnership with users and empower staff. For example, the first round staff survey demonstrated that the training process was too long and not very helpful. Three possible solutions were presented, and the winning solution was taken to a group of student workers who talked through the issue with the Studio planning committee. The training program was reworked and will be implemented in the near future. A student survey revealed that during finals there was a need to ration time on specialty computer stations. A sign up period was announced and will be instituted in the next finals session. The relative down time during the summer months is the most conducive time to build the survey instruments for the following year, making it is easier to implement them during the busy semesters.

Early Success

Within six months of its launch, the Digital Media Studio was helping about two thousand students each month. At this point, even as a secondary reference service point, over three hundred reference questions were being answered each month. Microtext initially experienced a bump in popularity, and at the six month point, approximately three hundred Microtext questions were being answered monthly. The Digital Media Studio's individualized tech appointments grew to about twelve per month. As a result of the Open House and marketing campaign, over twenty Digital Media Studio tours have been conducted at the six month point. The Library has received numerous positive customer service comment cards. Digital Media Studio personnel have made six software changes and have more planned. Digital Media Studio training and staffing models have been refined and popular equipment has been upgraded. A procedure has been developed for managing the busy times during the semester when students experience long waits to use computers. The Digital Media Studio has team leaders and Studio Assistants who conduct one on one technology help appointments. Studio Assistants contribute heavily to the staff blog, recording questions they get at the desk. Digital Media Studio personnel collaborate with anyone — users of all abilities and levels of interest. Assistance is provided to faculty and students from all disciplines. Those who know nothing about multimedia applications are welcome. Sometimes users start simply by printing a document, but when they see the other services offered, they come back later for help with complex projects. This did not happen by accident, because, as stated above, the Digital Media Studio is firmly interconnected with users. Additionally, other departments on campus are now seeking to collaborate with the Studio on software access. They see the value of the Library's traditional services in a light that they did not think applied to them. Further, campus faculty are asking that multimedia software demos and copyright tips be incorporated into traditional database demonstrations.

Standing Strong

The Digital Media Studio project demonstrated that the Library can internally create services of value to other campus departments and present new resources to the campus community. This gives the Library more control over future partnerships in a way that outsourcing tends to marginalize. The Studio is an example of how to ensure the sustained importance of the Library as a centerpiece of the MTSU campus. It shows that the Library can be a valuable and evolving partner to MTSU students, faculty, and staff. Middle Tennessee State University's accelerated growth has significantly impacted classroom space and faculty office space on campus. Both are at a premium at MTSU, but due to the Studio's success, the Library has tangible and statistical evidence to demonstrate that this space is spoken for, and that other spaces in the Library will also be repurposed to address student need.

The Studio in house project has demonstrated that the Library can undertake future solo initiatives successfully, having gained both confidence and practical knowledge from this project. The Studio project also strengthened internal Library departmental relationships as employees who previously did not work together now have a firm awareness, understanding, and appreciation of one another.

Summing Up: Lessons Learned

The Digital Media Studio project required a significant commitment to internal flexibility and adaptability. The planning committee had to understand that this project would undergo constant change whether it consisted of minor adjustments due to staff or stakeholder abilities or more substantial overhauls if monetary support fell through. While the Library is experiencing the rewards of an effective service point, there were significant challenges along the way. Even though the planning committee actively solicited user input and feedback, there were still some surprises. The slow pace at which users adjusted to open source software applications was unexpected. The planning committee decided to retain half of the open source applications in the Digital Media Studio despite the slow adoption and acceptance because the financial benefits and flexibility outweigh the constant upkeep of open source applications. Plans are underway to launch an aggressive faculty education campaign to further their awareness of open source and to encourage them to use open source for student class projects.

Another surprise was the volume of Studio user traffic in the evenings. In response to these issues, Library administration is working to sequester funding for more proprietary software and permanent full time night personnel. Users' demands for more training were anticipated, and the Digital Media Studio will soon launch a dedicated four-seat training room which will also double as a green screen interview and Skype/webinar space. Campus faculty will continue to be included in training and orientation sessions to services and technologies offered in the Digital Media Studio. In sum, the Digital Media Studio project resulted in several important lessons:

1. It is critical to have a clear vision of the proposed service as well as how it will enhance what is already provided.
2. Both users and staff must be included in all phases of the project management, launch, training, and continual evolution.
3. Feedback is critical to sustained relevance and success. When soliciting feedback it is important to be ready to respond to *all*— the bad, the good, and the unusual.
4. Do not start a program or service if there is no time to sustain it.
5. Do not underestimate the power of student workers and dedicated library users. They have a vested interest in ensuring relevance, and they are not afraid to share their opinions and ideas which are valid and useful!
6. Copyright, copyright, copyright. This challenge has been met by providing up to date copyright-free media resources, as well as copyright information sessions for staff and faculty. Copyright compliance is showcased in library training and instruction sessions.

Libraries have proven themselves flexible, forward thinking, and responsive to user expectations and needs. Sometimes, due to campus environments and funding, it is necessary to forge ahead alone. The Digital Media Studio is an outstanding example of entrepreneurial thinking and showcases what can be achieved through sound project management, perseverance, and collaboration with the Library's most important constituents— users.

Works Cited

Bailey, Russell, and Barbara Tierney. "Information Commons Redux: Concept, Evolution, and Transcending the Tragedy of the Commons." *The Journal of Academic Librarianship.* 28.5 (2002): 277–286. Print.

Cowgill, Allison, Joan Beam and Lindsay Wess. "Implementing an Information Commons in a University Library." *The Journal of Academic Librarianship.* 27.6 (2001): 432–439. Print.

Crockett, Charlotte, Sarah McDaniel and Melanie Remy. "Integrating Services in the Information Commons." *Library Administration and Management.* 16.4 (2002): 181–186. Print.

Fadel, Stephen. "Resources to Encourage Entrepreneurial Creativity and Innovation." *Online.* 34.1 (2010): 22–24, 26–30. Print.

Garner, Susan and Susanna Eng. "What Students Want: Generation Y and the Changing Function of the Academic Library." *Libraries and the Academy.* 5.3 (2005): 405–420. Web.

Houghton-Jan, Sarah. "Staff Participation and Buy-In." *Library Technology Reports.* 43.2 (2007): 26–28. Print.

MacWhinnie, Laurie A. "The Information Commons: The Academic Library of the Future." *Libraries and the Academy.* 3.2 (2003): 241–257. Web.

Massis, Bruce. "Academic Libraries and Information Technology." *New Library World* 112.1/2 (2011): 86–89. Print.

Matthews, P.H. "relevant." *The Concise Oxford Dictionary of Linguistics.* Oxford University Press (2007). *Oxford Reference Online.* Web. 29 July 2011.

McKinzie, Steve. "Library and IT Mergers: How Successful Are They?" *Reference Services Review* 35.3 (2007): 340–343. Print.

"Mission Statement." *Digital Media Studio Planning Document* 2010. Print.

Oden, Robert A. Jr., et al. "Merging Library and Computing Services at Kenyon College: A Progress Report." *Educause Quarterly* 4 (2001): 19. Print.

Schachter, Debbie. "A Resurgence in Our Relevance." *Information Outlook* 15.1 (2011): 32. Print.

Schonfeld, Roger C., and Ross Housewright. *Faculty Survey 2009: Key Strategic Insights for Libraries, Publishers, and Societies* ITHAKA S+R, 7 April 2010. Web. 6 June 2011.

Scott, John and Marshall, Gordon. "entrepreneur." *A Dictionary of Sociology.* Oxford University Press (2009). *Oxford Reference Online.* Web. 29 July 2011.

Stahl, Bil. "IT-Library Mergers Require Good Leaders (Letters to the Editor)." *The Chronicle of Higher Education (The Chronicle Review)* 54.3 (2008): A39. Print.

Sullivan, Rebecca. "Common Knowledge: Learning Spaces in Academic Libraries." *College and Undergraduate Libraries* 17 (2010): 130–148. Print.

Section III
Entrepreneurs

6 — An Interview with Mary Ellen Bates

Amy Archambault

Mary Ellen Bates is the entrepreneur behind the thriving and sought-after information business, Bates Information Services (BatesInfo.com). While she has made a successful business out of being a business researcher and analyst, her passion for what she does is so contagious that she started another successful venture — coaching. In addition to working with clients and mentoring, she speaks at conferences and workshops, has written six books, and writes two monthly columns, one for ONLINE, and until recently for EContent. With boundless energy, she also is quite active in AIIP (Association of Independent Information Professionals).

Mary Ellen, a dynamic power house, makes running her business look both easy and fun! Her passion and drive for what she does is obvious and impressive. Anyone who is thinking of going into business for themselves might want to consider copying these pages and pasting them to the bathroom mirror. In short, this may be your new manifesto.

The interview began before her speaking engagement at Wake Forest University's Conference for Entrepreneurial Librarians in early March 2011.

AA — What was your "ah-ha" moment where you said, "Hey, I can do this on my own and I really want to!"?

MEB — Honestly, it was one too many sales people coming up to me when I was working at the MCI library, saying "I want anything and everything on these 10 sales prospects." They were saying "don't-make-me-think, just retrieve material." In that context, I couldn't find out what would be most helpful to the requestor; it was really kind of an order. I felt like I should ask if they wanted a shake with that order. I realized it wasn't fun doing the same thing over and over again.

The other reason I launched my business is that I can't manage people to save my soul. No, seriously! Unfortunately it provided a negative incentive to start a business, which I tell people isn't a great idea, but the fact that none of my employees jumped me in a dark alley and just knifed me is a miracle. It would have been totally justified! I just can't manage people. I didn't see a career path that was going to work, one that was going to continue to be challenging and that didn't require managing people.

I could see myself as a reference librarian but that just didn't feel challenging enough for the long run. I guess I have a short attention span. So I saw the booth for the Association of Independent Information Professionals <AIIP.org> at an SLA conference and I talked to someone there. I also knew someone who had been independent for a long time. I had seen people who had started businesses, and had seen that they were normal people! I think that was when I realized that I had to do something different. Starting my business was the scariest thing I had done; I'm amazed that I did it, in retrospect. I was such a leap into the void! And now I can't imagine doing anything else. I just love it. It definitely was the best career move I've ever made.

AA — What were some of your early successes and failures moving into that venture, because I'm sure you had ups and downs?

MEB — I have to do something 100%. I can't just "try" something. I have to go whole hog, in order to evaluate whether it's going to work or not. Then I would evaluate the results. If it didn't work, I stop and do something else. While coaching other info-entre-preneurs, I see that one of the hardest things for people to learn is to just look at what they're doing and say, "Even though this is the most comfortable way to do this, it's not effective, so I have to do something else." Looking at myself in the third person helped me not make some of the stupid mistakes I could have made by just realizing that I wasn't getting any return for my efforts.

One of the best things I did was to allow my last employer to be my first client, at a reduced hourly rate. While I wasn't making as much, I had a steady source of revenue. Then the second best thing I did was fire my former employer after a year. Well, they didn't feel like they were being fired. I just raised my rates to the price I wanted to charge, and they decided they couldn't keep using me. The gig gave me a cushion for my first year, but it was holding me back from doing more lucrative work. Within two weeks of letting that client go, I had three other big clients come in.

AA — What were some of the other things you learned, specifically with budgeting?

MEB — First, people freak out about the thought of spending money and having a budget, and I sometimes wonder if that is an excuse for failing. For instance, my house-hold pays $1500 a month on health insurance. It's a lot of money, and it's just part of the overhead. It's my job to figure out how to design my business so I've got $1500 a month to go out for health insurance. It's not an impediment unless you allow it be an impediment. It doesn't cost that much to start the business and it doesn't cost that much to run it. It's mainly just being smart about your money and realizing that you have to have a service that is worth charging a lot of money for, because otherwise you'll never be profitable.

If you offer a lower-end service, and charge less, you'll never build your revenue. Don't worry about whether your current clients will pay your fee; just focus on building a service that is so valuable that people will pay you a lot of money for it.

I don't spend money foolishly and most of my marketing doesn't cost all that much money. That said, marketing is a part of my budget, the cost of doing business. I ask myself "How am I going to pay for something?" rather than being at the effect of the budget and saying "Oh, I can't afford to market."

AA — Did you find a marketing approach that worked better than others?

MEB — I tried direct marketing and cold calling, even though I had heard from every-one that it doesn't work. I had to try it myself to learn that lesson, apparently. Successful marketing is all about word of mouth. That's what I heard from everyone, and it's true. I get virtually all of my business from word of mouth.

Successful marketing is all about finding approaches that feel genuine to you and that reflect who you are, because that's what people are buying. It's thinking about how you can get in front of a lot of people at once. It's not chasing clients but instead developing mar-keting gravity. That's from Allen Weiss, who wrote *Million Dollar Consulting*.

Marketing is something you're always going to be doing. I've been in business for 20 years and I still market. About 20% of my time is spent marketing ... and always will be.

AA — You've written six books, you write 2 monthly columns, you present at workshops, conferences, you run your own business, you're doing coaching. With everything you do, how do you plan out your day, your month and get it done effectively and efficiently?

MEB — Having structure when your head is unstructured is hard. I am a total groupie of David Allen, who wrote *Getting Things Done*, which we groupies refer to as GTD. You either drink the Kool-Aid or you don't! Seriously, GTD is what keeps me sane, that weekly review. When I have a new task to do, I assign it a time slot in my calendar or my "to do" list. I know that I've put it where it needs to be and I don't have to think about it again until it's time to address it.

Procrastination is the enemy of time management, because when you're putting off one thing and working on something else instead, you're not as effective as you could be. So you're wasting time while you're not doing something else. Once I realized that and just do the thing that I want to procrastinate on, the time opens up for everything else. So you get things done.

Whenever I create content, I try to get multiple uses out of it. For example, I do a free monthly conference call for all the people I'm coaching. My clients love it, and it's only an hour of my time. I record it and listen to it afterward, so I can catch insights I had during the call. I'll write those down and now I have the foundation of a blog posting or an article or something else. And once I have an article about it, I can turn that into a presentation. That's how I get those things done — I'm working on them simultaneously.

The nice thing about using content in multiple ways is that it ensures that my marketing is consistent. If I notice that I am having to develop a lot of content from scratch, I think about whether I'm going off on a tangent or whether it's a strategic expansion.

AA — How do you keep yourself current? What do you do to grow yourself professionally?

MEB — Actually, one of the best reasons for doing public speaking is that it keeps me on top of the industry ... it gives me a structure of what to monitor. I've got file folders for all of the things I am currently talking about. When I travel, I bring print magazines, and I horrify my seatmates because I'm tearing out pages all the time and writing stuff down on them! Then, when I get back to my office, I sort those pages and that goes into the "value-added" speech, this goes into the "future of the web" speech, and so on. Then, when I am preparing a talk, I already have a folder of useful resources I can start with.

AA — Let's talk about your new venture: coaching. How do you grow your own business and help other people grow theirs in a way that's not competitive?

MEB — In 20 years, I can count on one hand the number of times I've figured out I'm competing with someone else for a job. It just doesn't happen. There isn't competition; there is more business out there than there are people offering high-quality services.

I happen to love this business and I keep thinking that here are probably lots of people like me who are miserable in their jobs and don't realize that there are lots of other things you can do that are so fun! And I learned about this because Reva Basch was staffing the booth for AIIP at the SLA conference and she was willing to share her expertise with me. And I learned a lot from Sue Rugge, who wrote the first book about how to do this business; she was very generous! A lot of us are former librarians so we have that collegial mindset any way; we all know that our profession is richer when there are more of us in it.

And it helps me to have other good information professionals out there. I have people I can subcontract to and who will subcontract with me. Plus, I love sharing what I know about being an info-entrepreneur ... it's just so much fun!

AA — What things do you think make for a good entrepreneur? What characteristics or skills?

MEB— To me, it's entrepreneurial skills, business skills and professional skills. The entrepreneurial skills are the recognizing the need, thinking from a client's point of view, defining yourself by your clients' wants rather than by what you want to do, thinking about the "why" and not the "how."

Lots of people have great ideas about starting a business. Ideas are necessary, but making the ideas happen is where the real work lies. Instead of asking myself "what can I charge for my services?," for example, I ask myself "what can I do that people will pay me this much for?" It is a business skill ... to ask yourself that question. "How can I make a living at this?" "What can I do that I can bill $175 an hour for?" That's what client focus looks like.

And then there are the professional skills. This is either you doing the research or you finding the people to do the research.

AA — How can people learn or develop some of these skills?

MEB— If you're the kind of person who tends to think inside the box a lot, then you start asking yourself "how do I get my right brain thinking more? How do I get beyond binary thinking? How do I default to a third option instead of AND, OR and NOT?" That may be where people need to work and that's something that isn't often on the surface. I think that ability to just think creatively must be done on an on-going basis.

There's the skill of being able to go outside your comfort level — not just the finding and organizing of information but also the analysis and distillation. That's something that makes you a better employee too because you're offering higher-value skills; you're making yourself more valuable to your client.

I was talking to a manager in a company that had a lot of librarians. They had just laid off a number of them and the manager said to me, "the people I let go were the ones who didn't have multiple skills. The ones who were willing to do anything and learned how to do everything, I kept on, because they're worth more to me." That is a really good lesson! Not only can it save you your job but it makes your job so much more fun because you're doing more stuff.

If you hope to just coast along, good luck with that! There are so many more jobs that are being outsourced; we have to make ourselves irreplaceable. So we have to ask ourselves "What do I do that someone who's being paid $15 an hour can't do?" And if you can't identify anything that makes you irreplaceable, then your job is going to go overseas, because you haven't made a case for paying your salary.

It's not a fear thing. I just think it makes for a more interesting career if you focus on building your entrepreneurial, your professional and your business skills. It gives you a bigger toolkit of things to do, whether you're an employee or a business owner.

AA — What can we, as librarians and information professionals, do to change the perceptions of the public about our roles and use the skills we've been talking about today?

MEB— We can't tell people that we add value. We have to just start doing it. So that means if we're in a library and someone feels intrapreneurial and wants to move it up a level, they start doing it. For every client, every patron who comes in, just start asking questions like "what can I do to make this information more useful for you?" Start raising your clients' expectations!

Our job is far more than finding information and organizing it. Those tasks are necessary but not sufficient. Our skills have to go beyond that and if we don't see ourselves as more than just finders and organizers, then we are going to be toast. It's the finding and organizing and THEN doing something amazing with it that clients value. That's our job ... it's doing amazing things with information. How can you not like that?

7 — An Interview with Tim Spalding, Founder of LibraryThing

Jeff Tiberii

On March 10, 2011, Tim Spalding, founder of LibraryThing, came to the campus of Wake Forest University to speak at the Conference for Entrepreneurial Librarians. While he was on campus, he sat down with Jeff Tiberii, anchor and reporter for the local NPR station WFDD, for an interview.

JT: Will you just say your name and tell me why you're here?

TS: My name's Tim Spalding. I founded a company called LibraryThing which is a social network for book lovers. I'm here talking at a conference for entrepreneurial librarians telling librarians how to be more entrepreneurial and perhaps become entrepreneurs.

JT: LibraryThing, as I've read a little bit about it, is it fair to call it an e-library, is it an online library or is it more of a database?

TS: It's a place where you can catalog your books. Once you've done that it connects you with all the people who also have those books. It can connect you with your friends and find out what they're reading, what they've got in their library. It doesn't have the books themselves; it's all metadata — data about data. Obviously, things are going to go that way as everything moves to digital form.

JT: So it doesn't have the books or it has the electronic digital versions of the books?

TS: Basically, it doesn't have the books; it has some links to the books. It's a way of cataloging for yourself and then sharing what you have, but you're still reading the paper or maybe you're reading on the Kindle. It's not a place to read the book.

JT: It's a place to go to...

TS: It's like Facebook doesn't actually have your friends on it.

JT: How old is LibraryThing?

TS: Five years, 5.5 years.

JT: The idea for this came about how, when, why?

TS: LibraryThing came out in 2005; there was a bit of an upsurge in social media sites about that time. LibraryThing is about a year younger than Facebook, for example. It started because I wanted to catalog my books and I'd always been doing so. I realized it could be done much better online — I wouldn't have to type the data in, I could get the data from somewhere. LibraryThing started out and still is getting a lot of the data from libraries which have the highest quality data — libraries know the most about books. It grew from there. Once you've got thousands of people doing it, then all of a sudden you see how people can connect around the same books—books they're reading, books they have. So the social grew out of a need to organize and collect.

JT: How many people are currently registered on LibraryThing?

TS: We have more than a million registered members, but a million people aren't showing up at LibraryThing every day.

JT: How many people are going to LibraryThing every day?

TS: I don't actually know, frankly. It varies a lot. Some people are only using it for its original purpose — they're only cataloging their books. Some people only use it to talk about books—they don't do any cataloging, just write reviews or something. More on the order of 50,000 are showing up every day.

JT: How many books are cataloged on LibraryThing?

TS: 61 million.

JT: That's a lot.

TS: Yeah, a couple times the Library of Congress.

JT: Is it profitable? Is this a money-making thing?

TS: It actually is, weirdly. LibraryThing the company really does 2 things. One is we have this service from which we've grown a business selling similar services and data to libraries. In various other ways we make money, one of which is we actually charge for the service if you use it a lot, which is a very rare model online. Usually the model is everything's free and then we're going to shove ads at you. On LibraryThing there are no ads for any member even if you haven't paid. The sum result of this is we're profitable; not Google profitable, but it's a neat company that didn't hit the ground.

JT: When you started, what was the plan, what was the vision? You said you wanted to catalog your books; there are now more than a million people cataloging their books and about 50,000 doing it daily. Was that the original vision?

TS: No. It's funny; when I started I had no sense of how many people would want to do this. Was it 100? 200? People around me, those who know and love me said, "Tim, nobody wants to do this. It's a crazy idea." Part of the thing about it is like so many social services, they get better as more people join. Cataloging your books—there are many people who do that, but on some level it's a weird OCD kind of thing to do. You have to have a lot of books to do that. But when you get from that the recommendations for new books, connections with people who like the same stuff, conversations about these books and authors, stuff emerges from that that's more than the total you intended. So all of that grew out of it. Within about 6 months I knew where it was going, but it was 6 months of sleeping with my laptop.

JT: Is it fair to call it a spider web, a library-focused Facebook?

TS: It definitely spread virally — people telling each other. We never bought any advertising. In many ways it's like Facebook but in many ways it's the anti–Facebook. Certainly you can connect with your friends, but there's something really neat about finding a person who shares 30 or 40 books with you. Wow, that person shares something significant with me, I don't actually know them, but maybe we should talk. Very often, when you do that you find out that they're unexpected in some way. They may share your love of Vietnamese history, but maybe they aren't American. Or they are not of the same political party as you.

There's a real opportunity to interact with people at an intellectual level. Some of these social services are too focused on friends.

JT: From an overhead perspective, what costs are associated with this? What do you have to pay for?

TS: That's one of the great things that happened. Somewhere in the 2000's, suddenly, it became really cheap to run websites. In 2000 it was expensive; by 2005 it had become cheap. It's a bunch of commodity hardware boxes sitting in a facility somewhere, and as we grew, we had to buy more, but we're talking about $100,000 of equipment, not a million. Then, [the other cost], it's employees, people who are good at programming, who can make it better.

JT: How many employees do you have?

TS: We have 8 employees.

JT: All in Portland, Maine?

TS: No. Only one other employee is in Portland, ME and that's another cool thing about it and about what's happening in business. We have employees in Tasmania in Australia and Seattle, and others in Connecticut.

JT: Do you have board meetings once a year?

TS: We have some, but we have one employee I've never met.

JT: Really, what are they doing at night?

TS: I don't know. The guy's in Australia, so.... But the great thing about start-ups is, standard companies measure your productivity by how many hours in the day you stick your bottom in a chair. A start-up can measure productivity much more closely because everyone's working together so closely and that's an exciting thing to be part of. That's what you get out of it.

JT: Not to totally stick to Facebook, but people are friends talking to friends, sharing email addresses and phone numbers, security issues, harassment, people poking each other.... What problems have there been, what security issues are there?

TS: Pretty minimal. So, the world has changed since LibraryThing came online; it changed toward the Facebook model. I'm attracted to the earlier model in which everyone was anonymous unless they chose to say who they were, where sites didn't know everything about you, they only knew what you told them. LibraryThing takes that to the extreme; I think because we were influenced by librarians who were upset by the idea that your reading would be known to other people — government, corporations, etc. LibraryThing doesn't even require you to provide an email address. Most people provide an email but not everyone uses their real name. I think we're better off under this model; we're moving to a model where Facebook has identity services spread out all over the web; you see their logo on CNN, etc. It's always tied to who you really are and there are advantages to that: there's less trolling, there's better accountability, but you lose something, too. I'm on the side of people who think you're losing something with Facebook.

JT: So, less attached at the hip to your identity?

TS: Yes. There's that old New Yorker cartoon "no one knows you're a dog" — today everyone knows you're a dog. They even know what breed of dog you are. And they're serving you based on that. There are different ways of going about this; maybe if I were starting it now the whole thing would be deeply hooked into your real identity.

JT: It could change in an instant. You could make that happen tomorrow.

TS: I think members would resist that. LibraryThing has several competitors, actually, and they've gone more that route. I love the sharing that comes out of sharing books. I was a graduate student in Classics and I love the atmosphere of a group of people who've all read the same thing sitting around and talking about it. I'm more attracted to that than the idea of knowing exactly what books millions of people have read. It scares me a little, or weirds me out, I don't know. So LibraryThing tends to zig when others zag. There's been this convention on the web that you're this little square box that has a picture of you. On LibraryThing, you're always a name or a word. I don't know, but whenever I see those boxes— maybe I'm too libidinous— but whenever I see a picture, I think "there's a cute girl" or "that guy's really old." I don't want to know that. I want to experience people through what they say, through what they read. I think that's a precious thing the internet can offer.

JT: Let's talk a bit more about what people are doing? They're sharing the titles of books. Are they sharing books? Are they meeting in group settings? Are they mailing books to each other? Are they having group chat sessions where they say, let's discuss the Grapes of Wrath, chapter 6?

TS: There's a ladder of commitment. At the bottom, you have people who are there just there to catalog their books. As you move up, you start reviewing, you start tagging your books. You start making book recommendations, you know, if you liked this you might like that. There are groups and there are groups divided by genre or location, so if you want to have a conversation about Kurt Vonnegut, you go to the Sci-Fi group and have a conversation there. And it keeps ascending. LibraryThing has lots of opportunities for helping the system out, contributing data. You can add information about series or awards, or the school an author attended, and people get involved in making the information beautiful and perfect. At the high end of it, we have people who have cataloged the libraries of famous dead people. So there are printed catalogs or maybe there's a manuscript out there where members will get together and catalog. They started with Jefferson but they've done Marie Antoinette, John Adams and Marilyn Monroe. We've got Tupac Shakur. We just did the International Space Station. It's because someone had a Freedom of Information Act request for a list of books on the space station. It's kind of neat. Because it's LibraryThing, not only is there now a way to find out what Jefferson had or what the space station has, you can figure out what your overlap is with them and who has the biggest overlap. So, people do that and there have been some real-world meetings or parties, and we've gotten together to catalog a library really quickly. We did the Rhode Island Audubon Society in an afternoon with a bunch of people. We've done a bunch of churches, a synagogue, and academic departments. We're talking about 50 or 100 people who've done that.

JT: Is that a volunteer effort?

TS: Yes, all volunteer, for the love of books. There are some people who think the idea of going to a church and giving them a library catalog in six hours is fun. It's a small group of people, however. As far as mailing books, there are some cool sites that do that. We connect now with ten of them. BookMooch is one of them. You can see how many copies there are at BookMooch which is integrated with LibraryThing, so while you're at BookMooch you can see what's going on at LibraryThing. So we're tied in with them, but there's a limit to the amount of code I want to write.

JT: In terms of more than a one million number of people, give me a sense if you can, what percent are Americans?

TS: We have versions of LibraryThing that are translated into a lot of languages, about a dozen of them are in good enough shape that you can use LibraryThing without speaking English. Except for Holland, which has done really well, most members are English-speaking. I think it splits according to population so we're 300 million and 80 million in England, plus Australia and New Zealand. LibraryThing reaches out to libraries and LibraryThing sells products to libraries, so I went to New Zealand and there are lots of fans there, but definitely, the majority of our members are American.   •

JT: What does this leave for you?

TS: Do you mean where's the company going or what the heck am I doing with my life?

JT: What are you doing with this company day-to-day? What is your role?

TS: I'm still actually heavily involved in the code. I started out as a programmer. I'm here to talk about entrepreneurial companies and librarians and so many of the best web companies were founded by programmers. I don't think Zuckerberg is still writing code all day long, but he could. I think Sergey Brin still is. So, I write a lot of code. Then, I manage people, which is hard when they're just someone at the end of a Skype connection. I do a fair number of conferences, either talking or selling to libraries. I have a great deal where LibraryThing has rented an apartment in a house that I own, so it's like I'm working in the house but using a different door. So I'm still working insane hours, but if my kid suddenly does something cute, I can run downstairs and see it. So it's kind of a neat deal.

JT: What are those hours?

TS: They're insane. I stay up really late. I drink a lot of Diet Coke and stay up late.

JT: What the heck are you doing with your life? You're in your late 30's or there about — where's this company going?

TS: There are so many cool things I want to do with the site, so many features I want to implement, features I want to improve. I made a decision early on not to do LibraryThing and then do MovieThing and then CDThing. I made a decision not to get into other areas. That avenue isn't completely closed; I think some of those are interesting.

JT: Why?

TS: Focus. I think it's hard. We didn't get and didn't try for huge Venture Capital (VC) money, so we don't have millions to burn. Focus. I think some of those are interesting for the medium term future, but mostly I'm just focused on making LibraryThing as awesome as it can be. About half the company is making software for libraries that relates to Library-Thing but it isn't LibraryThing and there's so much to do there. Library software is terrible, so there's much, much to do there to make libraries easier to use and so forth. I think the big thing on the horizon is e-books; it's changing everything. It's something I've thought a lot about; I'm still trying to figure out how it impacts LibraryThing. It's going to be an interesting decade.

JT: The future of libraries connects how to LibraryThing? They obviously overlap. How do you see LibraryThing helping the future of libraries, if at all?

TS: I do a lot of thinking about the future of libraries. I'm not a librarian, but Library-Thing has a strong library orientation. We get data from libraries and that means you can catalog books that aren't currently for sale at Amazon.com which is the other source of data about books. That affects our customers; if you're over 40 and you're not a Philistine, then you probably own some books that aren't currently for sale on Amazon. It's important to have really good data and it's also completely necessary if you're going to do anything in other languages that Amazon doesn't have. So we've been connected to the library world from the beginning. One answer is simply social: LibraryThing does social things. Libraries have traditionally not had anything social in them, right? So we provide software that adds tagging and reviews — putting social features into the library catalog. And then I think LibraryThing serves as something of a ... I'm interested in libraries I also follow what's happening in publishing and my wife is an author, there are all these parts of the book world that don't talk to each other. LibraryThing brings data together from different sorts of people and most significantly from our users. Our users contribute wonderful, wonderful data. They do it because they love it, they love each other through it, and because we have open data licenses on much of our data and I think a lot of that can go back into libraries, can enrich libraries and serve as an inspiration for what libraries should be doing with their data.

JT: What's the value of the company?

TS: I'm not going to sell it.

JT: Not at any point?

TS: Well, who knows? It's definitely not in my short-term plan. That's one of the differences between LibraryThing and other start-ups. If we had taken VC [venture capital] money, the investors would be demanding that we sell it now. Five years is kind of the limit on when a company should be prepared to return the original investment to its investors. LibraryThing is different because I still own a majority of the company. I love it. I enjoy it. It's not losing money; it's making money. The value is what it provides to its users and an awesome job for me.

JT: But you're happy. If someone came to you with a check for $2 million?

TS: No, but you can keep counting up. Not at $2 million, but at $20 million, probably.

JT: Any other future plans for LibraryThing?

TS: Libraries need to make a real quantum jump in how they do this stuff. Libraries are facing some really severe threats; I think e-books pose a severe threat, particularly public libraries, not so much academic libraries. I want to be part of the solution to that. I care about libraries, I care about where that goes and I want to be part of the solution to that.

As far as book lovers go, I think there are lots of interesting things going on there, too. I'd like to be part of the solution there, too. I guess the answer is we lose half of our bookstores. I guess the answer is we read a lot more stuff on e-books. There's going to be this huge process of adjustment and there will be opportunities there — opportunities to make money — and there will be dangers there as well, definitely. I'm anxious to ride that wave and contribute in any way I can.

JT: The future of libraries and LibraryThing, by the arbitrary year of your choice, will this all be digitized? Will there no longer be pieces of paper in libraries? Does that even affect you? Is the future of libraries going away from having many books at all?

TS: I think it's a matter of speed more than anything else. If something goes slowly enough, other things may intervene to change the course. In 20 years we might say: "Why were we talking about the future of books—these implants in our heads have changed everything?" I believe in a fast move to digital, though I'm not happy with that in many ways. I think it's going to be an accelerating process that feeds on itself. For academic libraries, the process will be fairly painless, just expensive. There are no real changes, just more money. For public libraries, I think there's a real danger that the public libraries may lose their relevance or have to pay exorbitant amounts to lend e-books. There's a core problem; physical books under law are physical objects and they can be loaned without permission. E-books are licensed objects. Publishers and authors realize that 40% of reads happen through libraries but only 3–4% of purchases are made to libraries and the publishers want that money. I'm really worried about citizens' ability to borrow books 10 years out.

JT: Is there anything else we haven't discussed?

TS: I should say that LibraryThing is free, until you have 200 books. After that, it's $10 a year or $25 for a lifetime account. And when you go to pay you'll discover it was all a big psych-out and you can pay us any amount you want. The cool thing about that is that we actually get more money than we ask for. That, I think, is a sign of a service that people actually want. I think people appreciate that even though it's so bizarre to pay for anything online any more, if you join LibraryThing you're a customer; that gives you certain rights and a sense of ownership. That's the type of relationship I like to be on the other side of. I don't think Zuckerberg wakes up every morning thinking of his customers. His customers are ad companies.

JT: Thanks, I appreciate it.

TS: Thanks.

8 — Market Research Service Partnership at the University of Kentucky

An Entrepreneurial Future?

PETER HESSELDENZ

Introduction

The concept of an academic library charging a fee for research services, though less common these days, has been widely employed in the past as a way to provide services which go beyond the "basics" and extend services to patrons outside of the main user group. Typically, academic libraries consider starting a fee-based service when a previously manageable program outgrows the ability of current staffing to handle the workload, forcing the librarians to choose between discontinuing (or severely curtailing) the service or finding a new funding source. This situation will soon be the case with the research work done by the Business Reference Outreach program at the University of Kentucky (UK). In the past, the program had occasionally assisted local entrepreneurs who were usually but not always, referred by the Kentucky Small Business Development Center (KSBDC). It has lately grown at such a rapid rate that soon, the two-person operation will no longer be able to keep pace. This growth coupled with an economic climate which precludes the possibility of additional staffing makes a fee-based solution definitely worth exploring.

In fact, the Business Reference Outreach program has already taken the first step toward becoming a fee-based program. At the beginning of fiscal year 2010-2011, the program's most frequent client, the Kentucky Small Business Development Center (KSBDC), agreed to pay the salary of a part-time (20 hours per week) student employee to perform market research for its clients and consultants. A library science graduate student was hired and, after extensive training, began researching at the beginning of August 2010 under the supervision of the business librarian. Not long after the graduate student started, KSBDC's administration distributed an announcement to all of its employees encouraging them to contact the University of Kentucky Business Reference Outreach program for research assistance. Since that email was sent, the number of research requests has grown steadily, causing the turnaround time to increase. This situation puts the program at a crossroads. This chapter will present a brief history of the program, analyze how it currently works, assess possible future directions and address some of the practical and philosophical considerations that will have to be examined before a fee-based solution is attempted.

Controversy: Fee versus Free

The idea of charging a fee for library services has always been a controversial subject capable of stirring "strong emotion" in librarians. Though they can generally agree on condemning anything that impedes free access to information and prevents librarians from providing optimum service, "considerable disagreement" exists about how charging fees for library service affects those two concepts (Nshaiwat 1). The root of this conflict lies in the convergence of two forces that are central to American society: capitalism and democracy (Lowell vii–viii). Just as these two concepts sit uneasily beside each other in the whole of society, so they do in libraries where information is seen by differing parties and at differing times as both a commodity and as a right.

The capitalist argument would assert that charging a fee allows for greater access to information and provides greater service because it enables programs to exist that would be difficult to afford without a fee (Sally 352). This issue came to prominence during the 1980s, when the number of libraries charging fees increased greatly. The impetus for the increase in fees was the introduction of electronic databases into the library world. If libraries were going to offer this expensive new technology free of charge, they would have to make drastic cuts in other areas. For the most part, librarians viewed the new format as a luxury, especially since viable alternatives, such as paper indexes, were available; for this reason, many libraries chose to impose fees for database use. In most cases, the basic services such as reference help and circulation remained free of charge. However, some librarians argued that the introduction of fees for database searching opened the door to allowing fees for many other non-basic services such as meeting rooms, video rentals, and reserves (Giacoma 6).

The crux of the argument against charging a fee for these services held that it violated one of the most cherished tenants of librarianship — that of free access to information. Much of the debate about the philosophical and ethical questions surrounding the fee-for-service question occurred in the public library arena. Perhaps this is because access to information from public libraries has traditionally been so closely aligned with democratic ideals. Public libraries have been one of society's great equalizers, allowing the same access to rich and poor. Many public librarians view information as a social good that should be available to all citizens (Sally 346). They see it as akin to fire and police protection and, like those services, easily justified because citizens pay for it with their tax dollars (Sally 351). However, beneath the surface lies a moral and philosophical issue that goes deeper than the funding source. Namely, it is the notion that the right to information is "the backbone of a free society" which allows people to understand issues, make decisions, and question any action which might seek to curtail freedoms (Warner 2).

History of Fee-Based Programs in Academic Libraries

The earliest examples of fee-based services in academic libraries began to appear in the early part of the 20th century and were aimed at serving the information needs of local businessmen (Sheehy 5). Fee-based services continued throughout the 20th century, growing in the 1960's and 1970s, while targeting both individual and corporate clients (Brooks 347). During the 1980s and early 1990s, the number of fee-based services in academic libraries grew to over 400, its highest level (Warner 21), necessitating an ALA/ACRL discussion group — FISCAL (Fee Based Information Centers in Academic Libraries). Many of the large ARL libraries featured some sort of fee-based service at this time (Josephine 48), although the type and depth of service varied a great deal between institutions.

The increase in fee-based services was mainly the result of expanding database availability, which occurred at the same time that budgets were shrinking (Nshaiwat 1). Effective use of these new online databases required extensive training, so academic librarians offered mediated search services for their patrons. Many of these services continued until the late 1990s and early 2000s when their need was lessened by the development of CD-ROM technologies and, later, less cumbersome online databases that were specifically designed for end-users (Diamond 190). After the turn of the 2000s, many of the long-running fee-based services shut down because businesses and individuals thought they could use the Internet to find all the information they needed (Fong, Ward, and Dearie 196).

Now, business patrons are beginning to realize that even though much of the information they need is online, it is not always easily accessible or freely available. The fee-based services that exist today specialize in convenience and efficiency. They provide high-level expert research quickly so that companies and individuals can use their resources differently (Fong, Ward, and Dearie 201). A few high profile services continue to operate at major academic and public libraries, such as Vanderbilt University, the University of Toronto, the University of Wisconsin, and the New York Public Library. Many independent researching companies and special libraries also continue to offer fee-based research services (de Castell 24).

Business Research at UK: The History

The roots of the current business research service at the University of Kentucky date back to 1982, when KSBDC was formed. The partnership started slowly with only scattered and occasional meetings and infrequent requests by KSBDC staff for reference advice, research consultations, and training sessions from the UK librarians. However, a greater partnership was inevitable because KSBDC's mission meshed so well with UK's. The idea for a Small Business Development Center originated as collaboration between the federal Small Business Administration, higher education institutions and economic development organizations across the United States. The center provided a way to encourage entrepreneurs and small business owners by offering free or low cost assistance; in addition to the location at the University of Kentucky, nineteen other centers and satellite offices were opened and currently operate in Kentucky, and most are also located on college campuses. Today's clients generally want to start new businesses or expand existing ones; occasionally, KSBDC advises clients whose businesses are in trouble and need expert advice.

With the hiring of several key people at the University of Kentucky, the relationship between KSBDC and the library began to blossom. In 2001, Lee Todd was appointed president of the University of Kentucky; he came into office promising to battle the social problems which plagued the state which he dubbed the "Kentucky Uglies." These problems included poor health care, poverty, and lack of education. He proposed that UK increase its commitment to promoting economic development as a way of addressing these issues. In his Top 20 Business Plan, he called for the University to work toward providing support for "more locally-owned businesses" and "improved economic vitality" ("Top Twenty Business Plan" 1). Shortly after Dr. Todd came into office, the UK Libraries hired a new director,

Carol Diedrichs, who made it a priority to increase both local and national collaborations. In this atmosphere, UK hired a new business librarian, Eeva Hoch, in 2002, the immediate predecessor to the current business librarian. She came to UK with considerable experience working as a business researcher, both in academic and professional settings. Following Diedrichs' directive, she initiated contact with KSBDC's director, who she found to have a keen interest in and great respect for the role that business research plays in economic development. From this convergence of forces came the first stages of the formal collaboration that exists today.

The early work was mostly limited to Hoch teaching entrepreneurs, referred to the library by KSBDC, to use UK's business resources to do their own research. She would meet with an entrepreneur for an extended reference interview and instruction session in which she would show the available resources to him or her. Often the entrepreneurs were amazed to learn about the wealth of information that could be found, but dismayed at the amount of work it would take to extract and synthesize it. In addition to her work with the entrepreneurs, Hoch occasionally worked directly for the administrators and consultants of the KSBDC on research topics; she also attended their continuing education sessions in a training capacity.

The collaboration continued in the same vein up to the point when Hoch left the University of Kentucky in the summer of 2009. Her replacement, the author and current business librarian, continued the collaboration until the spring of 2010, when the KSBDC director proposed the hiring of a graduate student as a dedicated KSBDC researcher. The idea was greeted enthusiastically by the library administration and the details were quickly worked out, including the decision that a Library Science graduate student would be best suited for the job since it consisted primarily of research and an intimate knowledge of library resources and databases would be required. Interviews were held and an appropriate candidate was hired.

Current Research Program

With the student in place, a new model for the partnership was started, which entailed that research requests would, for the most part, be received directly from the KSBDC consultants who would be asking for information on behalf of their clients. Meetings with entrepreneurs would be greatly reduced and, in effect, the KSBDC consultants would be doing the reference interview and then asking the researchers for the targeted information that they felt was necessary to continue with their business planning. This method has worked well, although maintaining good communication with the consultants requires continual effort. The researchers are able to use their time much more efficiently and target the information needed.

Once the research material is gathered, the process consists of organizing it into a logical order and then highlighting pertinent passages. Articles and reports are read or skimmed and important passages are marked. This part of the process is often the most time-consuming, but necessary as important information is often buried deep within an article. Invariably, new ideas or terms to search come to the fore in this phase, generating more research. Once all of the material is reviewed, the next step is to organize it into logical groupings (such as "trends," "competitors," "customers," etc.). This exercise is useful because it makes patterns, as well as "holes" in the research, easier to identify. After these processes are completed, the printed materials are then delivered to the requestors.

Why a Fee-Based Model?

KSBDC has indicated that they are satisfied so far with the research products they have been receiving. However, as the rate of requests has gone up, the turnaround time has also increased. In the business world, time is money, so a point will inevitably be reached in which the wait is no longer acceptable. Because of the multifaceted nature of an academic liaison's duties, the business librarian cannot increase the portion of his time given to this project. A fixed percentage of his time is devoted to outreach while other responsibilities in areas such as reference, collection development, and information literacy also have to be attended to.

So, the Business Reference Outreach Program finds itself in precisely the situation that Coffman and Josephine identify as the most likely reason for starting a fee-based service: "to accommodate the increasing demand for extraordinary services from businesses, professionals, and, in the case, of academic institutions, other non-university clientele" (33). At this point, the administration will need to be approached to gauge their receptivity to expanding the fee-based service. Many areas will need to be explored and many requirements put into place before the service will be allowed to grow and change. The service, which has supported entrepreneurs, could itself become an entrepreneurial endeavor. The researchers will need to use the resources and know-how they have employed in the service of other businesses on their own behalf. The remainder of this chapter discusses actions that will need to be taken to determine whether or not this direction is feasible and explore the hypothetical decision making process that would be needed.

Administrative Support

Before proceeding with a project like this, it is imperative that the administration of the library is enthusiastic and committed to the idea. Strong support is essential to the success of a fee-based service which will need administrative support and financial backing (Simons 211). The ultimate goal of the project would be to have the service pay for itself, but an initial investment will be required. The money involved would be significant and would be allocated to several different areas. In some cases, it would come in the form of employee time because a great deal of planning would be necessary in the early stages, which would take employees away from their current jobs (Warner 62). Once the planning is done, funds will be necessary to pay for a variety of start-up charges. The largest expense will be for salaries for additional project staffing, possibly student wages or perhaps a new permanent full or part time position. In addition to salaries, there could be outlays for equipment, such as office furniture, computers, printers, telephones or photocopiers and office supplies such as business cards, paper, pens, and mailing materials. Other start-up costs might include augmentations for the collection or licensing fees for database use. Finally, funding would also be needed for marketing and promotion efforts.

Before the administration simply hands over a significant amount of money, it will need to investigate the project in greater detail. Often a committee is formed to undertake this type of investigation and this would be the most likely solution in this case. To determine whether or not the service would be viable, the members would be charged with looking into the feasibility of expanding the operation and then producing a report recommending a particular course of action — either going ahead with the expansion, keeping the project the same, or possibly discontinuing it altogether. The persons on this committee could be library employees, employees from other departments at the university or a combination of both. Ideally, the committee would be made up of a balanced group of people from a variety of backgrounds, with expertise in areas crucial to setting up such a program, including knowledge about university financial matters, database licensing, and the research process.

One area the committee will need to consider early on is the impact this service would be likely to have on current library staff and services. The primary mission of an academic library is to serve the university community — the students, faculty and staff of the university. The committee will need to ensure that the other departments are able to continue without detrimental effects. Currently the business librarian and the graduate student working for the Business Reference Outreach program are housed in the Reference Department. If they continue to be housed there, space might become an issue as would the disruptions caused by increased conversation between staff member, clients, and others due to the physical environment which is made up of cubicles and lacking private offices (Warner 55). The Reference Department currently provides printing and office supplies, absorbing these costs.

Collection use could also be potentially troublesome. None of the business databases have a limited number of seats, so access to electronic resources would not be compromised. However, Business students and faculty might have to compete for paper resources with the Business Reference Outreach Service. The service would have to make sure that the materials were available when a faculty member or student needed them, perhaps necessitating the purchase of multiple copies of certain popular sources if conflicts regularly arose.

Though this project is likely to have its largest impact on the Reference Department, other departments in the library will also be affected. The Collection Development and Acquisitions Departments will have to assist in the ordering and licensing of the database materials. Cataloging, as well, will have to deal at times with an increased number of materials to process. Some of the branch libraries will, from time to time, need to be used and their librarians consulted. The most likely candidates would be the Science Library, the Medical Library, and the Engineering Library, but certainly any of the other 11 branch libraries at the University of Kentucky might be consulted as well on less frequent occasions. Policies about priorities might have to be prepared in order to avoid any confusion when conflicts arise.

The Business Plan

After these issues are resolved and the proposal is given the go-ahead by the administration, a business plan will be needed. A business plan is an "absolute necessity" for a fee-based program, as it outlines long and short range strategies and will serve as a guide or "roadmap" for the service (Warner 43). It provides specific information about the potential client base, start-up budget, staffing, marketing, competition, and institutional and legal requirements. In the business world, most funding sources will not provide money until they are satisfied with the soundness of the business plan. Certainly, the library administration will be no different, requiring a thorough and well-researched business plan before investing valuable resources (Cloutier 333).

The first question that a business plan should answer is what the goal of the service will be (Warner 44). The answer will have to strongly align with the mission statements of both the University and the library (Warner 44–45). Unlike the usual goal of a business, which would involve making a profit, the goal of a library research service at a public non-profit university would typically be to cover its own operational costs while supporting the educational and outreach missions of the library and the university as a whole. The University of Kentucky's mission consists of education, research and service and, while the first two aspects of the mission account for the majority of the effort put forth, the third is very important as well. The service mission is dedicated to improving the lives of Kentuckians through economic development, among other things. Therefore, the University of Kentucky's mission statement prominently requires providing aid in "recruiting and creating businesses" ("2009–2014 Strategic Plan" 11).

The University of Kentucky Library mission statement meshes well with that of its parent institution. It too contains statements which ensure that the library will promote "business information for economic and business development" ("UK Libraries Strategic Plan" 9). In practical terms, this policy allows for open access to the library resources for all members of the community. These privileges include free use of the library buildings and many of the services within them. Community patrons may use printed materials (in the library and for check-out), computers and the electronic databases (within the library building), and also receive reference assistance. This reference assistance can include extensive business help for entrepreneurs; however, it does not call for the librarian to do the research for the patron. If a fee-based system were imposed, the entrepreneur, or any business researcher, would have the option to receive enhanced service for a fee.

Services Offered

The business plan would have to detail exactly what services would be offered. The description would have to be very clear, so that customers would know exactly what they were paying for. Warner suggests that a new fee-based service should only offer a few basic services at the beginning because it is easier to make additions later than it is to take something away (50). Certainly, the basis of the program would be to offer "research services," but that term might mean different things to different people so an exact and unambiguous definition must be supplied. A good definition to adopt might start with the one offered by the University of Calgary, which defines "research services" as "the mediated use of online commercial databases, the Internet, or other research collections by library staff in response to an information request" (Cloutier 333).

The definition should include information about how the product will be delivered, including organization and format. Currently, the Business Reference Outreach Program delivers its products in paper, however, some customers might prefer to receive electronic copies, and this option could be made available. A basic timeline would also have to be established for each project as speed and convenience are two of the main reasons why customers choose to use research services in the first place (Fong, Ward and Dearie 205–206). Other value-added services might be considered at this point such as accompanying the research with a personalized report which synthesizes and synopsizes the information, pulling out the most salient points, and then presenting them in an easy to read bulleted format.

The service would need to establish a method for finding out exactly what information the patron is looking for and for making sure that both parties agree on the research plan.

As most experienced librarians can attest, many people have trouble articulating their information needs. The service would, therefore, have to come up with a flexible plan for reference interviews. KSBDC clients could continue to work through the KSBDC consultants, but if the program is to be extended to others, another method would be required for non–KSBDC clients. Guidelines for a thorough reference interview would have to be in place so that particular questions could be answered and research goals established.

Contingencies would have to be in place to deal with unrealistic client expectations. In some cases, UK Libraries might simply not have the appropriate resources to provide the requested information. Experience would tell the researcher whether or not a particular topic is likely to yield much information. This observation would be communicated to the client, who could decide whether or not to pursue the topic. If the client wished the service to continue, research time would have to be compensated even if no information was found. It would be best in such situations to be up-front with the client and offer to check in with him or her periodically before getting too far into the process and accumulating an excessively high bill.

Assessing the Need for a Service

The authors of the business plan would also assess the need for a fee-based research service. They would look at several factors, with emphasis placed on the state of the local economy. Current trends and future predictions would be necessary. The economy was far from prosperous before the financial crisis of 2008, but in subsequent years, it has been in a fairly dismal state. The few bright spots, such as the increasing number of high-tech jobs in Lexington, are more than cancelled out by the many jobs lost to the financial crisis in surrounding areas (Sloan C7). The hardest hit sector has been manufacturing, which once flourished across the state. At the time of this writing in August 2011, the loss of jobs in this area accounts, in large part, for the highest unemployment rates reported in Kentucky in the last 30 years (Troske and Jepson 2), and those jobs are unlikely to return when the crisis is over. Economists Ken Troske and Chris Jepson predict that "the recession has likely permanently impacted Kentucky's manufacturing" (7). This reduction in manufacturing also exacerbates the problem of poverty in Kentucky (one of Todd's Kentucky Uglies), which is among the worst in the nation, with only six states having a higher rates in 2009 (Fording 14).

The financial crisis' disproportionally large impact on Kentucky serves to underscore the importance of the research done in support of new entrepreneurship. It is often said that small business is an "integral part" of all local economies and that is certainly true for Kentucky (Pankl 94). The library research service provided by the University of Kentucky is a small, but important, component in the process of generating more high paying jobs in new and innovative fields that can replace the lost manufacturing jobs (Fording 15). Simon states that the ideal condition for starting a fee-based business research program would be in a healthy local economy (Simons 211). This will unfortunately not be the case with Kentucky in the foreseeable future, but an opposite argument can also be made that an economic downturn is a good time to start a business. In a downturn, there is less competition as many established companies close. With well educated, experienced professionals finding themselves unemployed for long periods of time, some decide to take that time to work on a business plan. Funding, as always, is the most difficult element, but certain businesses, such as service companies, don't require much initial capital (O'Sullivan 35–36).

POTENTIAL CUSTOMERS

Once the need is identified, then the next step is to specifically define the customers that the service will try to attract (Warner 52). Many fee-based research services have failed because they did not have a well-defined picture of their potential clients. A library which has many patrons vying for free information does not automatically translate into a prosperous business as the case at the University of Nevada, Las Vegas illustrated. In the early 1990s, that library's reference department was being overwhelmed by inquiries from members of the local business community. Though there was initial interest in the fee-based program they started, there was ultimately not enough business to justify keeping it in place, even though it was run on a cost-recovery basis. The initial business closed soon after it started. The lesson they learned was that they did not know their customers well, nor how to reach them (Simon 154–155).

It was only later when the librarians at UNLV realized there was a market for specialized searching for the gaming industry, that they found their true niche (Simon 155–156). Other academic libraries have had similar experiences. The University of Calgary directed its research services towards corporate interests in the petroleum industry, after their Geology and Geophysics library noticed an increase in walk-up traffic and telephone reference questions on petroleum-related issues from non-university clientele. After some investigation, the librarians found that a number of corporate offices in the petroleum industry headquartered in the Calgary area had downsized and closed their corporate libraries, creating an opportunity to serve a group who would be willing to pay for research from one of the premier geology collections in Western Canada (Cloutier 332). Similarly, the University of Akron saw an opportunity to serve the major rubber and tire corporations headquartered in that city. The library's strong collection of materials centering on the polymer sciences and polymer engineering fields and the existence of links between the rubber industry and the University of Akron libraries (via donated archival materials) made a business partnership very easy. Through their Corporate Services Center (CSC), they provide "specialized technical and research services" (Durbin and Calzonetti 74), working on a contractual basis with the firms who employ them.

Currently, UK Library offers enhanced services exclusively to the clients of KSBDC. A logical move would be to expand the service that is already provided for them, which could simply be accomplished by having KSBDC pay the salary of another employee or student. However, if a larger client base is desired, UK Library will have to investigate to see if a market exists. Since the program is already experienced in working with fledgling businesses, it could seamlessly branch out to work with established businesses as well who might need competitive intelligence. The program could investigate the receptivity of local businesses to this idea by conducting market surveys in person, by phone, and by snail mail and email.

The program also might try to specialize in research for industries which are concentrated in the local area, just as the Universities of Calgary, Akron and Nevada, Las Vegas did. Traditionally, the Bluegrass area has been home to the horse industry and the spirits industry. In the past, the Business Reference Outreach Program has done work in both of those areas for KSBDC projects. The program also might consider aiming at some of the newer industries which have recently moved into the area. These include medicine and medical device companies, high-tech industries, and despite the economic downturn, more manufacturing.

People already associated with the University of Kentucky would be another group to target. Alumni are certainly a group that should be considered. At a large school like the University of Kentucky, there will be many alumni working in a multitude of business areas. Alumni are good potential customers because they are already aware of the University and its Library and have an interest in maintaining contact (Ward, Fong and Camille 13). The alumni office can be useful in helping to find interested parties and in providing ways to contact them. Another possibility is to aim the services at specialized groups associated with the university. An especially fruitful area might be departments working on development projects that might need research on potential donors (Brooks 350).

Budget/Pricing

The business plan should include a proposed budget. The goal of the budget would be to cover the costs of the project — not to make a profit. A budget for a fee-based service usually has three main areas that have to be covered: salaries, supplies and licensing, and overhead or indirect costs. The amounts needed to cover salaries will be fairly straightforward; simply determine which employees will be working for the service and how much those persons will be paid and the cost of benefits. If an employee is not working for the project fulltime, calculate how much of the employee's pay plus benefits corresponds to the percentage of time that he or she is devoting to the project. Next, the cost of supplies and licensing will have to be factored in. These last figures will probably involve a bit of guess work and intuition in the first year, although an approximation can probably be determined by tracking the supply use by the Business Reference Outreach program. Indirect costs or overhead include building maintenance and utilities. The university will have a method for arriving at this figure which the planners can find by consulting with the budget officer for the library.

Once a final figure is determined, the program will have a target for the amount of money that needs to be generated before it will break even. Most research programs charge an hourly rate for research services. So, the program will have to be based upon the number of expected billable hours divided by the costs that have to be covered in order to calculate what the hourly rate should be. Not every hour that an employee is at work is a billable hour — some time needs to be spent on administrative work, continuing education, and other activities. The planners will have to determine what percentage of employee time will need to be dedicated to these areas.

Setting fees is a difficult process with which librarians are notoriously uncomfortable. The natural tendency of most librarians is to give information away for free. As a result, they often set the fees too low (Warner 10). Low fees can be a problem not only because the library fails to recoup its spending, but also because they affect the way customers view the services. Businesses see low prices as indicating low quality (Simons 212) and might not choose to use a low-priced service. Corporate clients are more willing to pay higher prices (Warner 65) so, if that is one of the target groups, prices should be set accordingly.

The literature offers contradictory advice about setting prices. Cloutier selected several benchmark services and looked at their pricing to determine her rates in order to stay competitive with the other services (333). Warner, however, claims that there is no such thing as the "going rate" so it is not necessary to check what other places are doing, but simply to use a formula that produces a figure that will cover the institutions' costs (63–64). With this variance in advice, it is not surprising to see a wide range of prices at different services. Generally the hourly rate seems to fall somewhere between $50 and $140 for services at academic institutions and public libraries (De Castell 24–25). Once a rate is determined for the proposed UK service, it would be advisable to meet with experts from the University's controller's office to make sure all are in agreement.

Once the money starts coming in, an accounting system will be needed. The business plan should provide a detailed overview of how the financial record-keeping will take place. A system will have to be in place for invoicing clients, depositing payments, and paying for supplies or other materials. These procedures will have to be integrated with the University's and the library's existing accounting system, although the service will also need to establish its own separate system for tracking and record keeping. The separate system will allow the service to know at any given moment where it stands financially without having to wait for numbers to be posted by the university. Many accounting software systems are available that could be used.

Competition

The business plan should address the idea of competition, which is not a subject that librarians generally have to think about. In this situation, competition would be viewed differently than would be the case with a conventional business. The library would want to consider what competition exists mainly in order to differentiate itself. Some fee-based services in academic libraries are careful not to duplicate services with other area business for fear that they will be accused of unfairly competing with a for-profit business (Cloutier 333). Warner, however, claims that competition is healthy and that potential unfairness is not a concern (50). Ward finds that it is good to establish contacts with similar businesses because they can be a resource when questions arise. Clients can also be referred to other services if their needs would be better met (Ward 165–66). Coffman and Josephine often even worked with the competition, subcontracting for services at libraries that have materials in their collection that are needed (34–35), though with far fewer services existing today, this might be a difficult strategy to pursue.

Staffing

Staffing is another important consideration that must be addressed in the business plan. The quality and dedication of the staff for any business are essential to its success. Ward strongly cautions that the staff of the fee-based service should not have other responsibilities; having responsibilities in other parts of the library is "a recipe for failure" (Ward 33). She also warns that any professional positions designated for the service should be non-tenure track. To be successful in this line of work, the staff member must be able to concentrate solely on this endeavor and attempting to get tenure at this time would create undue stress (Ward 33).

The most important staffing consideration at the beginning is determining who will manage the operation. Those interested in starting a fee-based research service must keep in mind that these operations are businesses and need to be run as such (Nshwiat 4). All of the issues that businesses regularly have to attend to such as hiring, marketing, promotion, pricing, quality control — are necessary in a fee-based library operation. Many projects which evolved from existing free services have failed because the principals entered into them thinking that they could just continue to do what they've always done. However, they soon find that running a business requires more than good researching skills.

Two managerial models are popular with fee-based services. The first is a manager who administers the project, but does not engage in the day-to-day research work for the clients. He or she does not have to be a full-time employee of the project. The second is a manager who is hands on in administration, but is also spending a significant amount of time working with clients. Both methods have advantages. In the first case, the administrator can usually have a better perspective on the service since he or she can view it from afar. In the second case, the full-time manager does not have that perspective, but can better spot trends and stay in closer touch with the needs of clients. Ward strongly recommends the second type — the hands-on manager, but acknowledges that for budgetary reasons, this model might not be feasible (Ward 34–35).

Many combinations are possible for the rest of the staffing mix. There can be full and part time employees, professional and staff positions, or graduate and undergraduate students. Professional staffing is desirable if the hands-on manager model is employed; however, it is essential if the administrative manager model is used. The professional staff member must have good researching skills. A business background is desirable, but not necessary if the professional staff member can be trained by a business expert. The remainder of the staffing needs can be fulfilled with graduate students. Library science students are "highly recommended" because of their dedication to learning researching skills (Josephine 51). In addition, they are usually enthusiastic, grateful to be gaining valuable experience, and willing to work for low salaries, with few or no benefits. The main drawback with utilizing student labor is that the turnover rate will be higher, requiring much time to be spent in training new employees.

Legal Issues

The business plan should address all legal issues which might arise in setting up a fee-based service. The first item to consider would be the licensing of the databases that will be used in the research. A provision in the database agreement will be needed allowing materials to be printed-out and repackaged for a non-affiliated third party. Different databases providers will have different licensing requirements, so this part of the process will require a significant commitment of time. The database subscriptions will require considerable maintenance, including irregular troubleshooting and annual renewals.

Copyright issues will also have to be considered. For this area, the best procedure for this particular proposed service is to contact the legal department at the University and have it review the situation and give its recommendation. Many services pay regular fees to the Copyright Clearance Center to cover all costs. This non-profit center acts on behalf of copyright holders and collects and distributes fees for all copies that do not fall under the fair use doctrine. Most university and library administrations have worked with this organization in the past and should already have accounts and contacts in place. Ward recommends that copyright fees be paid on all documents copied on behalf of a client. She finds that this is a murky legal area and that erring on the side of conservatism is better than having legal problems down the road (66).

Liability issues are rare in this type of work, but can come up. Liability would occur if the service inadvertently provided information that was wrong or inaccurate and this somehow damaged the client's business. To deal preemptively with this issue before the research work begins, some services have clients sign a form which relieves the service of all liability. If such a form is used, the service would have to develop it with the assistance of the university's legal counsel. Ward discourages the use of a form, feeling that it inspires a lack of confidence in the client. Considerably more liberal in this legal area than she is concerning copyright, Ward sees the possibility of being sued as very small, and thus recommends discussing any potential limitations in the searching upfront with the client during the initial reference interview. This is usually sufficient to relieve all liability issues (Ward 67).

Confidentiality is another legal issue that needs to be clarified from the start. Businesses are often in keen competition with others working in the same area and will want their research interests kept secret. The research service will need to have a strict rule of confidentiality. All employees, including students, should be aware of this policy and understand its importance. Librarians will not find such a policy difficult to follow as it is in keeping with the tradition of confidentiality which is deeply ingrained in the library profession. Clients probably assume that their confidentiality will be respected, but it would be advisable to make a statement to that effect on any promotional material produced. It goes without saying that no client lists should be published or clients' names made public unless they give their permission.

A last legal issue to resolve would be to give the service a name, which is registered and must be distinct from any other service. Beyond the legal requirements, a distinctive and easy-to-remember name will establish the identity of the service (Ward 68). Much has been written about this process. Warner suggests using simple, easy to understand words that convey exactly what the service does. She feels that the initials that many services use can be confusing to customers (53). If the name does not indicate that the service is affiliated with the university and the library, that fact will have to be made clear in any promotional material or supplies, such as letterhead and business cards.

Promotion

Marketing will be an important concern in developing a fee-based service. A detailed strategy should be presented in the business plan. Inevitably, some customers will find the service by simply stumbling onto it or through word of mouth, but a well-thought-out marketing and promotion strategy will maintain a sustained, steady flow of customers. Without publicity, a fee-based service will probably fail (Simons 211). Marketing failures often lie in the fact that librarians are not trained to work in this area. In fact, librarians and libraries in general have trouble with marketing any of their services, not just fee-based ones (Gupta and Sevard 3559). Professional library literature of the last few years has been filled with articles about the problems libraries have in marketing their free services. It is no surprise then that marketing is a particularly troublesome issue for fee-based library services.

Marketing needs to be a large percentage of the manager's job, separate from the researching portion (Simon 157). The manager should look closely at the listing of potential clients and then make sure that the marketing efforts are directed to appropriate venues. Advertising should emphasize the results that a client will receive from the services, not the process that the researchers go through. The client will likely not care how the information is found or about the strength of the collection, but will only be interested in the results.

Funds for initial promotion will need to be accounted for in the start-up budget, although the marketing effort can include a combination of low and high cost methods. This varied approach should use several different high- and low-tech media sources. A good web page will be essential. The university or the library will have specialists who can assist in creating an eye-catching page, which will have an interactive element allowing potential clients to contact the service and inquire about it. In addition to the web page, the service will also need a paper brochure, which can be handed out at different venues and events. It is important to strike the right balance between looking professional, but not too slick and explaining the service sufficiently, but not being too wordy. The university's graphic design unit can help in the design process. The brochure can be sent to a variety of places, including the alumni office, local chambers of commerce, and public libraries.

Free advertising sources that take advantage of word-of-mouth are also useful. Speaking engagements with local organizations, such as entrepreneurial groups and inventors' clubs are good places to engage with potential customers. Attending trade fairs can also be helpful, but if they are not local, then travel expenses might be prohibitive. Leading training or informational programs at public libraries or other organizations can also be a helpful opportunity for promoting.

Potential Pitfalls

In most cases, fee-based business research services are well received by all concerned, but can involve complications (Josephine 12). One potential pitfall can be in the area of public relations. Community members who have received help in the past might be confused by the new fee-based research service and think they can no longer receive free reference help. This type of problem can be avoided with good communication. If it is made clear that traditional reference help will remain free of charge and that only a new "enhanced" service will carry a fee, then most people will understand that they are not losing anything. They might be glad to find that they are gaining access to a new service, albeit one that they have to pay for.

Another potential pitfall that will need consideration will be the level of discomfort felt by the librarians working for the service. Charging money for services goes against the basic beliefs of many librarians, so staff members will have to be chosen carefully (Warner 5). They will have to be aware of the additional layer of pressure that comes with charging a fee. Pressure, if not too great, can be a good motivator; however, it can also easily lead to burnout (Warner 11). In most cases, the pressure comes from unrealistic expectations. Generally, a good cure for these issues is, again, communication. If both clients and librarians understand exactly what the expectations are, then there will usually not be any reason for confusion or complaint.

Potential Positive Side Effects

The many potentially positive side effects easily counter the few negative ones. Foremost among these are the creation of new and rewarding relationships with potential donors. Business owners who are clients of the research service might think of the library when considering financial donations. Donations can be unrestricted or also tied in some way to the research service, such as money earmarked for collection development in the business area or seed money to establish an assistantship for a graduate students who can work for the service. In any case, the donation, even if specifically designated, will benefit the library as a whole. Alumni who have been helped by the research service will be especially receptive to this type of relationship. Connections can be made with influential members of the community or local government which can translate into unforeseen benefits at a later date.

A service like this can also give the library a chance to publicize itself and gain prestige within the community and among other libraries. Successful service in this area raises the image of the library outside of the institution. The longer the program is active, the more the librarians working for the service become specialized and skilled. As the reputation of the service increases, so will the number of highly qualified graduate students applying for its positions, and this will further raise the quality.

Conclusion

Having experience working with budding entrepreneurs, the researchers of the University of Kentucky Business Reference Outreach program know that a fee-based service is not a prospect to enter into lightly. In effect, a research service would function as a small business inside of the larger setting of the academic library and the university. Though there are many potentially positive outcomes to any entrepreneurial endeavor, it must be remembered that for the fee-based service, like any other business, there will be just as many, if not more, potential risks. In spite of the many efforts small business entrepreneurs make — sacrifice, hard work, and careful management of resources — many start-up businesses fail. A very important element in that mix that is often neglected is thorough background research used to make informed decisions. If the University of Kentucky Libraries decides to pursue the idea of a fee-based business and it is a success, some amount of credit will have to be given to careful preparation and research. Though librarians have not traditionally been thought of as entrepreneurs, perceptions might be changing. In an age where information is power, the time is right for librarians to assert themselves.

Works Cited

"2009–2014 Strategic Plan." University of Kentucky. 14 Jan. 2010. Web. 11 April 2011.

Brooks, Andrea Wilcox. "Library Research on Campus: Examining a Fee-Based Library Service Within University Walls." *The Journal of Academic Librarianship* 36.4 (2010): 347–350. Print.

Coffman, Steve, and Helen B. Josephine. "Doing it for Money." Library Journal 116 (1991): 32–6. Library Literature & Information Science Full Text. Web. 10 Apr. 2011.

Cloutier, Claudette. "Setting Up a Fee-Based Information Service in an Academic Library." *The Journal of Academic Librarianship* 31.4 (2005): 332–338. Print.

De Castell, Christina. "Research-on-Call." Business and Finance Division Bulletin Winter 2009: 24–5. Library Literature & Information Science Full Text. Web. 10 Apr. 2011.

Diamond, Wendy. *Reference and Information Services: Internal User Community."* *Managing Business Collections in Libraries.* Westport: Greenwood Press. 1996. Print.

Durbin, Roger and Jo Ann Calzonetti. "Academic Meets Corporate" *Science and Technology Libraries* 24. 1 (2004): 73–85. Print.

Fong, Yem, Suzanne M. Ward, and Tammy Nickelson Dearie. "Emerging Trends in Fee-Based Information Delivery." *Journal of Access Services* 1.1 (2002): 193–210. Print.

Fording, Richard. "Poverty in Kentucky: A New Look at an Old Problem." *Kentucky Annual Economic Report.* Lexington.: University of Kentucky Gatton College of Business Center for Business and Economic Research. 2011.

Giacoma, Pete. *The Fee or Free Decision: Legal, Economic, Political and Ethical Perspectives for Public Libraries.* New York: Neal-Schuman, 1989. Print.

Gupta, Dinesh K. and Rejean Savard. "Marketing Library and Information Services." *Encyclopedia of Library and Information Sciences.* Third Edition. (2010). 13 April 2011. http://www.informaworld.com/10.1081/E-ELIS3-120044552

Josephine, Helen. *Fee-Based Services in ARL Libraries* (Spec Kit 157). Washington, DC: Association of Research Libraries. 1989. Print.

Lowell, Martin A. *Enrichment: A History of the Public Library in the United States in the Twentieth Century.* Lanham: Scarecrow Press, 1998.

Nshaiwat, Naila Awad Mijalli. *Issues in fee-based information service in academic libraries: Entrepreneurial characteristics and managerial activities.* Diss. Indiana University, 1989. *ProQuest Dissertations & Theses: Full Text.* Web. 10 Apr. 2011

O'Sullivan, Kate. "Failure to Launch?" *CFO.* Oct. 2009: 35–37.

Pankl, Robert R. "Marketing the Public Library's Business Resources to Small Businesses." Journal of Business & Finance Librarianship 15.2 (2010): 94–103. Library Literature & Information Science Full Text. Web. 10 Apr. 2011

Sally, Dana M. "Prostitution, Simony, and Fees for Service: Walzer's Theory of Justice and a Defense of Communally Funded Information against the Tyranny of the Marketplace" *The Library Quarterly* 71.3 (2001): 330–359. Print.

Sheehy, Carolyn A. "Historical Foundations." *Managing Business Collections in Libraries.* Westport: Greenwood Press, 1996. Print.

Simon, Matthew. "One University's Experience Starting Fee-Based Information Systems: Two Case Studies form UNLV." *The Bottom Line: Managing Library Finances* 10.4 (1997): 153–157. Print.

Simons, Linda Keir. "Reference and Information Services: External User Community." *Managing Business Collections in Libraries.* Ed. Carolyn A. Sheehy. Westport: Greenwood Press, 1996.

Sloan, Scott. "Venture Clue Finds Reason for Optimism — Survey Shows Boost in 2010 Revenue." *Lexington Herald Leader* 26 January 2011: C7. Print.

"Top Twenty Business Plan." University of Kentucky. 27 Aug. 2009. Web. 11 April 2011.

Troske, Kenneth R. and Christopher Jepsen. "The U.S. and Kentucky Economies in 2010: When Will the Recovery 'Really Start?'" *Kentucky Annual Economic Report.* Lexington: University of Kentucky Gatton College of Business Center for Business and Economic Research, 2011.

"UK Libraries Strategic Plan, 2010–2014." University of Kentucky Libraries. 05 March 2010. Web. 11 April 2011.

Ward, Suzanne M. *Starting and Managing Fee-Based Information Services in Academic Libraries.* Greenwich: Jai Press, 1997. Print.

Ward, Suzanne M., Yem S. Fong, and Damon Camille. "Library Fee-Based Information Services: Financial Considerations." *The Bottom Line: Managing Library Finances* 15.1 (2002): 5–17. Print

Warner, Alice Sizer. *Making Money: Fees for Library Services.* New York: Neal-Schuman Publishers, 1989. Print.

9 — Putting on a Race
for Funds and Fun

SUSAN SHARPLESS SMITH *and* ERIK MITCHELL

Introduction

Libraries have a history of seeking innovative ways to fund local program needs. Common approaches include book sales or book author lectures but libraries also turn to less traditional methods such as athletic events or corporate partnerships. In 2008, Z. Smith Reynolds Library (ZSR) of Wake Forest University, found itself seeking funding for a popular semi-annual event, *Wake the Library*, which requires up to $8,000 to support it each year. Originally, sufficient funding came from internal University sources. However, in recent years, departmental belts tightened as budgets shrank, and ZSR Library turned outside the University to find supporting funds. The "Wake the Library 5K and 1 Mile Fun Run" (WTL5K) was born as a way to raise these funds, but it was soon recognized as more. As the authors planned the first race, they identified a side-benefit: the race provided a chance to re-define the library's role in the community. This chapter will explore fundraising through athletic events and present a case study that chronicles the evolution in planning and organizing that leads to a successful 5K. This case study is contextualized with data gathered from other libraries that also use an athletic event as a fundraiser. Using our three years of race-director experience, the authors offer best practices — not only on the mechanics of race preparation, but also for marketing, establishing partnerships/sponsorships, recruiting volunteers and maximizing the bottom line.

Background

Libraries have, by necessity, been involved with fundraising for a long time. In recent years a decrease in financial support for libraries has become the norm, and fundraising has become an established practice in both academic and public libraries. Dewey (5) cites four major reasons for libraries to get involved with fundraising: the rising cost of technology, an imperative by the parent institution, limited support from the parent institution, and the rising cost of library materials. Libraries, of course, are not alone in using events to promote a need or service. Special events have been used in the United States as far back as the Civil War to raise money and awareness (Vander). As many libraries have discovered, even if the primary goal is fundraising, building and enhancing community support are just as important. Although major fundraising programs focus on long-term methods such as developing a donor base or becoming part of a capital campaign, many libraries supplement those efforts by taking an entrepreneurial approach using creative fundraising ideas to meet smaller funding needs. Every library user is familiar with the traditional book sale, and as an extension of this practice, innovative libraries seek new approaches that will attract new support (Balas 32).

In addition to raising funds through special events, building relationships with library users, the community, potential donors and businesses are key goals (Rader 95; Dewey 9). Not only can these events raise money, they can also create publicity, attract members and volunteers, and educate and enhance relationships (Seltzer 180). In her discussion of charitable giving and special events, Prater notes other opportunities: they can appeal to participants as a way to fulfill personal goals while contributing to a cause at the same time (Bekkers and Wiepking), offer the potential to convert the special event buyer to an annual fund donor (Wayson 79), and provide a networking opportunity for the organization to increase its community connections and enhance existing relationships (Prater 5).

Participatory sporting events such as 5K footraces and fun runs have grown in popularity in the decades since running was popularized as a healthy lifestyle in the 1970's. A 5K is the type of charity special event that can fulfill multiple purposes for a participant: it can help a cause while meeting a parallel need for personal fitness (Prater 5). The organization sponsoring a participatory sporting event has the potential to engage new supporters (Pacey 28) and generate a new energy surrounding its image while raising funds. This type of event has been growing in popularity with libraries. Examples include the "Racing to Read" Kenton Library 5K <www.kentonlibrary.org/race>, the "Race to the Rock" at Clemson University <www.clemson.edu/administration/president/race/> and the "Love your Libraries 5K" at the University of Tennessee Knoxville <web.utk.edu/~gss/funrun.html>. While not every event is coordinated within the library, each of these has its primary purpose as supporting library fundraising needs.

Although large scale annual endeavors such as the Susan G. Komen Race for the Cure can be international in scope and raise millions of dollars, the majority of running and walking events are smaller in scale, attract fewer participants and may raise limited funds (Prater 2). Smaller races may be due in part to the population of participants sought but may also be due to poor planning and organization. Professional fundraising organizations (Pacey 28; Wolf 6–8) emphasize the importance of careful planning and organization to increase the likelihood of a successful event. In addition to affecting revenues, a poorly planned and executed event can reflect poorly on the sponsoring organization and fail to engage new supporters (Pacey 28).

Survey of Libraries

While athletic events are a proven method for building community support and fundraising in general (Rader 93), and libraries have a history of benefiting from athletic support events (Neal 58), the review of literature indicated a lack of research addressing the motivations and approaches for libraries that organize 5K events. While the authors' experience of coordinating a 5K demonstrated that such an event could be largely successful on a small to medium scale, the extent to which smaller 5Ks served the goals of fundraising and community building were unknown. To address this question, in the spring of 2011 the authors conducted a survey of libraries that have coordinated athletic events.

The survey sought to answer three specific questions. First, do libraries use athletic events as a fundraiser? Second, for the libraries that do, what primary goals are they seeking? Finally, our survey sought to answer the question "How did libraries approach the coordination of the event?" The survey was conducted online using the Zoomerang platform, consisted of nineteen questions and gathered a mix of qualitative and quantitative data. The full survey is available in Appendix A.

Survey Responses

The researchers used multiple solicitation methods to gather responses. Solicitation emails were sent to numerous library listservs selected to represent a wide spectrum of libraries, including lists for public, academic, law, medical and general libraries and also listservs focused on topics including public service, IT, administration, resource services and digital-services. The researchers also sought out participants who were known to have conducted an athletic event. A broad search of race sites yielded twenty potential participants. Efforts were made to contact the race director associated with each of these races. In total, out of fifty visits to the survey, only eight libraries indicated that they used an athletic event as a fundraiser. All eight libraries held 5K events and one library held a Golf tournament in addition to a 5K. The low level of completion rate for the survey, despite a rather high number of visits, limits the ability to generalize the results of the survey but perhaps provides an interesting perspective on the small number of libraries that engage in this sort of event.

"Do libraries use athletic events as fundraisers?"

The types of libraries that responded were academic or academic health (3) and public libraries (5). No other library categories were represented (e.g. Law, Corporate, Special) in the survey results. Population size for six of the eight libraries was over 10,000 with five of the libraries serving populations of fifty thousand or more.

The average race size was 306 participants but with a wide variance in populations. The largest race had 803 participants and the smallest was 75. The median number of participants was approximately 200. Libraries reported a wide range of years in which the race had been conducted. The oldest event has been held for 19 years but five of the eight libraries had held their events from one to four years. A commonly held convention in 5K events is that a race can be expected to grow in numbers over time. In this survey race size did not appear to be tied to the number of years in which the event had been held. In fact, the one library reporting that this was their first year also reported a registration rate between 300–400 participants.

Although certainly not conclusive, the lack of responses to the survey indicates that the 5K is not a widely used fundraising method in libraries. Although some libraries visited the survey and indicated that they did not hold a 5K, a majority of respondents abandoned the survey without completing the initial questions. As a substantiating piece of information, it proved to be difficult to identify a wide range of libraries using athletic events as fundraisers in the authors' own search of the Web. Of note, no libraries completed the survey that had once held but had discontinued a 5K event. Although the initial results of the survey are inconclusive with regards to determining how popular 5K races are in libraries, opportunities exist to expand the survey and call for participation to discover how widely spread this type of event is and whether or not there are libraries that have discontinued use of a 5K as a fundraiser.

"What primary goals do libraries have in holding athletic events?"

The survey questions in this area focused on identifying the primary and secondary goals of libraries holding athletic events. Again, the low response rate of libraries means that inferential statistics cannot be used to generalize these responses but some interesting trends can be noted. The authors identified five primary goals for libraries that hold special events. These goals are fundraising, community building, fulfilling general or specialized programming needs, outreach to special populations and supporting other organizations. In order to gather this data the authors asked libraries to rate each goal on a scale from "Not very important" to "Very important." From this list it was apparent that fundraising was the primary goal for all libraries (88% listed fundraising as "Very important"). Despite this focus, survey respondents often concentrated on community building comments in response to open-ended questions, for example, "It's a lot of work, but seeing the huge crowd there on race day and the energy the runners and walkers bring makes it all worthwhile." "It was a great experience and it was the first time that the community got to participate in a University event." In fact, secondary goals (those listed as "Important") included "community building" (50%), and "fulfilling special or general programming needs" (50%). These results and associated comments indicate that the lasting impact of an event like this may outweigh primary event goals.

The survey asked a related question about whether or not libraries met their primary (e.g. fundraising) goals. Libraries who responded indicated that in general, their funds raised were relatively low, on the order of $2000 — $4000. The most successful race indicated that they had met their $8000 fundraising goals the last two years but that that success was due mostly to the generosity of departmental and student organization sponsors within the University. In general, the responses on fundraising were positive but displayed awareness of current fund-raising issues. "We have a great group of sponsors but are having trouble reaching a higher level even though race participation has grown tremendously in the past several years."

One library indicated that the primary goal of fund-raising was to ensure that the race was at least revenue neutral. They reported approximately $5000 as the general cost for holding the race. A larger event that took an "outsource" approach indicated that their budget was $12,000 and included all race services—"filing the barricade plan and proper permits with the city, providing food and water, the printing of the T-shirts. There were additional expenses: Porta Potty rental, as well as trophies and awards costs, but they were also budgeted for. The entire budget was almost $12,000." It is interesting to note that of the eight respondents, only one indicated having a formal budget set aside for the event.

"How did libraries approach the coordination of the event?"

The final question that the authors sought to answer was concerning the implementation approaches of libraries that held 5K events. As the literature review found, there are a number of options for event coordination, including in-house coordination, collaboration, external partnerships or outright outsourcing (Wolf 7; Road Runners Club of America 4). Further, the authors' analysis of approaches found that decisions on how to select a method is largely, but not always, based on internal factors (e.g. staff time, organizational expertise) as opposed to external factors (e.g. race site selection, community interest). The survey examined how libraries approached six key areas of race-coordination: race timing/event handling, graphics design, event planning, marketing, fundraising, and event-day staffing. Five of the eight respondent libraries completed this question. Table 1 shows broadly how the libraries approached this issue:

Event Aspect	Outsourced	Hybrid	In-house
Race timing	5	0	0
Graphics design	0	2	3
Event Planning	1	3	1
Marketing	1	2	2
Fund-raising	0	3	2
Event-day staffing	0	3	2

Table 1: Race Coordination Approach.

As Table 1 shows, most libraries chose to handle much of the race planning, fundraising and marketing internally while choosing to outsource race timing. It was interesting to find that, by far, libraries had partnered with other units within their organizations but separate from the libraries (e.g. student groups, friends of the library groups, university development) for much of this work. In some cases, particularly the student-run event at the University of Tennessee at Knoxville, the event was cast as a partnership between the library and external groups (in this case the Student Senate).

The qualitative data gathered in this section indicates that libraries form ad-hoc networks of expertise for elements that are conducted in-house or in a hybrid environment. For example, each library identified a particular person or department that was instrumental in graphics design or fundraising. In one case a library hired an outside graphics designer. Similarly, event planning was an area where libraries tended to turn for external expertise. "We internally planned the event and the LV Running Team handled the permits and barricade plans."

The low response rate and largely positive nature of the survey results indicates that conducting athletic events as fundraisers in libraries is a niche but popular activity. This expectation is supported by the authors' own search for libraries who could participate in the survey. The libraries that were successfully contacted were enthusiastic about sharing their experiences. The open-ended comments also show that this type of event is often not used as the centerpiece event at a library. Although some events indicated a good participant rate, overall the fundraising goals and low participant rates show that the decision to conduct an event such as this needs to include soft-costs (e.g. personnel time) and certainly indirect benefits (e.g. marketing, sense of community) as well as firm costs and goals. The authors of this chapter included this survey to either qualify or substantiate our own experience with holding a 5K. While the results showed some variation in how events were planned and conducted, it was interesting to see that the motivations behind and positive outcomes of these events were largely in line with our own experience. In the case study section of this chapter we explore the circumstances surrounding the ZSR Library's own event in more detail and discuss some of the details of holding an athletic fund raising event.

Case Study

The "Wake the Library" exam event grew out of student interest in expanded library hours during exams. In 2004, ZSR Library operated on a schedule where the library closed at 1:00 A.M. Sunday through Thursday. Student Government approached ZSR Library's Dean to ask her to keep the library open 24 hours during exam week.

The Library decided not only to stay open all night, but also to provide a study break and food for the students each night at midnight as a way to support their academic efforts. Library staff solicited campus departments for food for 250–300 students each night. The event was christened "Wake the Library" and was immediately successful, quickly becoming a semi-annual tradition (McGrath). After 4 years, internal funding began to dry up as budgets tightened across campus, but the interest of the students in continuing this event did not diminish so the Library needed to seek other funding avenues.

The genesis for a solution originated in 2006 when a group of ZSR librarians decided to form a running group and train for a marathon together. The experience was a positive one, so much so that the group continued to plan annual group events. The group's success illustrated the benefits of community building and because running events are popular and potentially profitable, the idea of a 5K was proposed in 2008 as a good way to raise the funds needed to support Wake the Library. Because the authors were the two staff members with the most experience participating in races, we were asked to take the lead on planning the event. Despite our experience as event participants, the authors discovered quickly that running races is not the same as organizing them, so we started with our core librarian strength: doing research! In this process we connected with local running and sports stores in town for ideas about how to get started. This was invaluable to not only understanding the logistics of putting on a race but also in staking a claim in the 5K race schedule. Next, we turned to other units at the University, leveraging connections with campus recreation and food service. Campus Recreation is a department with a wealth of experience running a variety of participatory sporting events. They were key in helping to plan the event and identifying requirements specific to Wake Forest University (e.g. police staffing, event coordination, insurance and marketing opportunities). The campus food service department brought extensive expertise in catering large events including managing food and atmosphere and helped the race directors secure supporters and provided event resources. Through this process, the authors discovered that planning the 5K allowed the Library to develop ongoing relationships both inside and outside the University. Part of the growth of these relationships was due to the opportunity to "share the stage" with partners and over time the Library has had the opportunity to reciprocate this support.

During the process, we also discovered unknown areas of event planning expertise within the library staff that contributed to the successful outcome. Over time, this expertise and support has enabled the planning committee to grow from the two race directors to an eight-person team. This support is seen to be a key factor in enabling long-term viability of an event that is outside of the core business model of the library. The Wake the Library 5K and 1 Mile Fun Run completed its third year in 2010. In that time the race committee learned a lot about the aspects of people management, race planning and race-day coordination. The following section discusses these areas and their related components. Included are the ways in which the elements evolved from year to year, resulting in local best practices.

People and Organizations: Forging Relationships

Organizing a sporting event is not something that can be accomplished by just a few people. It is a complex process, and one of the major considerations is how to build relationships that will enhance the success of the event and lay a foundation for the future. As indicated above, while the definition of the overall vision may fall to a few people, the wide range of tasks required means that there is likely to be hidden expertise in any organization that can be leveraged to make planning easier and the event more successful.

Partnerships

The authors (race directors) quickly realized that there were people with much more experience in both race and event planning and that it would be to our benefit to form partnerships with them to assist in the race. Shortly after selecting a race date, we contacted Campus Recreation (CR) and received valuable advice on issues ranging from course selection to t-shirt vendors. They also committed a staff member to coordinate race day activities and provided equipment including water coolers, traffic cones, and a starting gun — all things that would have cost additional money to procure. ARAMARK, the campus food service provider, was the inaugural race's first "named sponsor," but also supplied the finish line balloon arch, ice, and water. They worked with the race directors to place marketing materials in the dining areas and opened the campus coffee shop early on race day. In the first year, the race directors saw the value in forming a partnership with a local running store. The running store helped to identify important race planning elements, provided awards and race numbers, and helped promote the event. Libraries responding to the survey reported a use of partnerships as well, often distributing the work of race coordination, marketing and development across multiple people or departments. A key way to approach these partnerships is to both define organizations or internal units with which a collaboration would be fruitful (e.g. CR) or to identify areas of race planning that are unfamiliar (e.g. finish line services) and to seek partners to fill that need. The WTL5K also leveraged an initial partnership with the Student Council who requested the expanded library hours for ongoing support through the race. This approach to planning helps bring in participants and support. After the first race, a staff member at the university observed: "Involving others in departmental initiatives oftentimes reaps benefits in the lives of those who come alongside. Who would have thought that a few months back when you asked me to help with your 5K that I would continue with the running. Thanks again for not only your example of fitness but your ability to conduct a top notch race (Floyd)."

SPONSORSHIPS/FUNDRAISING

Sponsorships are a necessary and important way to underwrite the cost of a special event (Prater 23). For a running event, sponsorships can come in the form of cash, or in-kind gifts. Sometimes in-kind gifts can significantly defray cost of resources for conducting a 5K. For example, a grocery store manager often can commit to donating water and food at the local level, where a request for a cash donation would require going up the corporate chain. The race directors found that having a mix of sponsorships was optimal in the goal to cover the costs detailed in the budget section below. Soliciting sponsorships is a process that is best started months in advance, as potential sponsors often have an annual budget for donations and make commitments at the beginning of their fiscal year. Securing sponsorships is most often about establishing a relationship through a personal interaction and cultivating that relationship to increase the potential of extending the sponsorship to future years. It goes without saying that sponsors should receive formal thank you letters following race days that include race statistics to demonstrate the impact of their participation.

Depending on a library's parent organization, there may be restrictions on independent outreach to secure sponsors. At Wake Forest, there are organizations that contribute to the University on a high level, and it is counterproductive to approach them and ask them to specifically sponsor a library race. ZSR Library works with the larger University Development effort to coordinate solicitation. It also finds sponsorship opportunities through relationships with internal Wake Forest departments and individuals.

RACE STEERING COMMITTEE

During the first year, the authors, as co-race directors, tackled all aspects of race planning, only pulling in a few people to assist. The race was successful, but the race directors were exhausted. For the second year's race, we formed a WTL5K Race Steering Committee. In addition to the two co-directors, we brought in a volunteer coordinator, a member of the library's marketing committee, a person to head fundraising and a team of two to manage in-kind (food) donations. A committee approach has worked well for the last two races. Putting a separate person in charge of each distinct area facilitated the ability to meet goals much more efficiently.

VOLUNTEERS

Volunteers are an essential component for putting on a participatory sporting event. Volunteers can be used for everything from helping with registration, giving direction on the racecourse, assisting with finish line duties and staffing water and food stations. At ZSR Library, race directors recruited library faculty and staff, but quickly discovered that more volunteers were needed to adequately cover all needs. At an academic library, the pool of student workers is always a benefit; however, asking them to actually "volunteer" early on a Saturday morning during Homecoming weekend might not yield a very large pool. Race directors opted for asking them to "volunteer" for their normal hourly wage, breakfast and a race t-shirt.

A volunteer coordinator is an essential aspect of good volunteer management. Often volunteers can only commit to a few hours on the day of the race and may not have previous expertise. The directors found this to be the case with students in particular who had never been to a 5K before. Even in an event as small as the WTL5K a pool of 25 volunteers was required to staff the registration desk, manage the food, staff the course and assist racers as needed. As the pool grew we found that we needed several area-specific coordinators to coordinate volunteers. This simplified training and direction and ensured that volunteers had a direct connection to someone "in charge."

Planning for the Event

The Road Runners Club of America recommends that in-depth planning should begin far in advance of the race; at least 6 to 12 months ahead (2). Planning many months ahead will improve the probability for securing a good date and increasing sponsorships. Planning includes a number of aspects from budgeting and date/site selection to partner coordination, marketing and fund solicitation. This section reviews each of these areas in detail.

BUDGET

Even though the purpose of most running events is to raise funds, there are fixed expenses that will be incurred in putting on a race. It is recommended that a budget be put in place that will account for those expenses, whether or not registrations and/or sponsorships are collected. Expenses, discussed in detail below, include: permits, insurance, race timing, t-shirts, awards, race numbers, food and water, sound system, portable toilets, and marketing. Race directors must make commitments to these while having only estimates of race participation. A wide variance between budget and actual revenues can result in a failure to raise sufficient funds or ending up in the red.

For WTL5K's initial year in 2008, race directors focused on obtaining a major "named" sponsor, an organization that would donate enough cash to cover the expenses that had to be committed to at the outset. We were fortunate to accomplish that goal, and ZSR Library's first race was the "ARAMARK Wake the Library 5K and 1 Mile Fun Run." This served to provide a base-line level of money that we knew could be relied upon. In subsequent years, race organizers were able to use the residue from years one and two. Proper budgeting means also planning for race growth over time. Costs that scale with the number of participants (e.g. T-Shirts, printing costs, food costs and timing company fees) should be increased from year-to-year to accommodate expected growth. The authors' own experience is that registration fees should typically be designed to at least cover race costs so that sponsorships can be used to support the charity or program being supported by the 5K. Granted, certain costs such as in-kind food donations help defray the actual cost but should be included in a race budget just in case these donations are not realized.

DATE/TIME SELECTION

Selection of a good date and time has a direct impact on the event's success. Spring and fall are prime times to hold races in just about any area of the country. It is important when selecting a date to check potential dates against local race calendars. It is hard to get a foothold into the race calendar if a date is selected that is in competition with an already established race. In an academic setting, the school's events calendar must also be a consideration. For the *Wake the Library 5K*, race directors worked through the University Events office to get clearance to hold the race on campus. This office gets a sign-off from major functional departments (e.g. Athletics, Campus Police, and Facilities) before approving any event. Public libraries may find an equivalent process is required with local government. If the event is designed to be an annual one, selecting a consistent date that will work each year will contribute toward long-term success (Prater 22).

SITE SELECTION/COURSE DESIGN/COURSE MEASUREMENT

The Wake Forest campus is known for its beauty and is used often by other groups as all or part of race routes. ZSR Library is one of the original buildings on campus and as the image in Figure 1 shows, provides a perfect backdrop for the race's start and finish line. In addition, it offers abundant rest room facilities AND a coffee shop for the spectators!

Route design should include accommodation for both scenery and logistics. There are many different route possibilities, so race directors considered factors such as number of intersections, construction areas (recent years have seen many new buildings going up), and impact on the residential neighborhood that is adjacent to campus. The campus police require that officers be stationed at each intersection so a course with multiple intersections will cost more for traffic control. The first year, to reduce the cost of traffic control, we routed the course through the campus cross-country trail. While it appeared to be a good idea, this decision required caused extra course preparation tasks and increased the complexity of the event on race day.

Figure 1— Wake the Library 5K, October 2009 (photograph courtesy Thomas J. Fischer).

What is the optimal distance for a running event? This is a question carefully considered. A 5K distance is one that is an achievable goal for most people. With a bit of training, at the least, people can walk the 3.1 miles. However, directors also wanted to be family friendly, so decided to include a 1-mile fun run/walk component. This provided a way to include young children and parents with strollers. While longer events are popular (e.g. 10K, Half Marathon and Full Marathons), these distances require appealing to a wider population, more planning and more race-day logistics. Because a 5K appeals to a broader portion of the population and race day expenses and logistics are lower, the 5K can be a more efficient approach to athletic event fund-raisers.

In general, racecourse preparation should be left to someone with race coordination expertise. This includes course setup, measuring, marking and volunteer and water-table placement. With the popularization of global positioning systems (GPS), it seems an easy task to measure out a 1-mile and a 5K course. However, GPS accuracy is not a simple matter. An accurate course is important to veteran racers and an inaccurate course is quickly noted. Most timing companies will provide course measurement as part of their service. In addition to good measurement, you should rely on your racecourse manager to mark the course with directional signage either the evening before the race or early on race day.

PERMISSION/PERMITS

Unless your library sits on a very large plot of land, you will need to obtain permissions to use the property through which your course runs, which may involve requesting permission from local authorities and obtaining required permits. Building in a long planning window will diffuse tension and lower planning stress. The *Wake the Library 5K* is held on both the Wake Forest campus and the nearby Reynolda Garden estate. Although the property is owned by Wake Forest, it is under separate management and required a separate authorization. As mentioned in a previous section, directors also had to obtain permission from major units on campus. It can be difficult to determine from whom permission needs to be obtained but this is an important aspect of course preparation and planning.

INSURANCE

Having insurance to cover the possibility of mishaps is not optional. Not only do most race timing companies require some form of race insurance, the governing organization of your library is likely to be more supportive of an event if it is insured. In some cases the parent organization of the library (e.g. University or city/county government) has existing insurance that will cover the event. Timing companies will require proof of insurance to protect their activities on race day.

TRAFFIC CONTROL

Unless the event is being held on trails, traffic control requires major attention and will most likely involve a partnership with community police. The directors worked with campus police who have experience in knowing where officers needed to be placed. The police positioned personnel at each intersection so that traffic could be halted as participants came through. Even though they are experts in this area, it is important to meet with them early on and again just before race day, because they need to understand the goals of the event and the expectations for the day. The second and third years of the race were held in conjunction with Homecoming. This added complexity to the process of traffic control because there were hundreds of people coming on campus for other events. Consider using traffic cones to supplement police and make sure that your racecourse coordinator has a method for communicating with the officer in charge. If traffic will be coming through the racecourse roads, cones can be used to restrict a lane for participants and an open communication channel can help manage the flow of traffic.

WATER STATIONS

According to the Road Runners Club of America, water station placement depends upon the length of the race and the time of year (8). Since a 5K is a fairly short distance, directors opted for providing a water station in a spot where runners would pass it during the first half of the distance and then run by again during the last half. Water stations benefit from having their own coordinators and sufficient volunteers as the setup, staffing, and disassembly is time consuming and filled with brief periods of intense activity.

SAFETY/SECURITY

When planning an event where hundreds of people of all ages are exerting themselves athletically on courses that might be shared with vehicular traffic and cover multiple miles over varying terrains, ensuring the safety of all participants is a primary goal. Safety of the participants should guide site selection and course layout. Race organizers should inspect the racecourse for safety multiple times prior to race day. On race day, traffic control is key for safety. It is also highly advisable to have medical personnel on hand. For all of the race events, directors engaged the Wake Forest's student emergency medical team to station a person at the start/finish line and to have a person cover the course by bicycle throughout the race. In addition, they assigned a person to lead the race by pacing the fastest runner while riding a bike (see Figure 2). This ensured that racers did not get off-course. This person then continually rode along the course and acted as the sweeper to make sure the last racers got to the finish line safely.

Safety also includes informing participants of potential risks and being aware of current conditions. During the registration process, participants should sign a waiver. Standard waivers are easily located through a Web search. The directors turned to a local running club and adapted theirs. Although races typically take place rain or shine, race day weather should be a prime safety consideration. Races should be delayed if a thunderstorm is imminent and organizers will want to be prepared to aid runners on extremely hot or bitterly cold days.

FOOD

A race should provide food to help participants fuel their bodies prior to the event and/or refuel at its end. For a short distance, providing food at the finish line will suffice. WTL5K provided food that local businesses donated: donuts, bagels, and fruit are easy to manage and are good choices to provide. As one of the most time consuming parts of a 5K is the generation of race results after the race is completed, a well-stocked food table helps keep racers happy while waiting for results to be posted.

Figure 2 — Co-Director Ready to Pace Race Leaders, 2009 (photograph courtesy John Borwick).

REGISTRATION

Managing pre-race registrations can be a labor-intensive process. There are online options such as services offered by Active.com that can automate and streamline the process. Active.com is a free service if organizers opt to pass the company's processing charge (a few dollars per registration) to the participant. Providing a manual registration process as an alternative for participants is valued and was used by about 30% of WTL5K race participants. In addition to tracking registrations and collecting fees, Active.com made it easy to set up different race divisions, at different fees and could build a database of racers to be used for pre-race communications and to promote the next year's race to previous participants.

Since students often do not like to commit until the last minute, the directors chose to allow race day registrations up until a few minutes before the start of the race. This added a level of complexity to tracking race results, but netted many additional registrations.

Establishing the right cost is important to the success of attracting registrations. Over time directors found that it helped to set an early bird registration price ($20) that increased to $25 by race week. We found that offering a family rate for the fun run increased participation. In years two and three, we established a student rate of $10 to attract more undergraduate participation. This change resulted in an overall increase in student registrations but also flattened the revenues that were received from that portion of the population.

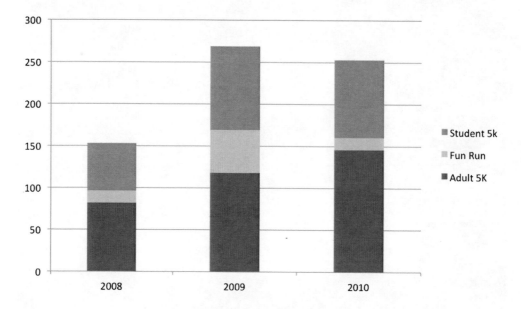

Table 2 — Registration Counts.

As Table 2 shows, student registrations rose dramatically from 2008 to 2009 due, in most part, to the change in race fees. In 2010 the race had a leveling off of student registrations. The bump of fun-run participants in 2009 was due to the addition of a "Library Book Challenge" that the library promoted with the public school system. The school with the highest number of race registrations was awarded a grant to purchase books for their library. The grant was secured through a book provider as a donation to the race. The increase in registrations was high enough that it impacted the overall registration revenue as well. Although this promotion was not run in 2010, an increase in adult registrations, as well as a maintained level of student involvement, helped the race keep pace with prior years.

The data from Table 3 illustrates the number of overall dollars raised through race registrations alone. As the data shows, properly targeted special promotions such as student registration fees or focused competitions can have a measurable impact on event participation. Other campaigns were attempted, including an alumni challenge and "Sleep in for

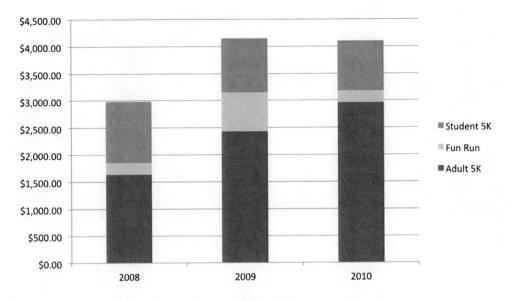

Table 3 — Registration Revenues.

the Library," an event that encouraged people who did not want to run but did want to support the library through race registrations, but these did not result in a dramatic impact on registration numbers or revenue.

TIMING THE RACE

As the survey results showed, race timing was the single element that all libraries outsourced completely by partnering with running clubs or race organizations. Race timing is perhaps the most fundamental of services and care should be taken to ensure that it is run well from course marking/setup, to timing splits to quick delivery of race results. In the WTL5K event, directors found that keeping the race categories simple helped facilitate timing. Likewise, we found that the decision to work with an online race registration service (e.g. Active.com) facilitated the relationship with the running club we used since a complete registrant database can be delivered to the timers.

MARKETING

The survey data showed that libraries tended to partner both with external organizations and also continued to focus on internal expertise for marketing. In the WTL5K races, the authors found that much of the participation came from Wake Forest's core community, meaning that race marketing activities needed to focus on attracting participants from this population. As part of this effort ZSR Library sponsored a number of race categories including a Greek Life competition, a public school competition and a homecoming weekend alumni participation competition. As reported in the section on revenue, these competitions sometimes boosted participation and other times did not. The most successful promotion involved the public school challenge where county schools competed to win books for their school library. This parent's comments and Figure 3 reflect the positive result of the challenge: "We had fun! I was so proud of my kids running that 5K! Chase was the youngest

Figure 3 — The Demon Deacon (school mascot) with Student Group, 2009 (photograph courtesy Z. Smith Reynolds Library).

who ran it and he was very excited about that! Chase also attends Southwest Elementary and we are very excited our school won the books contest! (Cannon)."

Over the course of the three years the Library also sought to identify marketing methods that were a match with its core populations. The marketing representative sought out coverage on student-run websites, the University newspaper and canvassed the university with brochures, flyers and table-tents. In a University setting, being able to advertise in residence halls and the cafeteria provides opportunities to connect with each student. In public library settings, the survey found that libraries often partnered with external organizations, businesses or news channels to advertise their races. Marketing efforts also utilized the ZSR Library website <http://zsr.wfu.edu/wtl5k>, and attempted to use social media including Facebook™ advertisements, Twitter™ and Flickr™ (Z. Smith Reynolds Library). While the group found that a large population of users saw the Facebook™ advertisements, it is unknown how many participants were enticed to register. Databases of known racers are a good source of targeted marketing. For example, the database of current and past race registrants in Active.com was another valuable method for outreach in marketing as was the distribution of several hundred race brochures through the local running club to its membership.

Packet Pick Up

Packet pick up is a central element of any race. Experienced participants expected the library to have race packets available for pick up on the day before the race. While somewhat unanticipated in the first year, directors found that by planning for this we could be better prepared for race day registrations. We also found that by moving the deadline for coordination back a single day to accommodate this, other elements such as volunteer training and coordination were facilitated as well.

T-Shirts

While seemingly one of the simpler aspects of a race, selecting a t-shirt provider and pulling together the required elements of price, sizing, sponsors, shirt design and logos in time can be difficult. This item also requires the collaboration of race directors (t-shirt quantities and sizing), marketing/graphics, and fundraisers. For a small race, the cost negotiated for t-shirts can make the difference between positive and negative revenues. The WTL5K directors found that estimating the number of shirts to be ordered for race-day registrations was difficult. In general, adding 30% to the current registrant list will provide a sufficient amount to cover most race-day registrants. It is also important to be sure to order shirts for volunteers. If funding exists, making these shirts different either through shirt color or graphics is important so that participants can easily locate help if needed.

RACE NUMBERS

Race numbers can be purchased by number companies, included as part of a sponsorship agreement with a running company, or solicited for free from companies like roadid.com. Obtaining race numbers early is easy and a good way to check off an item but it is important for order race numbers include the proper timing element (e.g. pull tab).

AWARDS

Awards can be difficult to coordinate, particularly if an event has a wide range of race categories. Although in the first year the race directors attempted to find cash or gift card prizes for first/second/third place winners in all age groups, in subsequent years we found that a nicely printed award certificate was just as much appreciated. Of course, award cat-

Figure 4 — Age group and Lenovo® laptop winner Helen Daughtry with co-director Susan Smith (photograph courtesy Z. Smith Reynolds Library).

egories depend on your race environment but typically, over-all male/female finishers plus age groups in five-year increments with male and female categories work well. If a decision is made to include prizes, it has been found more effective, as was confirmed in this case study, to aim for one big item rather than many small inexpensive ones (Wolf 7). For years two and three, ZSR Library secured Lenovo® as a sponsor that donated computers. The first year, two donated computers were awarded to the top men and women's finishers. The steering committee decided, upon post-race review, that this use of a large award did not really maximize the potential for expanding registrations. There are only so many people who really believe they might possibly win and then register in hopes of winning the top prize. The second time (Year three), Lenovo® donated one computer and the planning group decided to raffle it to all race participants who stayed through the awards ceremony. Figure 4 illustrates both the award certificate and shows the Lenovo® raffle winner in 2010.

RACE DAY COORDINATION

Race day is both exciting and stressful. On race day morning race directors will be trying to orchestrate all of the events and aspects that have been building in the preceding months. Delegation is important here, utilizing trained volunteers to be responsible for different areas. Key areas include course setup and monitoring, PA announcements and music, food/water, race desk registration and overall coordination. No matter how well the event is planned things will go wrong and on the spot choices will have to be made. On race day a good communication plan needs to be in place. While cell-phones can form a good ad-hoc communication network, a set of short-distance radios can also be useful in ensuring that individuals responsible for the different elements of the race stay in communication. It is particularly important to keep the timing company, police and volunteers up to speed on how many racers are left on the course and when the last racer is finished. While electronic communication devices are helpful, having a racecourse manager on the course monitoring conditions is the most useful way to ensure that everyone stays in touch.

Conclusion

The authors' review of literature, coupled with a survey and our own experience, support the idea that the ability to achieve key goals (e.g. fund raising and community building) in the first years of a race are primary motivators to continued development and support of the event. We have also found, however, that indirect costs such as staff time and library focus on this event, as opposed to other priorities, are significant considerations for organizations that choose to organize a similar event. Our review of literature and the results of the survey revealed that athletic events as fundraisers for libraries are neither widespread nor the most efficient means of fundraising in libraries. Regardless, the organizations that choose to use this approach report a wide range of positive outcomes including fundraising, community building, the ability to connect with new constituents and the ability to portray the library in a new light. For organizations considering this type of event as opposed to other forms of fundraising, key considerations include internal expertise/time, the alignment with the community's values, and potential levels of external support.

For ZSR Library, while immediate fundraising needs were met, the overwhelming benefit following three years of the event came from the goodwill it generated and the new relationships that formed. These participant comments capably sum up why it has been a valuable endeavor:

"We had an awesome time this morning. Thank you again for another great event! It has become a new family tradition.... This was Tatum's second run, although it was the first outside of the womb! She had a blast and squealed with delight the entire time. [Here] are the thoughts from the kids: "Thank you for letting us run in the Fun Run and for giving us the cows. We had a really good time. It was fun because I love running and that is pretty much the only thing you do at the Fun Run. We also liked seeing the Deacon! I would love to do it next year too. Thank you (Ellis)."

"I can't tell you how much my sister, her three boys, ... my family and I enjoyed the *Wake the Library 5K and Fun Run* on Saturday — it brought back a lot of good memories to run on our favorite college trail together through Reynolda Gardens with Wake Forest friends of all ages ... this was a great way to bring people together, promote good exercise, and support the library we all love. Having the Deacon there made my nephews' day! Not to mention the Krispy Kremes ... your staff gave all a warm Wake Forest welcome. Hats off to all of you on a terrific job ... your event provided a great way for families to be on campus together. We saw classmates we hadn't seen in 20 years and got our Homecoming Saturday off to a grand start (Wallace)."

Appendix A. Survey Instrument

LIBRARIES AND ATHLETIC EVENTS SURVEY

Question 1 — Choice — One Answer (Bullets)

What type of library do you work in?

○ Public Library
○ Academic Library
○ Corporate Library
○ Medical Library
○ Science Library
○ Special Library
○ Other, please specify _____

Question 2 — Name and Address (U.S)

What is the name and location of your library (feel free to share as much or as little information as you like)?

Name _____
Company _____
Address _____
City _____
State _____
Zip _____

Question 3 — Choice — One Answer (Drop Down)

What is the population size of your community?

○ 1–5,000
○ 5,001 — 10,000
○ 10,001 — 50,000
○ 50,000 — 300,000
○ 300,000+

Question 4 — Yes or No

Does your library coordinate, sponsor, or serve as a host site for an athletic event?

○ Yes
○ No
○ If so, what kind of event is it (e.g. 5k, triathlon, walk)

Question 5 — Open Ended — One Line

How many participants does your event draw?

_____

Question 6 — Open Ended — One Line

How many years have you held this or another similar athletic event?

_____

Question 7 — Rating Scale — Matrix

Can you rank how important the following objectives are in your event?

	Not Very Important	2	Somewhat Important	4	Very Important
Fundraising	❏	❏	❏	❏	❏
Community Building	❏	❏	❏	❏	❏
Fulfilling General or Specialized Programming	❏	❏	❏	❏	❏
Outreach to Special Communities	❏	❏	❏	❏	❏
Outreach to Special Communities	❏	❏	❏	❏	❏

Question 8 — Yes or No

Does your library coordinate the event internally?

○ Yes
○ No
○ If you do not coordinate it inside the library, who do you partner with?

_____

Question 9 — Open Ended — Comments Box

Can you talk broadly about the partnerships and collaborative efforts that are part of your event (e.g. timing companies, fundraising organizations, event management)?

_____

_____

_____

_____

Question 10 — Open Ended — One Line

Does your event have a title sponsor?

_____

Question 11 — Rating Scale — Matrix

Rate the success of your event

	Not Very Important	2	Somewhat Important	4	Very Important
Fundraising	❐	❐	❐	❐	❐
Additional Comments	❐	❐	❐	❐	❐
Community Building	❐	❐	❐	❐	❐
Additional Comments	❐	❐	❐	❐	❐
Fulfilling General or Specialized Programming	❐	❐	❐	❐	❐
Additional Comments	❐	❐	❐	❐	❐
Outreach to Special Communities	❐	❐	❐	❐	❐
Additional Comments	❐	❐	❐	❐	❐
Outreach to Special Communities	❐	❐	❐	❐	❐
Additional Comments	❐	❐	❐	❐	❐

Question 12 — Open Ended — Comments Box

Can you speak broadly about the demographics of your race participants (e.g. age, which segment of your overall community, participation goals)?

_____

_____

_____

_____

_____

_____

Question 13 — Yes or No

Does your event have a website? If so please include the URL below

○ Yes

○ No

○ Site URL: _____

Question 14 — Open Ended — Comments Box

Can you talk broadly about your fundraising goals and whether or not you met them?

_____

_____

_____

Question 15 — Open Ended — One or More Lines with Prompt

Can you talk briefly about how you addressed the following issues?

Race Timing _____

Graphics Design _____

Planning _____

Marketing _____

Fundraising _____

Race Day Coordination _____

Question 16 — Yes or No

Do you have an established budget line for your event?

○ Yes

○ No

○ Can you speak to what event elements are budgeted for?

Question 17 — Open Ended — Comments Box

Are there other comments about your event that you would like to share?

_____

_____

_____

Question 18 — Yes or No

May we include specific identifying information about your event (e.g. Library name, event name, event website) in our published results?

○ Yes

○ No

Question 19 — Yes or No

Would you like to see a summary of the survey data? If so, include your email address in the box below

○ Yes

○ No

○ Email address

Works Cited

Balas, Janet. "Fundraising: It's Not Just About the Money." *Computers in Libraries* 23.2 (2003): 32. Print.

Bekkers, René, and Pamala Wiepking. "Generosity and Philanthropy: A Literature Review." *SSRN eLibrary* (2007). <http://ssrn.com/paper=1015507>.

Cannon, Pansy. Message to Susan Sharpless Smith. 13 Oct 2009. E-Mail.

Dewey, Barbara I. "Fund-Raising for Large Public University Libraries: Margin for Excellence." *Library Administration & Management* 20.1 (2006): 5–12. Print.

Ellis, Andrea C. "Thank You." Message to Susan Sharpless Smith. 10 Oct 2009. E-Mail.

Floyd, Max. "Thank You." Message to Erik T. Mitchell. 02 Dec 2008. E-Mail.

McGrath, Kim. "Chasing Away the Exam Blues." Winston-Salem, 2011. *News Center*. Office of Communications and External Relations. 08 May 2011. <http://news.wfu.edu/2011/04/29/chasing-away-the-exam-blues/%3E>.

Neal, James G. "College Sports and Library Fundraising." *The Bottom Line: Managing Library Finances* 10.2 (1997): 58–59. Print.

Pacey, Megan. "Give Your Charity a Sporting Chance." *Third Sector* 2008: 28–28. Print.

Prater, K. N. "Participatory Sporting Events as Fundraising Vehicles." University of Oregon, 2009. Print.

Rader, Hannelore B. "Fundraising in Academic Libraries: The United States Experience." *The Bottom Line* 13 (2000): 93–99. Print.

Road Runners Club of America. "Guidelines for Safe Road and Trail Races." (2009). <http://www.rrca.org/downloads/event-directors/Race_Guidelines_for_Safety-DEC_2009.pdf%3E>.

Seltzer, Michael. *Securing Your Organization's Future: A Complete Guide to Fundraising Strategies*. New York: Foundation Center, 2001. Print.

Vander, Angela S. "Special Event Fundraising." n.d. Web. *Learning to Give*. 04 May 2011. <http://learningtogive.org/papers/paper60.html%3E>.

Wallace, Marybeth S. "Thank You." Message to Susan Sharpless Smith. 12 Oct 2009. E-Mail.

Wayson, Tracy. "Putting the Benefit Back into Fundraising Benefits." *New Directions for Philanthropic Fundraising* 1998.20 (1998): 79–92. Print.

Wolf, Jodi. "Event Planning Can Be Easier If You Follow These Steps." *Nonprofit World* 28.5: 6–8. Print.

Z. Smith Reynolds Library. "Wake the Library 5k & 1 Mile Fun Run." Web. *ZSR Library Flickr Site*. <http://www.flickr.com/photos/zsrlibrary/collections/72157622437127313/%3E>.

Section IV
Social and Cultural Entrepreneurs

10 — Unlocking the Treasures

Academic Library Entrepreneurs
Promote Collections and Raise Funds

SHAKEELA BEGUM *and* MANUELA BOSCENCO

Introduction

In the digital age, buzz words like *creative learning, connectivity* and *innovation* circulate widely. Public and cultural spaces like university libraries adjust to accommodate the ever-changing informational landscape. Traditional notions of access to exceptional library services are challenged by the methods and forms in which we look for and receive information and the speed with which these forms shift. With the push towards digitization, the inevitable rising costs of academic resources, and the nullifying impact of campus budget cuts, academic librarians are seeking ways to explore unconventional revenue sources while staying true to their social mission: to support research and enhance teaching and learning at the university. Expanding beyond roles as collection managers or research experts, librarians now take on the roles of savvy marketers, fundraisers, and entrepreneurs. This fundamental shift in the ways in which academic librarians approach their work allows the university library to remain relevant in the current global economy, providing quality services to their constituencies despite financial challenges.

Meaningful Marketing: An Entrepreneurial Shift

In 2007, at the University of British Columbia (UBC) in Vancouver, Canada, in a corner of the newly constructed Irving K. Barber Learning Centre, a team assembled to create an outreach tool that would cultivate a sense of community and rouse support from potential donors. This team from UBC's Library Development Office (LDO) was driven by the unavoidable truth that UBC Library's collections, particularly those housed in Rare Books and Special Collections, were being seriously overlooked as objects of value. Even worse, it seemed that users were not seeing these incredible resources at all. The team came up with an extraordinary way to showcase these collections, draw potential support and possibly respond to the demand for change that the academic library was facing. What became known as the UBC Library Vault began as a powerful and broad, but deceptively simple, development strategy.

The word "entrepreneurship" derives from the French word *entreprendre*, meaning "to undertake." Traditionally, the concept ties closely with the business sector, where commercial ventures drive innovation; entrepreneurs invest in revenue sources that deliver services tailored to customer needs and generate profits. Non-profit organizations are now borrowing elements from this business model to enhance the provision of programs more closely in tune with generating revenue while contributing to the greater public good.

In this spirit of entrepreneurship and innovation, the LDO set out to broaden their donor base. UBC Library Vault began as an online gallery of photographic images from UBC Library's "vault," a temperature-controlled storage space. The website's dual aim was to increase support for UBC Library among campus and community supporters, generating revenue and donations, while promoting the educational role UBC Library endeavors to play in the contemporary academic environment.

UBC Library Vault represented a first step towards crafting an inimitable outreach tool: an online showcase of illuminated manuscripts, early maps, music texts and vibrant historical photographs from British Columbia and UBC. Held in the storage facility and rarely seen by the public, the original manuscripts and artifacts remained preserved and secure; this element of mystery was captured by the initiative's tagline *Unlock the Treasures*.

This entrepreneurial concept was rooted in the Library's genuine strengths, projected natural growth, and the authentic emotive elements of image and story that had the potential to engage users from one-time donors to faculty, alumni, and current students. This was a project that was rooted in pride for UBC Library's place on campus and as part of an international framework.

"The Library Vault is a unique opportunity to reach out to those who value and support the second-largest university library in Canada. We are creating an online community that is interested in the Library's vibrant collections and want to learn about the story behind the spectacle," says Peter Ward, University Library Pro Tem, in November 2007 (Ward).

Library Development: Who Holds the Key?

Since its inception, UBC's LDO (Library Development Office) has sought to increase and diversify its support base in order to maximize fundraising opportunities for UBC Library. An analysis of its existing support structure revealed that engaging alumni in order to generate new sources of income had been overlooked. Alumni who choose to donate typically support their faculty, where their natural affiliation and connection with the university lies. There was no mechanism in place to assist UBC LDO in determining whether alumni have any interest in the Library to consider making a financial gift. As alumni were identified as untapped potential support, UBC LDO sought a way to make meaningful connections, inform users of UBC Library's resources, and to generate leads. UBC LDO had discovered an authentic alternative revenue stream which any entrepreneurially minded thinker would seriously consider.

The UBC Library Vault was the key to directly engaging with a broader donor base; this pilot project was the LDO's strategic long-term solution to the challenges posed by the fundraising environment in which it operates. Lacking a natural constituency, having an older constituency of supporters, raising smaller gifts in comparison to other faculties across campus, and attracting gifts-in-kind rather than significant financial contributions: all of

Inspired by *Alice's Adventures in Wonderland*. By Lewis Carroll, illustrations by John Tenniel. Courtesy UBC Library.

these elements put considerable pressure on the LDO to develop non-traditional methods in order to strengthen campus-wide support.

From Idea to Image: Launching UBC Library Vault

The LDO team at the time of UBC Library Vault's inception comprised of four members with a variety of backgrounds in fundraising (Shakeela Begum), marketing and web optimization (Courtenay Cox—co-op student from the Sauder Business School) and communications (Glenn Drexhage—Communications Officer and Meg Walker—Development Coordinator). Another key member and alumnae volunteer marketing strategist, Angelia Darnbrough, helped develop the framework for the UBC Library Vault from the very beginning and was instrumental in ensuring that the overarching goal of the site—"to create a database of self-identified subscribers with whom the UBC LDO could communicate over time and who were vested in the UBC Library Vault"—was primary to any decision made about the development of the site.

Making use of the donor pyramid, a proven model fundraising professionals refer to when discussing a development plan, the UBC LDO team, led by Director Shakeela Begum, set out to generate strategies that would actively target potential donors at all levels. This group of professionals, students and development officials strived to strengthen connections to the Library, inviting this new-found audience to involve themselves in exciting priority projects.

UBC Library Vault Website

As mentioned previously, UBC Library Vault was initiated in order to engage with the broadest group of donors. Entry-level donors who might give small amounts of money to UBC Library over time are traditionally engaged through library newsletters, direct appeal, telephone appeals, special events, online giving, annual campaign, bookplate program or/and a membership program.

Additional cultivation strategies for potential donors often include personal visits, invitations to meet with a senior administrator at the library to discuss the impact of their initial gifts, phone calls to thank them for their gifts, or private tours of the physical vault where special collections are held or of the permanent exhibit of the

Figure 1—Pyramid of Giving. Centre Point Advancing Non-Profit Management. "Theories of Fundraising."

Wallace B. and Madeline H. Chung Collection in the Rare Books and Special Collections area. Through further cultivation activities, the intent is to encourage these donors to increase their giving as they become aware of the needs of the Library and progress into the next level of giving in the pyramid.

The first step in engaging these potential donors in the UBC Library Vault was to provide a sophisticated, user-friendly website. Visitors to the main page were whisked off through the magical world of rare books: vivid illustrations of a Queen Triggerfish and other strange creatures from René Primevère Lesson's *Voyage de la Coquille*, 1824; excerpts of outstanding botanical diagrams from *Paxton's Magazine of Botany*, 1836; brilliant details of Abraham Ortelius's *Theatrum Orbis Terrarum*, thought to be the world's first modern atlas; Darwin's handwritten letters; art from a turn-of-the-century edition of *Alice in Wonderland*; hand-drawn maps of our province's early past and exquisite First Nations artwork created by aboriginal peoples in Canada.

Accompanying each image was a brief story revealing intriguing details about the author, date of publication, readership or historical background. Thoroughly researched with the assistance of the RBSC librarians, these stories contextualized the images and enhanced the website visitor's understanding of the breadth of the Library's collections. A link to the Library catalogue was provided as a convenient way of accessing more in-depth information about items in the related collection. The experience has been described as a memorable introduction to the Library and its vast resources.

Aside from the Vault image gallery, visitors were provided with Library News and Events, from conferences and lecture series to author readings, book fairs or exhibits. This feature was added as a way to keep the website dynamic to those first-time and renewal gift donors, providing additional opportunities to become engaged with the Library.

From September 2007 to November 2010, over 26,000 unique visitors were recorded, registering over 198,000 page views. UBC Library *Vault*'s link to the *Support UBC Library* website increased viewership of the Support website by 233% in the 2009/10 fiscal year. From November 2007 to July 2011, the *Support UBC Library* webpage has had over 4,000 visitors, with more than 11,000 page views. On average, traffic to the *Support* site has increased 300%; *Ways of Giving* was by far the most popular page viewed (3,536 times). These numbers demonstrate the effectiveness of UBC Library Vault's direct link in attracting and retaining potential donors to the Library. During the three year period between 2008–2011, donations secured increased by over 200 percent.

UBC Library Vault E-Newsletter

Donors who consistently give, and those who are considering major gifts, were targeted by the *eVault*. Launched in 2007, this electronic newsletter highlighted images and events driven by the Vault website. Interviews and articles with and by UBC Librarians were regularly featured. As a self-referencing tool, the *eVault* would draw readers back to the *Vault* and *Support* websites through cross-linking of content. This mechanism allowed subscribers to self-identify as potential library supporters by virtue of their interest in the library. Over time, it was thought that the *eVault* would create a qualified database of individuals who have a vested interest in the activities of UBC Library and want to help sustain its growth.

With UBC having over 240,000 UBC alumni in 120 countries, the *eVault* seemed an organic connectivity tool with obvious cost-analysis benefits. In the most recent UBC

Alumni Survey, alumni indicated that access to the library's resources after graduation was of utmost value. UBC Library Vault and the *eVault* were a natural way for alumni to remain informed about the availability of resources, providing incentive for donations to the library's capacity to serve them in their careers beyond the university.

From 2007 to 2010, the number of *eVault* subscribers increased from less than 200 to over 1,000, including faculty, staff, donors, students, and the larger UBC community. Due to the quality of content and engaging copywriting, the newsletter has maintained a stable open rate of 35% which is exceptional when compared to average open rates of 13.6% for e-mail newsletters ("Email Marketing Benchmarks"). These numbers demonstrate the sustained appeal and its effectiveness in cultivating and stewarding long-term relationships with UBC Library's loyal group of supporters.

Donor stewardship activity has resulted in public recognition for both UBC Library's resources and library donors, through extensive media coverage of key donor stories. The *eVault* profiled the world-class Wallace B. and Madeline H. Chung Collection in one of its editions, as well as UBC Library's acquisition of the archives of Douglas Coupland, author of the bestseller *Generation X*. Coupland and Chung expressed personal gratitude for the media profiles the UBC LDO generated regarding their gifts to the Library.

From December 2005 to November 2010 UBC Library Vault was profiled in more than 20 publications; 183 stories and press releases showcasing UBC Library and the value of its resources and services were published in local, provincial and national media including *UBC Press*, the *Vancouver Sun*, *Trek Magazine* and trade publications targeted at professional librarians and the information sciences community such as *BCLA Browser*, *Chronicle of Higher Education* and *CLA Digest*.

Extensive media coverage, spurred by stories delivered through the *eVault*, raised the profile of the Library, supporting ever-increasing fundraising targets and strengthening the Library image as a relevant source of information. In 2011, the *eVault* was rebranded as LIBFocus, a newsletter providing information about Library-wide events, services and programs. As part of the Library's broader communications and marketing strategy, readership will determine the need for a UBC Library communication tool as specialized as *eVault*.

UBC Library Vault Gift Line

In 2009, the LDO saw the need to expand UBC Library Vault naturally while appealing to the upper levels of the donor pyramid. Drawing on local sustainable resources, a line of note cards featuring Vault images was designed and produced. Another entrepreneurial concept, integrity branding as defined by de Chernatony in his 2009 online essay "Towards the Holy Grail of Defining Brand," aims to build on the authentic reputation and character an organization authentically maintains. The LDO sought to build a self-referential and trustworthy brand. The high-quality card sets had a gratifying effect: purchasing a set of cards offered a direct connection between a donor and the Library, as a portion of the proceeds from each purchase directly supported UBC Library's collections. Enjoyed or shared amongst friends, the UBC Library Vault note card left an immediate impression.

The success of the note card sets led to the design of an entire UBC Library Vault gift line, including matted prints, art umbrellas and cloth book bags. Sales from the Vault initiative continue to be valuable not only in raising revenues to sustain the program, but also in developing strong brand loyalty. UBC Library Vault merchandise is available for purchase at the Library's circulation desks, and at various other retail locations on campus, including UBC Bookstore, UBC Museum of Anthropology, cafés and gift shops. Repeat customers have connected with UBC Library and recommended its distinct gift line to other buyers. Each gift purchase creates the opportunity for one of our team members to interact with the customer and direct them to the *Support UBC Library* website to learn more about the projects that would not be possible without additional financial support.

To attract donors at the highest level of the pyramid, the *Canvas Treasures* program was launched in 2009. Featuring stunning reproductions of Vault images in a large-scale reproduction, canvases are currently available for lease or purchase and adorn the spaces of several UBC Library branches on campus.

UBC employs nearly 11,000 staff and faculty members, many of who may or may not use Library resources depending on the nature of their work. This core constituency identifies strongly with the university, and make for a natural support base. UBC Library Vault merchandise inspires this particular group of potential donors to explore the Library's treasures in depth, and offers them the opportunity to show their loyalty by purchasing "distinctly UBC" gifts.

Faculties across campus showed such an interest in the note cards that some contacted the LDO to inquire about having their own cards designed for special occasions. Shortly thereafter, the Custom Card Program was introduced, allowing customers to place bulk orders for art cards featuring customizable greetings, followed by the customer's own faculty or department logo. Over 10,000 cards were sold to faculties across campus in 2008 during the first year the program was offered.

The UBC President's Office has been a faithful Custom Card customer for the last 3 years; an exclusive President's Gift Line of ceramics and custom cards featuring Vault images has been custom produced and is given to dignitaries and key members of the international community during visits to the University and when the President travels internationally. This high-end visibility positions UBC Library as a valuable creative resource, and demonstrates how the social and cultural life of the academic library continues to flourish. The UBC Library Vault gift line continues to play a vital role in enhancing stakeholder engagement, raising awareness of the Library as a key campus and community resource, and increasing involvement in university-wide events and fundraising opportunities.

Promotional Items

When UBC Library Vault could support its gift card program, it was clear that promotional materials needed to be distributed, particularly to draw a connection with the approximately 43,147 students currently enrolled at UBC. Well informed about events within their faculty, students rarely receive specific news about UBC Library services or programs. Despite students' limited disposable income, it was made clear through events held at the UBC Student Union Building that the UBC Library Vault gift line is attractive to this constituency group. Even though they are unlikely to donate as undergraduates, students are potential donors after becoming graduates and alumni. The Vault provides an unexpected "behind-the-scenes" look at UBC Library, and encourages the notion that even a small contribution can make a difference.

To increase awareness as broadly as possible and in keeping with the integrated marketing approach to promote UBC Library's uniqueness, twenty-four assorted bookmarks were printed on high-quality card stock, highlighting the different branches and collections at UBC Library. Featuring our most popular images and their stories, the bookmarks are useful and extremely popular with all our audiences. We continue to distribute them freely both on and off-campus at different events, along with other promotional items such as UBC Library Vault stationery, and gifts featuring images of the Irving K. Barber Learning Centre.

Many of the Vault supporters are bookmark collectors and purposely seek us out at local fairs and annual conferences to stock up. We are regularly approached by student organizations on campus to provide them with bookmarks, which they use to entice members and supporters to their associations. This mechanism has allowed the use of the integrated marketing approach that drove target audiences to the Vault website. The Vault website address is printed on all Vault promotional items. This entices Library supporters to visit the site and explore the Library's spectacular collections. As more people engage with the Library online, the Library's community of supporters continues to grow online. The inclusion of our web address on printed materials such as the bookmarks, gift cards, and cloth bags, enticed supporters to visit the website and explore the story behind the spectacle, allowing the Library to cultivate a larger, ever-growing community of people to become engaged with the Library. UBC Library is now considered the go-to place on campus for one-of-a-kind gifts, strengthening cross-campus ties.

In addition, our award-winning Rare Books and Special Collections Package was developed specifically for key donor events and for cultivating donors with potential to make a major gift to UBC Library. This package consisted of a collection of high-quality reproductions of rare objects of value, allowing guests to hold a copy of a Sam Black painting or one of Darwin's letters and have an instant appreciation for the object itself. This was the first step in creating awareness and urgency to address a need to preserve these incredible and often fragile items, as well as determining a donor's personal ability and interest in becoming part of UBC Library's past, present and future.

Social Media

Complimentary e-cards were made available at the launch of the UBC Library Vault site to increase viral marketing opportunities through the image gallery. Between 2008/2009 and 2009/2010, the number of people viewing Vault e-cards increased by 31%, while the number of Vault e-cards sent increased by 56%. Overall, 1,800 e-cards were sent from the Vault website. This growth in e-card viewership is remarkable given the fact that, during the time in which these statistics were gathered, the selection of images available as e-cards remained fairly static in comparison to the growing number of images seen on the Vault site and merchandise was developed.

In a technique common to all types of modern entrepreneurial ventures, UBC Library also engages its audiences via popular social media channels such as Facebook and Twitter. Since May 2009, <twitter@ubclibraryvault.ca>, initially conceived as a way to promote the Vault project, now markets UBC Library as a whole, including its collections, services and programs, UBC Rare Books and Special Collections, and the Vault project. News, events, articles, videos and digital media are highlighted; digital collections and digital initiatives are showcased to the larger UBC community.

When UBC Library Vault's Twitter account was created, initial goals were to average two new followers per week and tweet at least twice per week. After one busy month, these goals were revised to tweet at least twice per day to gain new followers. Within six months, the Vault account had amassed more than 150 followers, and it currently exceeds 400 followers, including *Quill and Quire, CBC Learning* and EDUCAUSE. Second-order followers total more than 394,200. The *Vault* Twitter account currently averages five new followers per week; five tweets per day are posted. The numbers show a high level of activity, underscoring the effectiveness of social media tools in reaching out to new audiences and engaging them with the Library.

The most notable example of the success of this kind of engagement involved publicity surrounding Douglas Coupland's gifting of his archives to UBC Library: the initial tweet was re-tweeted five times, while ten other tweeters mentioned the UBC Library tweet in their tweets and five posted it to Facebook accounts or other blogs within hours.

One of the greatest achievements has been to build a marketing brand that allows anyone to gain an insider's view of UBC Library's collections and enjoy the narrative about select holdings. Our branded image gallery has provided an opportunity to license image rights to corporate supporters. In 2010, the UBC Library signed a licensing agreement with a vendor whereby Vault images with the Library's logo will be reproduced on journals that are distributed around the world. This allows an opportunity to diversify the project's revenue stream and to grow the target audience base by tapping into vendor's distribution channels.

UBC Library Vault's integrated fundraising strategies are being reassessed in light of the Library's broader communication and marketing strategy and the expectation is that any new developments in this area will strengthen opportunities for fundraising and outreach.

An Illuminating Experience: Celebrations and Awards

Within a year of its debut, the Vault initiative began receiving prestigious acknowledgements of its impact and potential. In 2007, the UBC Vault website won Gold for Best e-Innovation in University Advancement from the Canadian Council for the Advancement of Education (CCAE). Other acknowledgements from CCAE include being awarded the Bronze medal in 2008, and the Gold Medal for Best Print or Electronic Newsletter in 2009.

The Council for Advancement and Support of Education (CASE) presented its 2009 Gold Award to UBC Library's Special Packages for its innovative and creative Special Events publication containing facsimile reproductions of items held at UBC Archives and Rare Books and Special Collections. The package was presented as a gift to key Library supporters during the 2008 re-opening event of UBC Rare Books and Special Collections Division.

In May 2011, UBC Library Development Office was named the winner of the 2011 ALA Best of Show competition in the Fundraising/Print category. The competition is organized annually by the Library Leadership and Management Association (LLAMA) of the American Library Association and recognizes the very best public relations materials produced by libraries in the United States and Canada in a given calendar year. The winning entry from The Vault was a set of buttons featuring images from UBC Library's Rare Books and Special Collections. The buttons were launched September 2010 and were a huge hit, decorating the book bags, cardigans and jackets of donors, students, staff and the community. Certain button models were so popular that supplies were exhausted within weeks of introducing them. They continue to be available for purchase through LDO offices. Proceeds, as always, support UBC Library collections.

In coordination with UBC Library, the Vault distributed over 200 Library-related gifts and a record 2,000 bookmarks at The Word on the Street, a national book and magazine festival. After winning "Best Booth" at The Word on the Street in 2008, the Vault registered 161 new *eVault* subscribers, thereby expanding the network of potential Library supporters and facilitating their connection with the institution. In 2009, the Library continued to support the distribution of UBC's Community Borrower Library card at The Word on the Street, and in 2010 sponsored a local author, thereby empowering people to engage in meaningful literacy and learning opportunities in their community.

UBC Library Vault's crowning achievement was the *Canvas Treasures Launch* in 2009, which introduced our incredible giclée prints and the *Canvas Treasures* program to The Vault community of supporters and friends. Hosted by newly appointed University Librarian Ingrid Parent, the *Canvas Treasures Launch* celebrated UBC Library's remarkable collections with an exhibit of striking Vault art. Faculties across campus have since sought out our canvases to put up in public areas, and proceeds from the sale of each canvas support the growth of the Library's collections.

The *Canvas Treasures Launch* was followed by a reception and accompanying music; Library donors had a chance to socialize with alumni, senior Library administrators, staff and members of the wider UBC community. The event was publicized and covered in the local media. Local artist Patricia Richardson Logie, inspired by the depth and breadth of UBC Library collections, generously donated *Chronicles of Pride*, a collection of 31 First Nations paintings. UBC Library held a separate standing-room only event at the Irving K. Barber Learning Centre to celebrate the donation and honor Patricia Richardson Logie and her family. The University Librarian also announced the *Richardson Logie Chronicles of Pride Fund*, to assure future promotion and maintenance of this important collection. The gift of *Chronicles of Pride* to UBC Library demonstrates the Vault's capacity in engaging the wider community with the Library in a meaningful way.

Taking Stock: Grace and Gratitude

The road to success is not always a smooth one, and the LDO team encountered roadblocks that continue to be addressed. However, the good will and attention that went into growing the UBC Library Vault brand continues, and despite current technical and organizational setbacks, the authors consider this an entrepreneurial success story.

CURRENT STATUS AND ASSESSMENT

As more people connected with UBC Library's Special Collections online, the Vault website became the target of cyber-attacks and the IT department, in consultation with the LDO and Library Communications Office, recommended that the site be taken down. Presently, the website has been reprogrammed and is housed on an internal server and on a platform that is currently supported within the library.

While the website was being rebuilt, UBC Library and the LDO have taken this opportunity to review the project in its entirety. Like any great entrepreneurial venture, stock must be taken and practical decisions made regarding its value and function. The Vault

LDO team will take time to align brand and story across UBC Library's many branches and divisions, and tell this collective story in as many interesting ways as possible.

With changes to the organizational structure of UBC Library in process, an abbreviated version of the website became available as of August 2011 at <vault.library.ubc.ca/>. Once completed, the *Support UBC Library* website will include both electronic images and thumbnails of the physical collections, offering a comprehensive view of the collections as a whole and identifying the many rewarding giving opportunities available to support the library. The original project will merge with UBC Library's overarching promotional strategies so collections, both physical and electronic, can continue to be showcased in a unique and innovative manner.

At present Library news and updates are offered on the main page of the *Support UBC Library* website at <support.library.ubc.ca/>, along with descriptions of priority projects. Current initiatives include conservation, digitization and growth of the endowments, as well as collection acquisitions. Gifts and promotional items are distributed from the office in the Irving K. Barber Learning Centre, based on feedback received from our customers and supporters, who appreciate and recognize the value of our program.

The LDO is proud of its ability to have responded effectively to the complex issue of lacking a natural constituency of supporters. Our entrepreneurial approach has succeeded in growing a community of loyal friends who are interested in the Library and its outstanding collections, and are poised to extend their support towards sustaining its long-term care and growth. We are indebted to those who rally around the Vault and encourage staff involved with this project to persevere.

We look forward to the results of the assessment process, and continue to envision exciting new services, products and features (such as displaying Vault images on business cards, and potentially creating a mobile phone application that would enable users to download Vault images on their Blackberries and iPhones) to diversify the UBC Library Vault brand and respond to the evolving needs of our target audiences.

Future Constituencies

UBC Library Vault has so far reached out to a number of University constituencies, including Library supporters, students, faculty and staff. One segment of the University community that remains largely untapped is the parent community. Parents have numerous opportunities to engage in their children's education during primary and secondary school; once a child graduates from high school and enters college, there are limited engagement opportunities. UBC Library is actively collaborating with units on campus to create educational and interactive sessions, such as tours of the different library branches, workshops and presentations delivered by Reference and Instructional Librarians, as well as a tea event during *Imagine 2011,* the university's annual orientation week. Beyond these sessions given to incoming students and their parents, we hope to provide additional tours of exceptional Library spaces on campus throughout the year, as well as setting up a Parent Advisory Committee to help us consider additional opportunities to generate new revenue streams for the Library.

Finally, the UBC LDO participated at the 2011 Annual Conference of the Academic Library Advancement and Development Network (ALADN) in Flagstaff, Arizona by presenting a session on the Vault initiative and displaying Vault merchandise, which will no doubt inspire plans to welcome the world to ALADN at the University of British Columbia in 2012.

A Natural Evolution

UBC Library Vault is a powerful example of how librarians, working in harmony with fundraising teams, can position the academic library as a true collaborative force within the academy. By diversifying the support base to include alumni and international audiences, and by generating alternative revenue sources through sales of branded gifts, entrepreneurs behind UBC Library Vault demonstrated the program's potential as a flagship cultivation and stewardship tool and a key component of UBC Library's engagement strategy. We hope to inspire other academic librarians to emphasize the value of their own collections by utilizing technology to retain the institution's distinct identity well into the 21st century.

Works Cited

Berenbak, Adam *et al. Special Collections Engagement: Spec Kit (#317)*. Washington: Association of Research Libraries, 2010. Print.

Burnett, Ken. *Relationship Fundraising: A Donor-Based Approach to the Business of Raising Money.* 2nd edition. San Francisco: The White Lion Press, 2002. Print.

CentrePoint Advancing Non-Profit Management. "Theories of Fundraising." Chapter 2. 2011. Web. 26 July 2011.

Council for Advancement and Support of Education. *Donor Relations: The Essential Guide to Stewardship Policies, Procedures, and Protocol.* 2nd edition. Washington: Council for Advancement and Support of Education, 2005. Print.

De Chernatony, Leslie. "Towards the Holy Grail of Defining Brand." *Marketing Theories* 9.1 (2009): 101–105. Web. 27 July 2011.

Dees, J. Gregory. "Taking Social Entrepreneurship Seriously." *Society* 44.3 (2007): 24–31. Print.

"Email Marketing Benchmarks by Industry." *MailChimp Research.* MailChimp. 2011. Web. 14 May 2011. <http://mailchimp.com/resources/research/email-marketing-benchmarks-by-industry/>

Ratcliff, David, and Dr. Una Osili. "Charitable Behaviors and Motivations of Wealthy Donors." National Association of College and Business Officers NACUBO. Webcast. Vancouver BC, 2011.

Rosso, Hank A., and Associates. *Achieving Excellence in Fundraising.* 2nd edition. Ed. Eugene R. Tempel. San Francisco: Jossey-Bass, 2003. Print.

Sargeant, Adrian, and Elaine Jay. *Building Donor Loyalty: The Fundraiser's Guide to Increasing Lifetime Value.* San Francisco: Jossey-Bass, 2004. Print.

Saul, Jason. "The End of Fundraising: How to Raise More by Selling Your Impact." Association for Fundraising Professionals. Web conference. Web. Vancouver, BC, 2011.

University of British Columbia. "Place and Promise: The UBC Plan," 2009–2010. Web. 29 March 2011.

UBC Library. "Report of the University Librarian to the Senate," 2009–2010. Web. 31 March 2011.

Veeraraghavan, Vimala. "Entrepreneurship and Innovation." *Asia-Pacific Business Review* 5.1 (2009): n.pag. Web. 26 July 2011.

Ward, Peter. "Personal Interview." November 2007.

11— Value-Based Return on Investment in the Entrepreneurial Disposition of Library Materials

SHARON K. CURTIS, DORALYN ROSSMANN
and MOLLY C. A. ANDERSON

Introduction

Although integral to library management, the disposition of withdrawn or surplus resources requires librarians and library staff to navigate an often thorny interplay of normative, political, and economic matters. As library commentator Will Manley laments: "It's the hardest thing in the world to explain to taxpayers why we are throwing away perfectly good books" (80). Yet alternatives to the dumpster — including recycling, storing, selling, or giving books away — all require the careful balancing of staff, material, and financial resources. The entrepreneurial library continues to explore new venues for disposition without compromising its core values or its relationship with its patrons and community. It is important to explore the relationship — and tensions— between core library values and the selection and employment of disposition methods. A return-on-investment (ROI) model aids libraries in determining and defending disposition choices. The Montana State University Library's entrepreneurial exploration into disposition alternatives provides a case study into finding the right balance of preserving library values and providing optimum return on investment of staffing and resources.

Libraries, particularly those that receive public financing to serve academic institutions or broader populations, are defined by their relationships with their patrons and communities. This bond of service is given expression in statements of core values and principles by library professional organizations and reaffirmed in the mission and policy statements of individual institutions. A vital component for fulfilling this service imperative is ongoing evaluation and maintenance of collections in order to provide an "active library collection of current interest to users" ("Evaluating Library Collections"). Libraries must determine how to dispose of materials withdrawn from their collections and what to do with donated items that are outside the scope of their missions. Yet the necessary disposition of materials can be daunting as libraries face the practical limitations and political implications of their chosen disposal methods.

Literature Review

Dilevko and Gottlieb's survey of weeding practices and attitudes in American and Canadian libraries provides a good summary of the challenges associated with disposition practices. The study reports that book sales—including Friends of the Library, in-house, or online transactions—are the most common method of disposal. The added income from such sales, in combination with the fact that the books find a good home, makes this an appealing option for many libraries. However, book sales can be resource-intensive, requiring short-term storage of materials and staff time to organize and conduct the sales. Further, selling books can be tricky to navigate politically where institutions face unclear restrictions on the sale of surplus public property or public misperceptions about the purpose and outcomes of sales.

Faced with these challenges, it is not surprising that the dumpster was the second most frequently reported fate of weeded materials. Yet growing environmental awareness and scrutiny of wasteful government practices has made trashing books increasingly untenable; moreover, many library professionals see the need for their institutions to play an environmental leadership and education role in promoting green practices (Miller vii; Penniman and McCole 32). Secretly moving books to "locked dumpsters" while "under the cover of darkness" (Dilevko and Gottlieb 85) goes against the profession's longstanding commitment to honesty, public service, and social responsibility ("Core Values"). However, as recycling may not be available in all areas at a feasible cost, libraries may have to be creative in identifying alternatives.

Donating materials is a means of extending the use value of withdrawn or unwanted materials without the ethical considerations of generating a profit. Local public and non-profit organizations, schools, and other libraries may benefit from a larger institution's discards. Many charitable organizations will accept donated materials and then sell or distribute them to support national and international causes. As with book sales, donation programs can require an investment of staff time and short-term storage. Additionally, library professionals report ethical concerns with passing along outdated or worn materials to underprivileged communities (Dilevko and Gottlieb 86). Alternatively, in-house free book tables can avoid some of the overhead costs and provide an opportunity to foster positive community relations, provided they comply with an institution's surplus policies and do not raise concerns about library "waste."

While libraries have various disposition methods available to them, each comes with its own implications for the political, financial, and ethical environment. Underlying the choice of disposal outlets is the inherent library value of being a good steward of staff, material, environmental, and financial resources; finding an appropriate balance between resources, rewards, and values may require much experimentation with various disposal methods. An ROI model can aid libraries in determining and defending disposition choices. ROI broadly refers to the value received from an investment in an asset. Library scholars and practitioners increasingly look to ROI as a means of communicating the value of a library as a public or institutional investment (e.g., Kaufman and Watstein 226; White 5; Scotti 22; Kyrillidou and Cook 900; Sidorko 645–646). For a politically-heated operation such as disposition, ROI provides a means of communicating the connection between the organization's expenditures and the overall goals of an organization. Where ROI models fall short are in the commonly agreed-upon measurement of social good; here, libraries will need to make tough decisions in prioritizing the use and availability of resources in relation to values.

The next section of this chapter describes a case study of a publicly-funded academic institution's entrepreneurial efforts in the disposition of materials. In each approach to the book disposition process, value priorities and conflicts come to the forefront as do varying levels of ROI. Following the overview of the case, there is an exploration into the tensions between values and ROI encountered and a discussion of the future implications for related entrepreneurial efforts.

Property Management and Library Exceptions

Before embarking on any sale or disposal of library materials, it is important to be aware of surplus property regulations your library may have to follow. For example, Montana State University (MSU) has a "Property Management Procedure Manual." The section which is relevant to the library collections states:

> **XIV. SURPLUS PROPERTY**
> State Statutes, specifically MCA (Montana Code Annotated) title 18-6-101, provide specific ways in which surplus state property must be disposed of, regardless of whether it is being sold or junked. It is to the advantage of the department purchasing capital property to use current property for trade-ins as much as possible.
> **Under NO circumstances should individual departments attempt to dispose of State property on their own.** This includes all State property that is not consumable, costs more than $25, and lasts longer than one year. **Never** trade, cannibalize, or dispose of property purchased with government funds without prior approval from Property Management. Contact Property Management for procedures to dispose of inoperable or unwanted property.
> **Special Note:** Library material, books and software are excluded from the surplus property regulations ["Property Management Procedure Manual"].

It is essential to be familiar with institutional policies and regulations governing the disposal of library materials, both so that the library will operate within them and be able to answer questions about disposal actions. With this information in hand, the MSU Library explored many options for maximizing return on its surplus materials while balancing its expenditures in these efforts, as is described in the next section.

Case Study Background

MSU is the land-grant institution for Montana — a state which has a large geographical area (fourth largest in the United States), a small population (fewer than one million people), and poor personal income (43rd lowest household income) ("2010 Census Data"). MSU serves over 13,000 students, 2,400 employees, and the citizens of the state ("Quick Facts"). Located in Bozeman, it is one of 108 schools on the Carnegie Foundation's list of top research institutions ("Carnegie Classifications"). The MSU Library has over 775,000 book volumes and subscribes to more than 15,000 serial and databases. Its employee base includes seventeen librarian faculty members, two professional staff, thirty-three classified staff, and twenty-five students; it operates on a total budget of approximately seven million dollars ("Statistical Profile"). The MSU Library Collection Development (CD) Team manages the organization's book selling and disposing efforts. This team manages collection acquisitions, weeding, disposition, serials, and government publications. It consists of four full-time technical staff members, one student assistant, an Electronic Resources Librarian, and is led by the Collection Development (CD) Librarian. Two of the technical staff and the student assistant lead the majority of the book selling efforts, with the CD Librarian providing oversight and input, as needed.

Book Sales

Like most libraries, the MSU Library holds book sales in order to dispose of unwanted gifts and withdrawn items. As an academic library, our gifts are not as numerous as many public libraries; further, the limited weeding necessary to alleviate pressures from space constraints and maintain relevant collections does not produce large amounts of materials for book sales. Thus, for many years it was sufficient for the MSU Library to hold a bi-annual sale offering an average of three to four thousand items. Sales revenue ranged between two and three thousand dollars, a welcome supplement to the collections budget. Yet preparing for and administering the sale—particularly in the week leading up to the event—was stressful for participating staff. Further, the lack of disposition alternatives meant that books left over from the sale ended up in the dumpster. Throwing away books raised ethical and public relations concerns, but even worse, it was demoralizing for staff members who had invested a great deal of effort into the sale.

In 2007, the CD Team started taking a fresh look at the book sale to identify how to reduce investment and increase returns. Since the book sale process required a lot of staff time and effort for minimal return, the CD Team decided to reduce the scope of the sale, relocate it, and refocus it for a local market. Completely canceling the book sale was barely a consideration owing to its appeal to regional book resellers and success as a vehicle for good public relations. Through an iterative process, the CD Team revamped the book sale to reduce staff stress, connect customers with the subjects they sought, and optimize the return on the Library's investment. The implemented changes and lessons learned include:

TIMING

Instead of waiting two years, the CD Team decided to make the book sale an annual event. This reduced the number of books needing to be stored and sorted at each sale.

LOCATION

The volume of items at previous sales required the Library to utilize an off-site venue. Scaling down the sale allowed the CD Team to bring the sale back into the Library, saving staff much time and effort in moving books to another location. Moreover, reconnecting the event to the physical library was expected to bring students, faculty, staff, and community members through the Library doors.

TARGETED SUBJECT OFFERINGS

While changing the location and frequency of the sale reduced the stress on library staff, the volume of titles remained difficult to manage. The CD Team refined the items offered at the sale by identifying subjects which had traditionally sold well because they were of interest to our local patrons. Subjects such as literature, history (particularly Montana and Native American history), art, architecture, gardening, and some sciences received top billing at the sale, with some items specially priced to reflect their relatively higher value. This method reduced the volume of books for sale by several thousand, resulting in less effort, less waste, and about the same monetary return as in previous years.

SPECIALTY PRICING

Within the targeted subject areas, a CD Team technician identified higher-value items for specialty pricing. These materials were offered for more than the standard three dollar hardback and one dollar paperback price, but for about one-third of their value in the online market. Offering these items during the book sale required less overhead than online venues; however, explaining the specialty pricing to book sale customers proved difficult. Local and regional book dealers expressed dissatisfaction that higher value items had been priced closer to their market value. Individuals from the general public were surprised that the library would charge more than a few dollars for any item being sold. The longstanding expectation that library book sales should underprice other outlets can conflict with public perception of a non-profit or government agency making a profit. The MSU Library encountered this tension via criticisms expressed to book sale staff by patrons or, more troubling, in attempts to "cheat the system" by tearing off price tags for specially marked items and passing them off as regularly priced items at checkout. Consequently, the MSU Library now limits its book sales to regular hardback and paperback items and sells specially priced items via other venues.

While library book sales have a long entrepreneurial history, they represent one of many options for maximizing profits on the sale of these items, particularly with the options created by the online market. Considering the significant investment of staff time for low revenue generation, the CD Team reevaluated its procedures and looked for ways to yield higher profits.

Selling Through Third Parties

In light of our book sale's limitations, the CD Team conducted trials with local and regional book dealers, national auction houses, and high-volume online resellers, with mixed results. Libraries considering similar outlets may benefit from our "lessons learned" with third party sellers.

SELLING THROUGH LOCAL AND REGIONAL BOOK DEALERS

To alleviate the book sale surplus, the CD Team decided to look for a book dealer who would either buy more valuable books outright or manage the sales and return a share of the profits to the library. Finding the "right fit," however, with a book buyer can be difficult. Initially, the CD Team sought a local buyer who understood the markets for specific geographic, cultural, and historical materials. However, dealing with local buyers can have implications for donor relations, particularly in small communities. In one situation, a previous MSU Collection Development Librarian sold materials to a local book dealer. This dealer, unaware of the original donor of the materials, contacted that very same donor to find out if there was interest in adding these materials to that person's collection. While the MSU Library's gift policy is clear in the disposition possibilities, this situation was, nevertheless, uncomfortable.

More broadly, business relationships with local book dealers can be tricky to navigate. While the MSU Library encourages local dealers to come to its book sales, the Dean of the Library asks that any other exchanges with book dealers be with those outside of Montana, which can be unpopular from a public relations standpoint. This approach intends to avoid possible perceptions of giving more business to one local book dealer than another. However, out of state book dealers generally will not buy materials without first examining them; most are unwilling to travel far to make such an assessment. Moreover, no matter how much we expanded our search for book dealers, we found that buyers routinely offered pennies on the dollar for our materials. In sum, the public relations pitfalls and disappointing financial returns made dealing with local and regional book buyers untenable for our organization.

Auction Houses

Another option we explored was working with an auction house. We sent one auction house a list of 300 titles worth over 200 dollars each. They expressed interest in only two books, which we sent to auction and which made a fair profit for the library. Nevertheless, we were disappointed to be left with so many valuable, but unsold, items. Having learned that these initial approaches were not ideal in their return on investment, we recalibrated and ventured forth with other third party options.

High-Volume Resellers

The CD Team discovered several high-volume resellers which offered a better business model for our situation. These companies would store our stock, list items for sale on several Web sites, ship titles when ordered, and share a portion of the profits with us after recuperating costs. These companies offered an ideal process: very little effort on our part (simply shipping materials to them), and a reasonable return based on the worth of the items. However, our working relationships with two companies— resulting in two very different experiences— offered lessons in system failures, both global and organizational.

The CD Team initiated trial runs with two high-volume resellers, shipping five boxes, or approximately 150–200 books, to each company. One company listed our books immediately and we started seeing returns right away. Given this early success, we immediately sent off the rest of our stock. This proved to be a profitable process with very little staff time expenditure; indeed, the company seemed to meet the MSU Library's needs perfectly. Sadly, our relationship was cut short when the company did not survive the recent economic downturn and closed shop in 2009.

Working with the other vendor began with disappointment. We sent them older books, which did not have ISBNs, and followed the company's instructions for special handling of these items. Nevertheless, upon receiving the items, the warehouse accidentally recycled all the books instead of forwarding them to the appropriate department. The company eventually reimbursed us for the loss, but at a value lower than we estimated for sales. After this experience, we started sending books to them again, but this time we only sent more current materials that had no significant value. Even though this approach does not result in considerable revenue (out of an inventory of 1419 books, 626 have sold for a return of $932 over two years), it provides us with a method of discarding many books which are not attractive to local buyers in the book sale. It has the advantage of providing an environmentally-friendly disposal method, adding to our good stewardship of the environment, even if it detracts from our profits.

Using third party dealers is beneficial in that it alleviates some of the staff time it takes to handle items and offers the selling expertise that librarians may not possess. Working with an individual book dealer, who may buy items outright or sell items on consignment might be a productive system, if the right dealer can be found. However, most book dealers want deep discounts in order to guarantee maximum profits. In addition, working with too closely with one dealer may present a public relations challenge. Our venture with an auction house proved profitable. However, the nature of their business leaves them only interested in very rare books and the staff time spent identifying and listing such books for possible auction may prove too much overhead for many libraries. Companies that work as general listing agents offer a fair return and an easy system which does not necessitate an excessive staff time investment. However, these companies operate with varying degrees of success. Also, they limit their business to newer, popular titles and they have no interest in textbooks of any age.

While none of the third party options proved ideal from the start, this exploration highlighted the importance of doing a trial run of any venture before fully committing to a process. At each step we considered our time investment, our returns on public relations, and the impact on the environment. To gather data needed to make this judgment, we started every new venture with a trial run. Each third party seller we approached received a list of our books or would receive a few boxes of items to sell. This approach allowed us to evaluate our return on investment before committing too much time, effort, or resources. Because we initially made a minimal commitment, we were less invested in that selling method and were more nimble in our reaction to the situation. Initial hiccups might cost a few books or a little investment of staff time, but after analysis adjustments can be made in how libraries use these services.

Selling Directly Online

Considering the alternatives and experiences described, the CD Team became a book seller for its most valuable items. Third party selling experiences provided the impetus to venture out on our own for certain items. Initially, there was concern of investment versus return. For example, what was the staff time needed to list items, to ship sold books, and to work with customers? Eventually, space constraints and a backlog of valuable items prompted us to explore this option.

We queried the best known providers to identify potential hosting services. We were looking for a system that provided ease of listing, low fees, and a method of receiving sales proceeds which worked with the billing and payment structure of MSU's accounting system. In addition, the items we had for sale would be unusual. Hence, we wanted to have the ability to create our own listings, instead of being locked into a database of items which might not include many of our titles. Most outlets required a bank account for direct deposit and many of them would not allow us to create our own tailored listings. Eventually, we chose a service which offered, for a low fee, the ability to create unique listings and to receive payment in the form of a check. We began listing the books in our storage room.

Initially, listing books required quite a bit of time, simply because of the large backlog of items in our inventory. We numbered each shelf for finding ease, processed a shelf at a time, listed the items on the website, and then returned these items to their shelf in the storage room. For shipping, we worked with our Interlibrary Loan department to use their UPS shipping system. This made shipping easy and less expensive because we received a discount through our state contract.

Our book-selling name—our store name if you will—was the subject of much discussion. We were worried over possible perceptions about a non-profit library seeking to sell books for a fair profit. While we were guaranteed a certain amount of anonymity outside our state, we were wary of angering the local patrons and book dealers who were major customers at our book sales. However, we did not feel the need to deceptively conceal our online selling, as we are freely entitled to use this method. Balancing these concerns, the CD Team selected a name that was associated with our university (our team mascot name) and created an appropriate logo outside of official university brands or graphics.

Some insights gained from selling books directly online include:

FLEXIBILITY

We are able to determine which items will best be sold online: those that appeal to a different audience other than our local customers (particularly foreign language and unusual science titles) and rare items that are not of interest to local customers. We have a fairly low overhead in that many of our items are gifts, we get a state discount for shipping, and our shipping supplies are recycled from our regular library business. This allows us to set our prices low and still make a profit.

TIME AND SERVICE INVESTMENT

We have had to deal directly with unhappy customers who have had lost or misdirected shipments and with a hosting service whose processes are not always foolproof. Setting up and listing items is time-consuming for staff at first, but diminishes until all that is required is daily general upkeep. Also, there is the consideration of storing items. Selling directly means sometimes waiting years before an item is purchased.

EASE OF USE

Selling directly online is not as difficult as expected. Even though we have had some problems which resulted in a financial loss, the ability to list unusual or rare items is a great benefit. We found that our low overhead allows us to be competitive in the used book market. By keeping our "store" name different from our institutional name we limited the public relations problems with our current book sale patrons and other third party selling communities.

Current System

With many avenues explored and lessons learned, we currently have an approach which seeks to balance our investments with our returns. This system of dealing with withdrawn books and unwanted gifts consists of a somewhat complicated, but still workable approach as far as staff time, return, and ease moving items through the process. Unwanted items go to our storage room. This work is done by either the CD staff member who is processing gifts or, in the case of withdrawn items, staff members on the cataloging team. Items are stored for the annual book sale and are sorted on shelves for quick retrieval. Another range has space for subjects that are not part of the book sale; these items are separated into two groups—items with and without ISBNs. Books with ISBNs are usually new enough to be sent to our third party seller. Books without ISBNs (and items of particular worth from all shelves) are evaluated for their suitability for sale directly online, with one staff member reviewing items every few weeks.

Items that are not valuable enough to be sold online and are not appropriate for the book sale go onto a large book cart which is labeled "free books." Members of the CD team roll the cart out in front of the library on random days. This approach has proved a bonanza with students and faculty; most days, staff members have to gently shoo patrons away from the cart in order to bring it back inside at the close of business. Even though most of the titles are less than exciting (e.g., old business and education titles, pamphlets from government agencies, foreign language novels), it has become very popular and generated goodwill among our patrons. Beyond these efforts, we recycle and donate items, when appropriate, and dispose of our few remaining items.

Recycling and Disposal

While we use a variety of methods for selling and giving away items, there comes a point in the process when disposal or recycling is the sensible next step. Loose periodicals, unbound paper, and shipment boxes go into our campus recycling, using bins located near our dumpsters for maximum convenience. With no local options for removing books and bound periodicals from their bindings for recycling, we realized that the alternatives of sending books elsewhere or buying large, expensive de-binding machinery were beyond our budgetary means. Consequently, some of our materials do end up in the trash.

Recycling is not limited to print materials. Recently we decided to weed a large collection of microfiche because these items are now available online. These items are not suitable for sale or exchange because most other libraries are in the same situation. Given that some of this material could have hazardous contaminants and it was such a large amount of material, we decided to explore our recycling options. Our University's Environmental Services Manager, who handles computer disposal and other hazardous waste, found the following caveats with regard to microfiche types: if you have a large quantity of silver halide microfilm (original film) it might be worth offering the material to a silver recycling vendor for reprocessing and to receive payment for the silver. Microfiche copies (identified by a white band along the top edge), purple, and multicolor microfiche do not contain enough silver to be hazardous waste and can be disposed of normally. Microfiche copies can also be recycled for their plastic content. Libraries will find that these same vendors recycle other media such as CDs, DVDs, video cassettes, floppy disks, and microfilm. Our recent recycling project of over 4,200 pounds of microfiche cost $1,000 after credits for silver content and included pickup and shipping by the recycler. MSU's Environmental Services got price quotes from vendors, arranged for pickup, and provided the labor to pack these materials for shipping. This situation has proved a very successful partnership using existing campus resources and even resulted in an MSU News article heralding the event.

While recycling may have a negative financial return, it has the advantage of positive public perception and good environmental stewardship. From our experience, the public appreciates the library exploring and being aware of recycling options and articulating why these options are used or not. Being a good steward of resources includes being fully aware of the disposal tools at hand and choosing the option most aptly suited for the situation.

Gifts to and Exchanges with Other Libraries

As Montana has a small population and a large geographical area, there are a number of remote libraries serving small populations. When we have items which are appropriately suited for other libraries, we try to offer these items to those entities. For example, we have donated materials to a variety of places including a new law and justice center library, a school library which was rebuilt after a fire, our city public library, and our sister MSU campuses. We take advantage of our state library conference and other meetings requiring travel to deliver materials to avoid shipping costs. Another avenue which should be noted, but which we have not used because of the time and staff overhead, is the Backserv list. This list "is devoted exclusively to the informal exchange of serial back issues and books among libraries. Backserv provides a public forum for the listing of both available and desired serial issues and books in all non-medical subject areas" ("Backserv").

The biggest drawback to exchanging items with other libraries is the staff time required for communication. Contacting other libraries and, in some cases, needing to provide lists of potential titles, can be very time consuming. When we donate to other libraries, we prefer to donate whole groups of materials, with the recipient library deciding what to add, dispose of, or sell. This process takes minimal staff time and has the positive value of helping other libraries serve their populations at a lower cost than if they had purchased these materials.

Discussion of Value Tensions and Future Implications for Entrepreneurship

We recount the above experiences of the MSU Library not because our situation is universal but to illuminate tensions present in any good faith effort to maintain high-quality, dynamic library collections while sustaining good public relations. While more scholarly attention may be paid to determining which resources to weed, deciding the fate of withdrawn or surplus materials can be equally daunting. The entrepreneurial library must weigh the potential political, social, environmental, and financial ramifications of disposition alternatives; moreover, as with the case of the MSU Library, this reflection must be done in real-time and with enough flexibility to make adjustments to processes when things do not go as planned. To aid peer institutions wanting to explore or refine their disposal practices, we employ a return-on-investment model to assess the resource inputs and outcomes of available disposal mechanisms used by the MSU Library. Throughout our discussion in this section, we fill in the gaps left by traditional economic analyses by looking at the institutional values that inform the evolution of the MSU Library's disposal practices.

As noted in the introduction, contemporary library scholarship praises return-on-investment as a tool for telling the story of how libraries contribute to their communities and society at large. On a macro-level, connecting public and private investment in libraries to positive economic and social outcomes is critical for institutions facing budget cutbacks and declining support. At the micro-level, ROI allows institutions to tell the story of how specific policies and practices reflect institutional values. This story addresses both internal and external audiences; ROI analysis can help an institution set and evaluate its collection maintenance policies and communicate the values and purpose behind specific policies to patrons and other stakeholders. Applied to the case of the MSU Library, ROI provides a framework to connect quantitative and qualitative metrics and gain perspective on the impacts of our disposition practices. In short, it allows us to tell the story of how our collection maintenance policies foster good stewardship of public resources in harmony with institutional values.

In an era of shrinking budgets, publicly-funded libraries, in particular, find themselves under the fiscal microscope. Increased budgetary scrutiny can be a catalyst for reassessing current disposition practices to ensure the best allocation of staff time and resources in balance with revenues from sales. Disposition costs will vary depending on the size, scope, and location of individual libraries; however, the MSU Library's experience provides a good sampling of the types of investment to consider when looking at alternatives. Table 1 shows the costs and returns that the MSU Library considered when exploring disposition options. As is seen here, traditional cost-benefit analyses sometimes reveal that book sales are not cost effective (Fenner 166); thus, libraries should be careful to consider qualitative such as goodwill produced as well as quantitative data such as financial cost incurred when assessing disposition practices.

The benefit of an ROI model which includes both qualitative and quantitative components is that it encourages the inclusion of non-economic factors in the story of a library's disposition practices. While an institution may be able to calculate the cost of staff time

DISPOSAL METHOD	Costs and Returns								
	Staff time	Service fees	Mailing or off-site delivery required	Long-term on-site storage required	Dedicated bank account required	Inventory management system included	Produce revenue	Environ. friendly	Add to public good-will
Online Auction A	X	X	X	X			X	X	?
Online Auction B	X	X	X	X	X	X	X	X	?
Selling directly online option A	X	X	X	X		X	X	X	?
Selling directly online option B	X	X	X	X	X	X	X	X	?
Selling through 3rd party online	X	X	X			X	X	X	?
Book sale	X						X	X	X
Free book table/cart	X							X	X
Backserv and other donation programs	X		X	X				X	X
Trash	X								
Recycling	X	X	X	X				X	X
Donation to other libraries	X		X					X	X

Table 1— Comparison of Disposal Methods, Costs, and Returns.

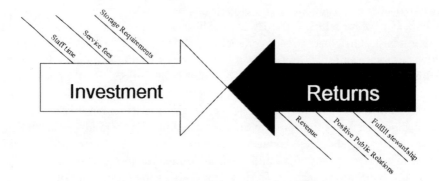

Figure 1 — Balancing Investments against Returns.

devoted to arranging and implementing book sales, economic analyses may be too blunt to account for qualitative factors such as positive or negative public relations. As is reflected in Table 1, conflicting public expectations of what a library does with its discarded materials may or may not result in public goodwill in the various methods employed. A library using an ROI model which incorporates underlying values could use this approach to explain to the public why it uses multiple methods for disposing of materials. Table 2 illustrates the quantitative and qualitative metrics which can be combined to tell the library's story. Investments such as staff time, service fees, and storage requirements are weighed against returns like revenues, positive public relations, and being a good steward of resources. The ability to articulate these considerations to the public and administrators will lessen tensions over the choices made.

So, how might one tell a story using ROI? As is reflected in the case study, we use a variety of entrepreneurial approaches which seek to balance investments with returns.

Investments

Quantitative measures easily apply to investments of staff time, service fees, and storage requirements, and these elements are described in more detail in the following sections.

STAFF TIME

An important consideration in an ROI measure is the amount of staff time spent handling items versus the return on investment in that effort. Work done by support staff versus that of a librarian will incur a lower cost per hour based on different rates of pay. At the MSU Library, once the Collection Development Librarian (higher hourly salary) deems a book to be inappropriate to retain in the collection, library support staff (lower hourly salary) manage the withdrawal and disposal processes, including any decisions on selling, gifting, or giveaways. One staff time metric is the total number of man hours expended times wages per hour.

SERVICE FEES

Selling items directly online or through third party vendors generally includes a flat service fee or a percentage of the overall sale. Once these fees are applied, libraries may find that the costs of selling items in these venues outweigh the net profits. One service fees metric is the total of all costs incurred per sale (a sum of postage fees, listing fees, percentage of sales proceeds retained by the vendor, shipping material costs, etc.).

STORAGE REQUIREMENTS

While difficult to quantify, storage requirements should be considered in an ROI model. Storage may include using an existing, available space which incurs little or no additional cost. Alternatively, storage may include overhead from maintaining environmental controls (such as air conditioning or managing humidity levels) or off-site space rentals. Storage can be measured as costs per square foot for storage which would otherwise not have been incurred by the library (a sum of environmental control costs, rent, security, etc).

Returns

Measuring returns with regard to book disposal includes both qualitative and quantitative measures, and is described in greater depth in the next sections.

REVENUE

With regard to financial return, revenue is defined here as income received for an item before any expenses (such as staff time) are deducted. Revenue can be measured as X amount of money received for an item. Considering environmental return, revenue may be measured by the least damaging carbon footprint when comparing alternatives (fuel surcharges, packing/shipping supplies, costs for removing book bindings, time for breakdown of materials in landfills, etc.).

POSITIVE PUBLIC RELATIONS

When the library gives away books for free or offers these items at a negligible price, positive public relations may result. This scenario may play out in a story such as the good feelings a patron receives after donating books to a library, knowing that the library will be responsible with these materials. This measure is more difficult to quantify as it is based on human emotion and may yield results which are difficult to correlate, such as financial donations from individuals in the future, based on past positive experience. This measure can be qualified when looking at negative financial returns weighed against positive public perceptions.

FULFILL STEWARDSHIP

As the library is generally viewed as a champion of information resources, as a public good, and as environmentally friendly, qualitative and quantitative measures of fulfilling these stewardship roles can be used in telling the ROI story. Stewardship can be measured as number of books sold or given away, numbers of books kept out of the landfill, or financial losses incurred in exchange for societal and environmental benefit.

Using a combination of these returns and investments, libraries can demonstrate their entrepreneurial efforts which generate only a profit, only goodwill, or both a profit and goodwill. Using the MSU Library case study, here are some examples of the ROI story.

FREE BOOKS

Certain books may be given away for free. This approach saves on trash hauling fees, storage, and staff time and effort spent trying to sell these items. But once staff time in the mere handling these materials is added to the equation, there is an overall financial loss in the exchange. At the MSU Library, we average about thirty minutes of staff time, at a salary of ten dollars an hour, to process a cart of 500 books given away. Indeed, there is "no such thing as a free puppy" and every item a library staff member touches incurs a cost. However, qualitative measures of value held by individuals who consider the library as a "place that finds homes for orphaned books" can increase support for the library and perhaps have a positive financial impact in future considerations of the library budget allocation and donations. This is a story of good stewardship of materials and the environment with minimal staff time invested.

WEB SALES

Items listed on a Web site for sale by a library may show a net profit which outweighs staff time invested and storage costs. On average, the MSU Library makes a minimum of fifteen dollars per rare or valuable book sold through direct Web sales, after expenses (including staff time of approximately ten minutes per book, shipping costs, listing costs, etc.); profits can be much higher depending on the book's value. This method requires more staff time investment and yields a high financial return. For common items sold via the Web, earnings average closer to one to ten dollars per item sold, after expenses. This approach involves minimal staff resources and returns a small profit. In both Web-selling situations, there is the story of an organization which employs entrepreneurially-savvy revenue production methods in keeping with its values to maximize returns to support library collections.

BOOK SALES

The book sale combines features found in the other sections; it generates revenue and produces goodwill. For every book sold, the MSU Library sees a profit of about twenty-five cents, after expenses (including staff time of approximately one minute per book and book sale advertising costs) and generates goodwill in the community. The library book sale creates perceptions that the library is a good steward of public resources and the environment with the added benefit that the public has access to items at a low price.

Both the literature and this case demonstrate a tension between the library as an effective entrepreneurial entity and buyers' expectations. Traditionally, libraries have been places where donated items can find further use and where the library's unwanted items can be obtained inexpensively or for free. When the library organization exhibits behavior which might contradict these experiences, especially when money is involved, there can be unexpected resistance. As the book sale case study exhibits, both book vendors and members of the public express surprise when items are priced closer to their market value and when the sale is honed down to those items the library expects will sell. Likewise, numerous anecdotes of these tensions can be found easily on book dealer message boards online. While it is understandable that people anticipate a pattern of past book sale experience to continue, it can be difficult to break out of this expectation in a manner satisfactory to buyers.

The entrepreneurial library seeks to maximize revenue to support library activities while minimizing costs in these transactions. Again, using an ROI model can help tell the story of the library's various approaches to selling. While buyers might not like libraries exploring multiple selling venues for maximum ROI, it is a model that is sensible and defensible as it is in keeping with the values and mission of the library.

Another tension which is a more recent development is ROI and environmental responsibility. There is increasing public pressure to reduce negative environmental impact, reuse materials whenever possible, and recycle what cannot be reused. Here, the import given towards being a good caretaker of the environment can be at odds with the significance placed on being a good steward of financial resources allocated to the library. These competing ideals can be politically charged depending on which value is placed more highly by individuals and the community. Again, the ROI model can be used to show the investments and returns for each of the material disposal practices employed by the library. For example, a total environmental cost assessment may demonstrate that the carbon footprint for throwing away materials is less than the environmental impact of shipping the items to a recycler. Presentation of the various methods used can be combined to tell the story of the many efforts made by the library and how the library is being most entrepreneurial with the resources available.

What are the future implications for entrepreneurship that can be gleaned from these experiences and what conditions might change the future marketplace? As many libraries face budget cutbacks, maximizing return on investment becomes increasingly important. At the same time, the market for used books is likely to see a significant shift for several reasons related to the growth of the e-book market. Patrons may donate more print books as they clear out their personal print collections in favor of e-books. Secondly, libraries may weed their print collections as they convert to e-books. Either of these changes could markedly increase the supply of used books. At the same time, increased interest in the electronic format may have a negative impact on the demand for used books through all channels, whether online book sellers or traditional library book sales. This scenario may increase the amount of staff time required to deal with donations and weeded books. As supply increases and demand decreases, prices are likely to fall and ROI will suffer, perhaps requiring another reassessment of disposal processes.

Conclusion

In this changing environment, the entrepreneurial library will need to continue to identify investments and returns and how to balance these ROI factors with core library values. The cheapest and perhaps easiest route for libraries would be to toss unwanted materials into the landfill. However, many librarians and library supporters find this solution untenable. The library as custodian of materials and the environment as well as dependable users of patrons' gifts counteracts any actions taken solely for financial reasons — there is a duality of mission. We have tried to provide, through our case study, not only examples of actions taken in our quest to minimize costs and generate some revenue to support library activities, but also an entrepreneurial paradigm through which we have navigated into a system of disposal. We have used the principles of ROI at each step in order to judge the concrete and ephemeral costs and benefits of our actions. Each library has a set of unique circumstances which may make some of our actions inapplicable. However, entrepreneurial libraries seeking a better method of disposition of unwanted materials may find the use of ROI, as applied to any situation, of benefit as we seek to resolve the often difficult situations encountered along the way.

Works Cited

2010 Census Data. U.S. Census Bureau, 21 December 2010. Web. 9 June 2011. <http://2010.census.gov/2010census/>.

"Backserv." *Swets.com.* Swets, 6 April 2011. Web. 6 Apr. 2011.

The Carnegie Classification of Institutions of Higher Education. Carnegie Foundation for the Advancement of Teaching. Jan. 2011. Web. 9 June 2011. <http://classifications.carnegiefoundation.org/lookup_listings/institution.php>.

"Core Values Task Force II Report." *ALA.org*, 2003–2004. American Library Association. PDF. 24 Feb. 2011.

Dilevko, Juris, and Lisa Gottlieb. "Weed to Achieve: A Fundamental Part of the Public Library Mission?" *Library Collections, Acquisitions, & Technical Services* 27.1 (2003): 73–96. Print.

"Evaluating Library Collections: An Interpretation of the Library Bill of Rights." *ALA.org*. American Library Association, 2 July 2008. Web. 24 Feb. 2011.

Fenner, Audrey. "Library Book Sales: A Cost-Benefit Analysis." *Library Collections, Acquisitions, & Technical Services* 29.2 (2005): 149–168. Print.

Kaufman, Paula, and Sarah Barbara Watstein. "Library Value (Return on Investment, ROI) and the Challenge of Placing a Value on Public Services." *Reference Services Review* 36.3 (2008): 226–231. Print.

Kyrillidou, Martha, and Colleen Cook. "The Evolution of Measurement and Evaluation of Libraries: A Perspective from the Association of Research Libraries." *Library Trends* 56.4 (2008): 888–909. Print.

Manley, Will. "Will's World: Readers Need Weeders." *American Libraries* 34.10 (2003): 80. Print.

Miller, Kathryn. *Public Libraries Going Green*. Chicago: American Library Association, 2010. Print.

Penniman, Sarah, and Lisa McColl. "Green Weeding: Promoting Ecofriendly Options for Library Discards." *Library Journal* 133.15 (2008): 32–33. Print.

"Property Management Procedure Manual." *Montana.edu*. Montana State University, November 2010. Web. 5 April 2011.

Quick Facts. Montana State University Office of Planning and Analysis. 4 Apr. 2011. Web. 9 June 2011. <http://www.montana.edu/opa/quickfactsindex.html>.

Scotti, George J. "Proving Value and Return on Investment." *Information Outlook* 14.4 (2010): 22–24. Print.

Sidorko, Peter Edward. "Demonstrating ROI in the Library: The Holy Grail Search Continues." *Library Management* 31.8/9 (2010): 645–653. Print.

Statistical Profile. Montana State University Library. 7 Jan. 2011. Web. 9 June 2011. <http://www.lib.montana.edu/about/statprofile.php>.

White, Larry Nash. "An Old Tool with Potential New Uses: Return on Investment." *The Bottom Line: Managing Library Finances* 20.1 (2007): 5–9. Print.

12 — Librarians as Sustainability Advocates, Educators and Entrepreneurs

ANNE M. LESS, BETH FILAR WILLIAMS
and SARAH B. DORSEY

Introduction

Sustainability is a hot topic these days. Demand for professionals and scholars who are knowledgeable about sustainability topics is growing exponentially. As with any nascent multidisciplinary subject area, sustainability students, scholars and professionals cope with the challenging imbalance of disorganized information abundance, coupled with knowledge scarcity. Questions far outweigh solutions and the pursuit of new knowledge abounds. For entrepreneurial librarians, environmentally conscious or otherwise, this is the perfect storm. Adept with much-needed research and organizational skills and a pre-existing ethic of collaboration and transparency, librarians are needed in this space. Motivated by their own personal passions and the needs of their patrons and institutions, entrepreneurial librarians demonstrate great leadership by carving new and essential niches for themselves in the emergent areas of scholarship and practice that embody sustainability.

The librarians highlighted in this chapter provide examples of how the leaders in this field employ the principles of social entrepreneurship in order to help solve social and environmental problems. Some get out from behind the reference desk in order to advocate on behalf of environmentally friendly libraries and institutions, bringing issues like transportation and energy efficiency to the forefront of the conversation. Others educate their communities and empower them to make lifestyle changes that are less resource dependent. Still others bring new value to their organizations by creating systems and programs that uniquely blend the strengths of librarianship with sustainability efforts. Regardless, like true entrepreneurs, all are changing the shape of librarianship and sustainability by challenging the status quo and expanding their job descriptions.

Librarians and Sustainability

Common trends were identified when the authors of this chapter surveyed sustainability entrepreneurs on why they think libraries and librarians are uniquely positioned to contribute to sustainability solutions. With a solid understanding of the information challenges in sustainability-related disciplines, many of the librarians interviewed during our research echoed the sentiments shared by Sarah Volpe of the California Center for Sustainable Energy, "In a busy world with so much information, people often come to libraries to seek direction on what is new and important, particularly for emerging topics, such as sustainability" (Volpe). Expanding on this, Fred Stoss of the State University of New York — Buffalo contends that librarians empower others to think outside of their traditional boxes, which allows entrepreneurial avenues to be explored (Stoss, "Re: Answers"). Andrea Minniear Cherney of the Energy Center of Wisconsin comments that "Today, energy issues are at the forefront of political conversation and we have an obligation to provide our users with accurate data..." noting that communities trust libraries and librarians as providers of accurate information (Cherney). This opening allows library professionals the opportunity to provide value to their communities by reducing user frustrations and increasing efficiencies, which saves both time and money. Furthermore, thinking of how communities maximize the use of their tax dollars to the benefit of future library users, Rebekkah Smith Aldrich of the Mid-Hudson Library System, proposes ways in which libraries play a role, "We are raising a generation of kids that will come to expect highly energy efficient buildings, low toxicity in building materials and adherence to 'reduce, reuse, recycle.' The library is one of the best places in the world (literally!) to demonstrate that commitment to sustainable choices. Kids grow up to be voters, politicians and policy makers and when they think back to who 'got it' early and who invested funds to make significant investments in sustainable options, I want libraries to stand out as early adopters" (Aldrich).

Librarians have been involved in the sustainability movement for decades, but the literature did not begin to reflect this until the 1990s. Since that time, library literature on sustainability and environmental concerns falls into four major categories:

- Sustainability of scholarship and collections
- Green library operations and practices
- Green library buildings
- Measuring and improving sustainability [Jankowska & Marcum].

An article by Monika Antonelli, published by the *Electronic Green Journal* in 2008 entitled "The Green Library Movement: An Overview and Beyond" provides a thorough summary of the green library movement through 2008. In this article Antonelli states that green libraries are approaching a tipping point creating a "true green library movement," which aims to not only save energy and money, but approach solutions from a comprehensive standpoint, including avoiding toxic chemical cleaning products which can trigger asthma attacks, developing recycling programs beyond the library into the community or campus, providing more environmental resources, offering local expert panel discussions and talks, creating sustainability book clubs and fairs, and even in a few instances continuing education courses and workshops on eco-librarianship.

One of the earliest articles on green libraries appeared in 1991 in the *Wilson Library Bulletin's* special section on "Libraries and the Environment" with James and Suzanne LeRue contributing the lead article entitled "The Green Librarian" (Antonelli, "The Green Library Movement"). A few other articles were also published in that same issue on topics related to making environmentally sustainable choices at home and in the library, developing environmental information resources, and the 20th anniversary of Earth Day. The intent behind this special issue was to bring these concepts to the forefront of the profession.

The creation of the *Electronic Green Journal* not only demonstrates entrepreneurial librarianship, but also marks an important milestone in sustainability research and publication. Started in 1992, *The Green Library Journal: Environmental Topics in the Information World* was formed by founder and editor Maria Anna Jankowska of the University of Idaho

Library "to create an international exchange forum for librarians, information consultants, civic groups, organizations, educators and individuals" (Jankowska, "From Print to Gopher"). At this same time, the American Library Association Task Force on the Environment (TFOE) formed and collaboratively supported this new journal, which eventually switched to an open source system and became the *Electronic Green Journal*.

The next round of green library research and publication did not reappear for another 10 years. In the early 2000s, *Library Journal* consistently began publishing on the topic of greening library buildings, with numerous articles such as "The New Green Standard" by Bill Brown, which focused on the concept of green building design. Starting in 2007, the Oregon Library Association published an entire issue each quarter, called "Going Green: Libraries and Sustainability," which covered a wide variety of subjects, such as environmental auditing in your library and transportation alternatives and resources (Stotak).

Today, sustainability-related subjects and approaches are increasingly woven into many libraries' services, resources and activities, as well as librarians' job descriptions and titles. Indicative of the increasing importance and relevancy of this area within the library arena, there are too many published works on sustainability and libraries to mention them all. Previous articles have described how librarians learned to adapt strategies from other disciplines, examined green facilities and collections and highlighted sustainability resources and data. This chapter looks at the subject from a new angle, by sharing stories of how individual librarians use their strengths to implement nontraditional and entrepreneurial sustainability programs that re-frame how value is assessed and delivered in libraries.

Social Entrepreneurship and the Triple Bottom Line

A formal definition of social entrepreneurship has only recently started to emerge in the literature despite the fact that its practice has a long, albeit informal, history in the non-profit world and the public sector. Interest in social entrepreneurship is closely linked to an expanded definition for business success called "The Triple Bottom Line." This concept is commonly defined as "an expanded baseline for measuring performance, adding social and environmental dimensions to the traditional monetary benchmark" (Elkington, "Glossary of Terms"). "The Triple Bottom Line" is often informally referred to as the three P's: people, planet, and profit. Organizations, companies and individuals that adopt "The Triple Bottom Line" develop innovative strategies and solutions that contribute to human quality of life and environmental protection, in addition to the more traditionally and narrowly defined economic "bottom line." The outdoor apparel company, Patagonia, provides a good example of this approach in practice. As a company, Patagonia has made a commitment to not only promote safe working conditions and fair labor practices throughout their supply chain, but also to "cause the least harm to the environment," all while, of course, pursuing a profitable business ("Company Info: Corporate Responsibility," "Environmentalism: What We Do"). Patagonia illustrates "The Triple Bottom Line" in action, because it pursues an economic bottom line alongside social and environmental goals. Economic success increases the impact of its social and environmental goals, and they in turn help to drive the company's economic success.

Social entrepreneurs are individuals who use the principles of entrepreneurship to apply "The Triple Bottom Line" within their communities, businesses and organizations. An entrepreneur, by definition is "one who undertakes innovations, finance and business acumen in an effort to transform innovations into economic goods" (Thachappilly, Gopinathan). Therefore, a *social entrepreneur* can be defined as one who undertakes innovations, finance and business acumen in an effort to transform innovations into *social, environmental and economic goods*. Social entrepreneurs are "leaders or pragmatic visionaries" who "often seem to be possessed by their ideas, committing their lives to changing the direction of their field" (Ashoka; Schwab Foundation for Social Entrepreneurship). Social entrepreneurs share common traits, including:

- An unwavering belief in the innate capacity of all people to contribute meaningfully to economic and social development.
- A driving passion to make that happen.
- A practical but innovative stance to a social problem, often using market principles and forces, coupled with dogged determination that allows them to break away from constraints imposed by ideology or field of discipline, and pushes them to take risks that others wouldn't dare.
- A zeal to measure and monitor their impact. Entrepreneurs have high standards, particularly in relation to their own organization's efforts and in response to the communities with which they engage. Data, both quantitative and qualitative, are their key tools, guiding continuous feedback and improvement.
- A healthy impatience. Social entrepreneurs cannot sit back and wait for change to happen — they are the change drivers [Ashoka; Schwab Foundation for Social Entrepreneurship].

History is filled with famous leaders who fit this description, yet due to the very recent development of social entrepreneurship as a formal discipline, most would not have self-identified as social entrepreneurs. The field of librarianship provides numerous examples of unknowing social entrepreneurs in action. By nature, libraries exist for the benefit of the common good and librarians operate under the assumption that the bottom line should benefit society. They also, of course, endeavor to maintain the stability of their programs and institutions. Therefore, they were already two-thirds of the way to the "Triple Bottom Line," when this concept started gaining traction in the 1990s. Similar to progressive members of the business community, for a growing number of librarians, elaborating upon the existing ethic within the field has been an obvious extension of librarians' roles and responsibilities within knowledge communities. In the past few decades, leaders in the library profession have transformed their institutions, patrons and general purpose by adopting the final "line": environmental sustainability. Many librarians demonstrate the spirit of social entrepreneurship and make an ongoing commitment to "The Triple Bottom Line" as sustainability advocates, educators and entrepreneurs.

Methodology

In order to understand the current sustainability trends and activities in librarianship, as well as identify notable leaders in the field, the authors sent out a call to our community of practice. The call was distributed to over twenty listservs and blogs whose audiences include all types of librarians and information professionals. This initial information-gathering activity connected the authors with approximately fifty librarians who are engaged in sustainability-related initiatives. Each of these individuals was invited to respond to an online interview that provided the authors with an in-depth understanding of how their work reflects entrepreneurial and sustainability ethics. The questions asked were:

- How do you think librarians and information professionals are uniquely qualified to contribute to the sustainability movement?
- Do you feel you have created a new innovative idea, program, approach or strategy that wouldn't exist in your area/institution otherwise?
- Have you recruited others to join in your cause or collaborated with other groups?
- How have you taken risks in order to establish and advocate for the existence of your program, idea, etc.?
- Do you consider yourself a change agent? How so?
- Have you come up with innovative solutions to resource limitations?
- How do you measure success?
- What would you do differently (if anything) when you look back?

The entrepreneurial librarians highlighted in this chapter were selected because they exhibit the characteristics of social entrepreneurs, as defined by Ashoka and the Schwab Foundation for Social Entrepreneurship. Each of these individuals demonstrates the myriad ways in which employing the principles of entrepreneurship helps librarians to tackle complex issues related to sustainability.

It is important to note, however, that this analysis is limited by time and length and does not provide a comprehensive landscape of librarians' involvement in the field of sustainability. There are certainly many examples of important leadership that are not, for one reason or another, included in this chapter. However, as a result of the connections created through this research and the discovery that entrepreneurial sustainability librarians had a need to connect with one another, the authors built an online network on LinkedIn for sustainable entrepreneurial librarians and all of the librarians we surveyed are represented there. Here, librarians will share stories and best practices with one another, momentum will continue to build, and others will be inspired to join the movement.

While each of the stories represented in this discussion is unique, the authors identified a few common themes, which inform the structure of our analysis. Therefore, the librarian leaders referenced herein are organized by the following common traits: Advocates, Educators, Entrepreneurs and Embedded Librarians.

Advocates

This section highlights examples of librarians advocating for sustainability practices in the profession, throughout their communities, and on their campuses. Leaders in the library profession serve a wide variety of communities, from institutional to local to national, which reflect their range of impact. Some librarians are sustainability advocates within the larger profession. These individuals attempt to instruct other librarians and to affect broad change in their field by creating committees, events, programs, and disseminating resources about sustainability. Those in academic environments get involved as sustainability leaders on campus; they work within student groups, create action-oriented campus teams, or market sustainability knowledge and resources to faculty and students. Still other sustainability leaders take an active role in their home communities by serving on non-library committees, advocating for libraries, using their expertise in creative ways and collaborating with others.

Frederick Stoss, the Associate Librarian for the Biological, Environmental Sciences & Mathematics at the University at Buffalo SUNY, is a key example of a social entrepreneur, an advocate and one who "cannot sit back and wait for change to happen" (Ashoka; Schwab Foundation for Social Entrepreneurship). Stoss has a driving passion to make a difference; educational degrees in biology, zoology and library studies; and eight years of research in toxicology and environmental health. He got involved in the sustainability arena over 25 years ago. His first job as a librarian was at the Center for Environmental Information in Rochester, New York, where he developed and managed the Acid Rain Information Clearinghouse. The only librarian to chair environmental sections of the American Library Association (ALA) and the Special Libraries Association (SLA), Stoss is now a recognized sustainability leader within both associations. As one of the original members, past Chair, and Co-Chair of the ALA Task Force on the Environment, Stoss has been active in developing programming and resources on environmental issues, which many libraries today use regularly. Involved in ALA's "Libraries Build Sustainable Communities" project, Stoss advocated for sustainability by creating print posters, guidebooks and a website of useful resources for library professionals and the general public. He has also created the Green Libraries Community on the ALA website, which brings sustainability librarians together in one place to share ideas and to network. Today, he still helps keep his fellow librarians up to date on sustainability initiatives through his regular publications in ALA's Social Responsibilities Round Table (SRRT) Newsletter and the *Electronic Green Journal*. He focuses on "a wide variety of free and low-cost data and information resources, that were and are underutilized, simply by not being widely known in non-research settings," such as data produced by World Data Centers, ecological research institutes, and other ecological and environmental data repositories in his publishing (Stoss, "Re: Answers"). For example, he has written helpful articles like "Librarians Taking the LEED and Sustainable Communities" (Stoss, "Librarians") and "The Roles Libraries and Librarians Play," which are useful to many librarians (Stoss & McCook).

Entrepreneurial leaders like Stoss take risks to advocate for their beliefs. In 1999, he successfully introduced a resolution to ALA's Social Responsibilities Round Table in support of the establishment of the Environmental Protection Agency's Office of Environmental Information (OEI). The OEI's goal was to make the agency's environmental information more easily accessible to the public — one that should be a natural desire for any librarian to advocate (Stoss, "Editorial"). In 2006, when OEI was hit with substantial budget cuts that threatened the existence of the EPA's National Library Network, Stoss and others at ALA and SLA proposed resolutions and recommendations in support of restoring funds to OEI "to continue support during extremely stressful times, when it appeared that generation of, access to, and dissemination of critical and essential environmental data and information was in jeopardy" (Stoss, "Re: Answers").

Stoss' leadership is recognized outside of the library community as well. He facilitated library workshops for the 2001 National Council for Science and the Environment Conference, whose recommendations were later presented at the 2002 United Nations World Summit on Sustainable Development. Furthermore, in 2007 and 2010, he was trained under Vice President Al Gore and The Climate Project to present Gore's slide show that served as the basis for his award-winning book and documentary film, *An Inconvenient Truth*. Stoss has subsequently given this presentation at too many places to list (Stoss, "Re:

Answers"). His leadership, risk-taking, publishing, teaching and hard work illustrates that Stoss is an influential and inspirational sustainability advocate, educator and entrepreneurial librarian.

Rebekkah Smith Aldrich, Coordinator for Library Growth & Sustainability for the Mid-Hudson Library System, was named a *Library Journal* "Mover & Shaker" in 2010 for her dedication to helping libraries secure sustainable funding. This publicity helped to launch her career in sustainable library building design and operations (*Library Journal*). Aldrich is currently a public library consultant who helps over sixty public libraries in New York find funding and governance solutions for green library facilities. Demonstrating the characteristics of a social entrepreneur, Aldrich uses practical innovations and marketing techniques to alleviate ideological constraints and deal with social and environmental problems, which are common traits of social entrepreneurs (Ashoka; Schwab Foundation for Social Entrepreneurship). Whether Aldrich is garnering community support or finding green building solutions, she is always helping libraries to achieve their goals of developing facilities with lower operating budgets and healthier environments for staff and patrons. She uses sustainability as a marketing tool, a way to change behaviors, and a motivating factor for employees. For example, Aldrich created a friendly team competition by challenging her staff to come up with innovative ways to save on electricity, paper, water and money within their library. Aldrich also networks with her local chapter of the U.S. Green Building Council, the New York State Preservation League, the New York State Energy Research and Development Authority, and politicians involved with the state Energy Committee to build networks to further her work in a more integrated manner. Her outreach, marketing, and advocacy demonstrate value to her libraries providing them more integrated sustainability services (Aldrich).

There are a number of web-based efforts by librarian entrepreneurs to provide free and open access to information reaching an infinite number of people. Green guru Monika Antonelli of Minnesota State University Libraries, has made a laudable commitment to resource-sharing, as she has created the well-known online directory called *Green Libraries: A Website for Information about Green and Sustainable Libraries.* Dedicated to documenting the greening of library facilities in North America, this site keeps a running list of libraries that were built with green building principles and archives resources that have helped people to green their libraries. In addition, Antonelli currently serves her home community as a member of the Greater Mankato Envision 2020 Energy Conservation Task Force and as the web administrator for the online discussion group, "Sustainable Mankato" (Antonelli, "Green Libraries").

An entrepreneurial team of librarians at Tufts University in Medford, Massachusetts got together for the first time in 2009, when Reference Librarian Laurie Sabol spearheaded the Tisch Library Sustainability Team (TST). Upon completion of her Tufts Eco-Ambassadors Program training — an optional environmental stewardship training for staff at Tufts University — Laurie advocated for the official chartering of TST, whose goal is to educate library staff and students about making sustainability a part of everyday choices. The team blogs and uses Twitter to share news, information, and ideas with campus community members, covering topics such as using eco-font, local recycling, and energy saving methods. TST also collaborates with other campus eco-ambassadors, the Library's Special Events Committee and the Office of Sustainability in order to promote practical, but innovative solutions to social and environmental problems. In just two short years, this group of sustainability librarians has developed programs that inspire eco-friendly habits and behaviors.

TST initiated programs such as: collecting recyclable chip bags, wrappers, and writing utensils, in order to send them to Terra Cycle for up-cycling; switching to filtered tap water around the library to reduce consumption of bottled water; and becoming the host site for the second Community Compost Bin on campus. TST also created the Bring Your Own Place setting (BYOP) campaign to the library, which encourages library staff to bring in plates, mugs and silverware from home, in order to reduce the need for disposables at meetings and events (Thompson).

Academic Programs Librarian, Kristen Bullard, an active member of Northern Arizona University's Environmental Caucus, is another campus sustainability leader and advocate. Recognizing the need to address transportation in a more comprehensive way, Bullard founded and chairs the Transportation Action Team (TransAT) of the Environmental Caucus. Bullard's Transportation Action Team quickly grew to become the largest action team on campus, bringing together people from all parts of campus, not just Environmental Caucus participants. Some of the group's successes, in less than one year, include: installing of electric car charging stations; establishing bike storage areas in garages and lockers on campus; conducting transportation surveys and creating action plans from the results; and promoting a campus ridesharing program. The group had three student interns during the 2010-11 school year, both Public Health and Environmental Sciences majors, who focused on projects concerning carbon offsets, the Bike Friendly University application, and education programming about sustainable commuting choices. TransAT also merged with the campus Bike Safety Committee, and collaborates with Flagstaff community organizations for events like Car-free Day and Bike to Work Week. TransAT has neither the authority nor a budget to implement these initiatives, but this passionate group demonstrates a "healthy impatience" nonetheless— an inspiring trait amongst social entrepreneurs (Ashoka; Schwab Foundation for Social Entrepreneurship). Rather than sit back and wait for change to happen, social entrepreneurs, like Bullard and TransAT, leverage the institutional roles, knowledge, and passion of individual members to achieve their sustainability goals.

Recently, Bullard was honored for her important work as a sustainability advocate by being awarded her campus's 2011 Environmental Caucus Sustainability Leadership Award. She demonstrates the value of librarians proactively taking risks to make changes in their campus communities. Bullard suggests that sustainability initiatives like these "are increasingly viewed as tools for extending campus resources in creative ways to meet student needs and enrollment growth," which is a value that academic libraries are often asked to provide (Bullard). More and more college students are demanding green campuses and seek out colleges that value sustainability. Integrating the library into both academic and non-academic life helps to demonstrate how relevant, useful, approachable, and helpful the library and its staff are. Connecting with students in these non-academic ways brings them into the library when their academic and research needs arise, allowing for librarians to expand their roles from advocates to educators.

Educators

Whether their patrons are students, the general public or colleagues, librarians are natural educators, researchers, information sharers, and awareness-builders. Moreover, the library buildings themselves offer a neutral venue to promote educational opportunities such as workshops, film nights, local speaker events, book clubs, contests, fairs, and art exhibits. Entrepreneurial librarians, possessed by their commitment to change through outreach, partnerships and education, are now educating with sustainability themes, resulting in some unique programs (Ashoka; Schwab Foundation for Social Entrepreneurship). As a result, there are numerous inspiring stories of entrepreneurial librarian-educators building awareness and sharing knowledge within their communities.

Librarians often organize and host educational events with local experts, and they collaborate with external partners in order to build powerful educational experiences for constituents. Increasingly, we are seeing a sustainability theme for these programs and experiences. While working at Craven Community College, librarian Julia Mielish organized a green team, which built environmental awareness each month by hosting local expert talks, workshops, and films on that theme. For example, a showing of the documentary *Fresh* followed by a talk on vegetable gardening, inspired students to petition the president of the college for a campus garden. Additionally, she started a Green Fair supported by her library, in which 36 local sustainability-focused organizations and businesses were invited to showcase their products. This partnership benefited the library, businesses and the community (Mielish). Mielish's educational events demonstrate that she possesses the "healthy impatience" that commonly describes a social entrepreneur (Ashoka; Schwab Foundation for Social Entrepreneurship).

Another example of an educational sustainability film series developed by an entrepreneurial librarian can be found at the University of North Carolina — Greensboro where Sarah Dorsey, one of the co-authors of this chapter, is Head of the Music Library and the 2010 UNCG Champion of Sustainability. Dorsey created a film and discussion series five years ago that is still going strong with a loyal campus and community audience. Before each film, there is an opportunity for community advocates to share information with arriving audience members. Each film is followed by a group discussion led by experts to apply the film's theme to local initiatives. For example, following the showing of the film *Bag It*, community members started an initiative to reduce the use of single-use plastic bags in Greensboro, and "in the process restoring our local community's commitment to environmental sustainability." The local Sierra Club is working with the city council, colleges, churches, and grocery stores to promote this campaign.

In 2011, the second annual UNCG sustainability short film competition was held with prizes given to filmmakers who created sustainably-themed films under 10 minutes in length. Highlights from these competitions include a film on sustainable burial (*A Natural Death*), and one shot entirely from a bicycle (*Balance*).

Additionally, the Green Libraries Group that Dorsey and others created in 2008 to educate library colleagues and encourage green behavior has (among other things) adopted a local stream and started a Green Book Group. Through these educational events, Dorsey's leadership has educated her campus while connecting it to the wider community of Greensboro. This helps to cultivate a healthier culture based on sustainability.

Social entrepreneurs are proactive about collaboration as a means to create educational programs that build awareness in their communities (Ashoka; Schwab Foundation for Social Entrepreneurship). An example of this can be found in the "Brown Bag, Green Book" lunch-and-learn series created by Emily Ellis, Reference Librarian at Knox County Public Library. Ellis built partnerships outside of the library in order to develop "Brown Bag, Green Book," a free, library-sponsored, community event. Each event features discussions on sustainability-related publications led by community leaders, such as a city councilman, a downtown developer, an architect, a university professor, the founding president of the Friends of the Smokies, and a local TV meteorologist. Books in this series cover a variety of topics including environmental economics, consumerism, product design, climate change, nature deficit disorder and the food system. Ellis approached the city's Office of Energy and Sustainability to ask for financial support and assistance in finding a venue to host the events closer to the hub of downtown. As a result the City of Knoxville joined as a co-sponsor. After several venues were tried, the series established itself at the East Tennessee History Center's auditorium, two blocks from the centrally located Market Square in downtown Knoxville. The library's Communications Department pitches in by developing marketing materials for the programs and the Friends of the Library buys each speaker a personal copy of the book and gives introductory remarks at each event. The reach of these events extends far beyond the actual discussion as the conversation continues virtually, and Ellis' colleagues podcast the events to allow a broader reach to those who cannot attend live. Ellis' collaborative entrepreneurial efforts have resulted in invaluable environmental educational experiences for her community.

On another level of education, Irene Reti, Director of the Regional History Project at the University of California at Santa Cruz Library, has completed a unique oral history, *Cultivating a Movement: An Oral History of Organic Farming and Sustainable Agriculture on California's Central Coast*. This educational project is entrepreneurial due to the enormity of the plan, the variety of stakeholders involved and the many disciplines it supports. There are fifty-eight interviews included in the online archive for this project, with stories from farmers, community activists, researchers and educators. One of the narrators in this diverse oral history is María Inés Catalán, a migrant farm worker who entered an organic farming program in Salinas, CA in 1994, becoming the first Latina migrant farm worker to own and operate a certified organic farm in California and the first Latina in the country to run a CSA(Community Supported Agriculture). She is an activist working to improve food security for low-income communities and educating students who learn through residencies working at her family garden. Another narrator is California State Assemblyman Sam Farr, a "political hero for the sustainable agriculture movement" and the author of the California Organic Food Act of 1990 (Reti, "Oral History ... Farr"; Reti, "Oral History ... Catalán").

In addition to the website and events that brought positive publicity to the campus and the library, popular exhibits of related artifacts are mounted at the University's Science and Engineering Library and McHenry Library. Furthermore, a book that includes excerpts from the oral history will be published by the UCSC Library in the fall of 2011. Reti hopes the book will be used in various college courses such as a history of social movements, agroecology and environmental studies. As Reti says herself, "I consider myself a change agent and see this project as participatory research where the library partners with a community in creating knowledge ... [which] becomes a resource as the movement journeys forward and serves as a link between past generations of sustainability activists/environmentalists and the younger generation of college and even high school students engaged with these issues" (Reti, "Re: collecting").

The influence of this project is spreading. In the Midwest, a historian is working to embark on a similar venture with the Wisconsin Historical Society. Writers and environmental documentarians seek Reti's advice and organizations like the International Federation of Organic Agricultural Movements (IFOAM), Slow Food, the Ecological Farming Association, California Certified Organic Farmers and the Oral History Association are publicizing their work. At a recent meeting of the national Ecological Farming Association, *Cultivating a Movement* was "praised ... as a model of the kind of project that should be done by libraries across the country" by recent president of the Organic Farming Research Foundation, Bob Scowcroft (Reti, "Re: collecting").

Reti's work to bring this unique undertaking to fruition exhibits entrepreneurial energy at its best. The power of this diverse community united over time through this project will continue to "cultivate a movement" inspiring local histories to be collected and preserved elsewhere.

Entrepreneurs

By definition, a start-up is "the act or an instance of setting in operation or motion, a fledgling business enterprise" (Merriam-Webster). Establishing a new initiative within a library or community of practice, along with its associated services, is no different from starting a company. These ventures are entrepreneurial by nature, requiring gap analysis, business and financial planning, stakeholder engagement, marketing and constant iteration. Social entrepreneurs possess "an unwavering belief in the innate capacity of all people to contribute meaningfully to economic and social development" (Ashoka; Schwab Foundation for Social Entrepreneurship). Examples of this attitude and approach are popping up increasingly in the sustainability movement, where opportunity abounds. Librarians are beginning to capitalize on this trend as well, by carving important niches for themselves and their expertise within their communities and institutions. The entrepreneurial librarians highlighted in this section are demonstrating leadership through their efforts to bring the principles and strengths of librarianship to sustainability-related efforts.

The Richmond Grows Seed Lending Library is the first of its kind to be housed within a U.S. public library. As the Co-Founder and Coordinator of the Richmond Seed Lending Library, Rebecca Newburn is a leader amongst green librarians. After hearing about the Bay Area Seed Interchange Library (BASIL) in Berkeley, California, Newburn was inspired to begin a similar initiative in her own community, in order "to create local resilience and a community of sharing and abundance" (Newburn). Newburn seized the opportunity to reintroduce seed saving to her community and attract patrons to the public library with a distinctive offering. The concept behind Richmond's Seed Lending Library should be familiar to librarians and archivists alike; deemed important to the preservation of local heritage and culture; unique artifacts (seeds) are collected and shared with future generations. However, unlike a traditional library or archive, in a seed lending library, the artifacts are literally alive and often edible. Entirely operated by volunteers, this library engages the community by collecting, preserving and sharing local seeds. Furthermore, only a year after its inception, community demand and support from the public library have driven the program's expansion. According to Newburn, "the project has benefited from being linked to a library because lots of people can see and access the seed library. We've been able to direct people to resources in the library to support them in learning about seed saving and the library staff has been very receptive to building their collection of seed saving books to support our community. We also recently assumed responsibility of the community garden at the library and are recreating it as a community seed garden where we will have educational signs about seed saving and work parties engaging the community in seed saving while growing quality seed for our community" (Newburn). Newburn's initiative provides an inspiring example of how much can be accomplished with nothing more than a passionate individual and an important cause.

For entrepreneurial librarians who are passionate about sustainability, their dream library might look something like this: a collection that focuses on energy efficiency, climate change, transportation, urban forestry, renewable energy and green building, with a tool lending library that lends energy meters and thermal imagers to the public, free of charge. This was exactly what Sarah Volpe, an inspiring entrepreneurial librarian, imagined. The best part of Volpe's story is that she was the person who brought all these elements together at the California Center for Sustainable Energy (CCSE) in San Diego, California. CCSE is a nonprofit organization that helps individuals, businesses, municipalities and others to adopt greener practices and save energy and money through rebates, technical assistance and education. Volpe submitted a plan for completely revising the Energy Resource Library at CCSE, which outlined a work plan for new library resources as well as predictions for its success. Her proposal also made the case for why she would be the right person to implement the plan. Volpe's proposal was accepted and CCSE's Reference Library and Tool Lending Library was realized. As a result of Volpe's entrepreneurial approach to problem solving, an invaluable set of services now contributes to the greater mission of her organization. According to Volpe, "the symbiotic nature of the library with the offerings of the Energy Resource Center provides a unique opportunity for our visitors. They can attend a workshop on a particular technology, see the display of that technology in our showroom and visit the library to check out a book or DVD to learn more about it and then borrow a tool to see how they can implement that technology in their own home or business. And it's all completely free of charge" (Volpe). This is social entrepreneurship in action.

While they are holistic in their thinking and global in their reach, it is important to note that social entrepreneurs are also rather attuned to finding and delivering achievable solutions. In fact, one of the common traits shared amongst social entrepreneurs is their tendency to work toward "practical but innovative solutions to social problems" (Ashoka; Schwab Foundation for Social Entrepreneurship). "Practical but innovative" is a very fitting description for Beth Filar Williams, Distance Education Librarian at the University of North Carolina — Greensboro and a co-author of this chapter. Filar Williams has made a point to leverage her role in distance education in order to advocate for environmentally-friendly education delivery solutions that more effectively and efficiently serve distance students. As a result, Filar Williams' program is much more efficient in terms of customer service *and* energy; it reduces transportation costs and carbon emissions by eliminating the need for students to travel to the library to use the resources, and the need for vendors to ship books to the library. Still, Filar Williams does not stop there, because she understands that virtual services can drive up energy costs. The collaborative efforts with her colleagues in the library Information Technology department, in which she works, are truly exemplary of an entrepreneur who aims to solve a larger social problem with a practical solution. Filar Williams' group has implemented server virtualization, which greatly reduces the energy demands associated with online services. That she steps outside of the traditional role of a librarian in her situation in order to contribute to this larger issue is certainly exemplary.

Heather Cunningham, Reference Librarian and Web Coordinator of the Gerstein Science Information Centre at the University of Toronto, provides another example of a librarian who has found "practical but innovative solutions to social problems" (Schwab Foundation for Social Entrepreneurship, 2011). In 2009, sustainability was not a primary priority for Cunningham's organization, until she took the lead and found a solution to a common problem: paper use. Cunningham initiated a partnership between the library and the University's Sustainability Office to decrease paper waste through green printing policies and paper reuse. The program became so successful that it was implemented throughout the central libraries on the University of Toronto campus. As a result of this effort, the Library has reduced paper use by over a half a million sheets per year. Furthermore, in 2010, Cunningham and her colleagues shared what they had learned with the library community by publishing a paper on the topic in *Computers in Libraries*, "Paper Cuts Don't Hurt at the Gerstein Library" (Cunningham, Feder, and Muise). Through sharing their story with others, Cunningham and her team have made an impact at their own institution, and inspired others to initiate similar programs within their own organizations.

Providing access to information and creating opportunities for continuing education have long been primary elements of the ethic of librarianship, and librarians often leverage related principles in order to tackle complex sustainability issues. However, one notable entrepreneurial librarian rises to the top in this area — Maria Jankowska, Social Sciences/ Government Information Librarian at the University of California — Los Angeles and founding member of the American Library Association's Task Force on the Environment. Librarians were very rarely involved in publishing on topics outside of librarianship and formal journals on the subject of sustainability were limited in the early 1990s. Demonstrating that she truly possesses a "healthy impatience," Jankowska saw a gap and took the initiative to fill it (Schwab Foundation for Social Entrepreneurship, 2011). At this time, Jankowska started the *Electronic Green Journal (EGJ)*, a scholarly publication that aimed to "to assist in international scholarly environmental communication by providing a quality, unbiased, and freely accessible forum for the exchange of environmental information as an alternative to the costly, commercially produced scientific journals" (Jankowska, "Re: Interview questions"). This growing field of sustainability librarianship has Jankowska to thank for the continuing existence of this important resource. In 2002, *Library Journal* recognized Jankowska for her leadership in this area by naming her one of the fifty "Movers & Shakers" in the field. She continues to inspire others through "her scholarship, work on synthesizing information for Web access, promotion of environmental ethics and information, and national and international activities" (Jankowska, "Re: Interview questions").

Embedded Librarians

Embedded librarianship, a quickly growing trend in all sectors, aims to serve patrons in the context in which their information needs arise. This approach "focuses on the user and brings the library and the librarian to the user, wherever they are — office, laboratory, home, or even on their mobile device" (Kesselman and Watstein). Sometimes the role of embedded librarians is intentionally created; for example, an academic library initiative that embeds librarians in university courses or in residence halls, in order to assist students in their own spaces. However, equally as important, sometimes the role of embedded librarians develops organically, resulting from initiatives started by entrepreneurial librarians. Sustainability-related initiatives and teams are inherently interdisciplinary and ever changing, with abundant knowledge gaps and opportunities. Entrepreneurial librarians who work on sustainability efforts are uniquely positioned to propose and experiment with embedded librarianship on interesting projects that seek to change the way the world approaches issues related to energy, the environment and public health. The librarians noted in this section demonstrate that embedded librarians can help organizations efficiently and effectively achieve rigorous sustainability goals while displaying a social entrepreneur's "healthy impatience" (Schwab Foundation for Social Entrepreneurship, 2011).

Many entrepreneurial librarians are bringing the concepts of sustainability to their libraries and institutions, but for those organizations that are already focused on sustainability, sometimes what they need is a dose of librarianship. The efforts made by Betsy Herzog at the Rocky Mountain Institute (RMI) demonstrate the value that librarians bring to sustainability-related businesses. RMI, a nonprofit think-and-do tank, is well known in the sustainability world for its innovative solutions to some of the world's greatest energy problems ("About RMI"). When Herzog, now Librarian and Knowledge Manager, was hired as an intern in 2008, she saw an opportunity to fill an essential gap at RMI and subsequently created a role for herself. RMI's researchers, consultants, communicators and fundraisers create new knowledge on a project-by-project basis, but unfortunately, as at many organizations, that knowledge is sometimes lost at the end of each project cycle. Herzog set out on a mission to capture RMI's rich knowledge. She developed a database that catalogs all of RMI's past work, communities of practice, project documents and individual expertise and skill sets. This knowledge management tool is now an invaluable resource that helps to build new and inspiring sustainability initiatives. Moreover, Herzog's program has changed the culture of her institution, as she says, "my organization treats their internal knowledge, institutional memory, and research skills as important values for an organization to maintain. Prior to my tenure, the organization did not have an advocate for these ideas" (Herzog).

The U.S. Green Building Council (USGBC) is most commonly known for the LEED (Leadership in Energy and Environmental Design) rating system, which is a benchmark for energy-saving buildings that use resources responsibly ("Intro—What LEED Is"). Similar to the Rocky Mountain Institute, USGBC's purpose is strongly based upon the principles of sustainability and the Triple Bottom Line. As a result, the organization was not lacking a sustainability advocate, but rather, a knowledge management advocate. That was until Anne Less, a co-author of this chapter and formerly USGBC's Knowledge Center Specialist, saw an opportunity to share her skills as a librarian and knowledge manager with the organization. She envisioned a system that fosters cross-departmental communication internally, and member collaboration and education externally. Less outlined all of this in a proposal to the organization's management team. With a great level of trust, a new position was created for Less to execute her plan for a Knowledge Center at USGBC's Headquarters in Washington, DC. Less oversaw the development of the organization's first library, from design and construction through collection development. She also developed an internal education program in which she taught classes on online searching and RSS feeds and hosted a sustainability movie hour each week. Through these efforts, like Betsy Herzog at RMI, Less helped to foster a culture of knowledge-sharing and professional development. Furthermore, Less extended the reach of her program by creating the first freely available digital library focused exclusively on green building. This online catalog, comprised of over 600 reports, websites and research papers, became a useful tool for green building professionals, state and local policy advocates and also other sustainability librarians.

Social entrepreneurs possess "a dogged determination, that allows them to break away from constraints imposed by ideology or field of discipline" (Ashoka; Schwab Foundation for Social Entrepreneurship). Breaking free from constraints is precisely what embedded librarianship is all about. In her current work on Google's green building team, Anne Less has found that the benefits of stepping outside the traditional bounds of librarianship and joining an interdisciplinary team far outweigh the risks. As a consultant to Google, Inc., Less creates and implements resources that support the company's goal to eliminate toxic chemicals from the workplace, while challenging the market to provide healthy products whose contents are fully transparent to consumers. Unfortunately, building materials do not have "ingredient labels" on them in the same way that food does. Therefore, consumers do not know when they could be unintentionally bringing harmful chemicals into their offices and homes. Less bridges this information gap in order to enable her teams, which are comprised of architectural designers and construction professionals, to successfully design and build offices that are toxin-free. Less has relied on her background in librarianship to develop guidelines for healthy building material selection and creating a digital library of toxin-free building materials. As an embedded librarian, Less not only has something unique and valuable to offer her team, but more importantly, by learning from team members from other professions, she has been exposed to a diverse set of problem-solving techniques. This systems approach to sustainability problems results in innovative, entrepreneurial solutions that would never be discovered if experts stayed safe in their professional silos.

Social entrepreneurs cannot sit back and wait for change to happen—they are the "change drivers" (Ashoka; Schwab Foundation for Social Entrepreneurship). The effort Cindy Davis has made to bring green building practices to her architecture firm provides notable examples of how "healthy impatience" incites positive change and influences others. Nowadays, it is common to hear about buildings that have achieved LEED certification and about design and construction professionals who are LEED Accredited Professionals (LEED APs). In the early 2000s, this was not the case. The building industry had yet to adopt the principles of the Triple Bottom Line, and instead focused on the bottom line in its most conservative definition. However, there were some leaders in the industry willing to take risks in order to learn more about building green. At Callison, a Seattle-based architecture firm, a team of innovators, including the firm's librarian, Cindy Davis, developed a Green Research Team, which set out to transform the way the organization designs and builds. Since architects and construction professionals who work on LEED projects are required to possess the LEED AP professional certification, the first step Callison's Green Research Team took was to be the first in their firm to become LEED APs. Davis was certainly an unprecedented leader in this regard, as she was likely the only LEED Accredited Librarian at that time (Davis). This step in Davis' career not only changed how her firm approached building projects, but it also altered her own career path. Since Davis became a LEED AP in 2002, Callison's Green Research Team has inspired over 130 employees to become LEED APs, and the firm has completed over 20 LEED-certified projects. Davis' role in the organization has evolved beyond managing the Research & Information Center to now include management of the LEED certification process. Davis teaches classes on the LEED Rating System as a part of the firm's professional development program, and she helps to organize LEED study groups. Most importantly, Davis' green leadership is continuously rewarding, particularly when she sees "some of those skeptics I have encountered make a 180 degree change in their position" (Davis).

Andrea Minniear Cherney, Senior Project Manager at the Energy Center of Wisconsin, is committed to strategic "doing" as well as strategic planning, which she reveals continuously through her work. Her driving passion makes Cherney an excellent example of an entrepreneurial librarian, for she has carved a special niche for her expertise in an interdisciplinary environment (Schwab Foundation for Social Entrepreneurship, 2011; Ashoka, 2011). The Energy Center of Wisconsin is dedicated to reducing energy use and developing the next generation of solutions to clean energy challenges. This nonprofit organization, which engages in research and education and operates in a cross-disciplinary manner, is comprised of engineers, evaluators, planners, economists, an architect, communications professionals and librarians. Cherney's willingness to take on new challenges has allowed her a wide variety of opportunities, from managing the Center's research library, distributing energy efficiency materials and portable energy meters to public libraries in Wisconsin, developing an electronic information clearinghouse, to managing a conference for professionals in the residential building industry. Each of these experiences has influenced Cherney's most recent accomplishment — leading the creation of a revenue-generating distance learning program for professionals in energy-related industries. This program, which aims to make energy efficiency knowledge as accessible as possible, has impressed both internal and external stakeholders, raising the level of support for Cherney's work. Other energy organizations have noticed the impact of this program and now hire Cherney's team to deliver content through their channels. The interdisciplinary approach the Energy Center of Wisconsin takes to problem solving, along with Cherney's desire to "rely 100% on [her] librarian roots," has fostered an entrepreneurial spirit in all of her projects.

Academic institutions are also starting to embed librarians within their sustainability-related disciplines and efforts. The University of Nevada–Las Vegas is fortunate to have Marianne Buehler as their Urban Sustainability Librarian, perhaps one of the first of her kind. One of Buehler's main tasks is in creating digital archives to build UNLV's Institutional Repository (IR), which allows global access and the electronic preservation of such items as: faculty and student's e-theses and dissertations; conferences and campus events; and sustainability research from Brookings Mountain West and the Harry Reid Center. In this regard, Buehler serves as a bridge between the university and constituents with related sustainability goals, such as city, county and state agencies and local and national nonprofits. In concert with these organizations, Buehler works to bring topics like transportation, energy, water and land conservation to the forefront of state and local conversations. One of Buehler's projects involves gathering what is often buried government documents, local reports, conference materials and digitized lectures, in order for citizens to more easily locate sustainability resources in the IR. Her focus on collaboration and relationship-building has afforded Buehler successes that would never have been possible if the university had approached these issues alone. Buehler's dedication to cooperation and resource sharing provides Nevadans with the opportunity to learn about and join in the quest for sustainable solutions (Buehler).

Buehler is also a member of UNLV's Urban Sustainability Initiative Council. Their most recent project has been completing the University's STARS rating (Sustainability Tracking Assessment & Rating System) for the Association for the Advancement of Sustainability in Higher Education (AASHE), which is an organization that aims "to empower higher education to lead the sustainability transformation" (AASHE). In addition to UNLV receiving STARS credits for the Sustainability Librarian position, the IR was instrumental in garnering points as a vehicle to showcase UNLV faculty and student sustainability research efforts archived in an open access environment. As a STARS Research Technical Advisor, Buehler is part of a team that regularly reviews and updates research credits for content related to faculty and student sustainability-related research activities (Buehler).

Exhibiting a trait of social entrepreneurs who "break away from constraints imposed by ideology or field of discipline," the most rewarding aspect of her work involves working with academics in order to reveal the advantages of open access to those individuals who are most accustomed to traditional modes of scholarly communication (Ashoka; Schwab Foundation for Social Entrepreneurship).

Conclusions and Opportunities

The accomplishments of the sustainability librarians and leaders mentioned in this chapter are not only inspiring, but also demonstrate the variety of ways in which growth in the sustainability movement provides librarians with a wealth of opportunities. Librarians who seize upon these opportunities are true entrepreneurs. Moreover, in an uncertain economic climate, these librarians are actively demonstrating their relevance and institutional value. Librarians who carve out a niche for themselves in the sustainability movement demonstrate that their roles and libraries bring additional value to their organizations and institutions, something that is increasingly demanded of them by funders. Entrepreneurial sustainability librarians are positioned to re-frame how value is assessed and delivered in libraries. An esteemed leader in our field, Maria Jankowska says, "libraries still have a long way to go in adopting the holistic view of sustainability ... [we] need hard data on how much energy, water, and money goes into making and storing our print collection versus how much goes into creating and storing electronic resources. We need an objective assessment of not only environmental sustainability but also economically and socially sustainable practices in our libraries" (Jankowska, "Re: Interview questions"). Libraries will achieve an important milestone when they embrace the performance metrics of "The Triple Bottom Line," in lieu of traditional tenure expectations, circulation statistics, funding models, and number of reference questions answered.

The examples that have been provided here are worth replicating in other institutions, but there are other opportunities that have yet to be explored. For example, we anticipate that library schools and professional associations will offer subject-specific training in sustainability. Additionally, librarians can and should advocate for laws that favor sustainability initiatives at the local, state or federal levels. It is our hope that sharing these stories will inspire others in the field to take advantage of the ample opportunities for librarians in the sustainability movement. No matter who you are, there is a place for all of us in this ever-growing field, as Cindy Davis of Callison has found, "you can be influential without necessarily being in a leadership role" (Davis). Moreover, entrepreneurial initiatives are always more successful if approached collaboratively, so if you are inspired but hesitant about where you can make the most impact, take the advice of the Tisch Library Green Team, "seek out a group of like-minded individuals to identify some potential areas of improvement for sustainability practice and related communications within your workplace" (Thompson). Still, the most common thread amongst all of the wonderful, inspiring librarians featured in this chapter is that they are not afraid to cross barriers. If each of us in our own small way took Fred Stoss' advice, the authors sincerely believe that anything is possible: "take advantage of the opportunities placed in front of you and NEVER look at them as burdens, hurdles or barriers. Things placed in front of you are challenges to overcome: walk around them, crawl under them, jump over them, break through them — it makes you smarter and stronger" (Stoss, "Re: Answers").

Works Cited

"AASHE Mission, Vision and Goals." aashe.org. AASHE, n.d. Web. 27 June 2011.

"About RMI." Rocky Mountain Institute, 2011. Web. 10 April 2011.

Aldrich, Rebekkah. "Re: Interview questions for Green Entrepreneurial Librarian Book Chapter." Message to Beth Filar Williams. 1 March 2011. E-mail.

Antonelli, Monika. *Green Libraries: A Website for Information about Green and Sustainable Libraries.* Web. 13 April 2011.

_____. "The Green Library Movement: An Overview and Beyond." *Electronic Green Journal* 1.27 (2008): n. pag. Web. 10 April 2011.

Ashoka. "What is a Social Entrepreneur?" Web. 10 April 2011.

Brown, Bill. "The New Green Standard." *Library Journal* 128.20 (2003): 61. Web. 11 Apr. 2011.

Buehler, Marianne. "Re: Interview questions for Green Entrepreneurial Librarian Book Chapter." Message to Beth Filar Williams. 3 March 2011. E-mail.

Bullard, Kristen. "Re: Interview questions for Green Entrepreneurial Librarian Book Chapter." Message to Beth Filar Williams. 17 March 2011. E-mail.

Cherney, Andrea Minniear. "Re: collecting Green Librarian stories." Message to Anne Less. 22 February 2011. E-mail.

"Company Info: Corporate Responsibility." Patagonia, 2011. Web. 10 April 2011.

Connell, Virgina. "Greening the Library: Collection Development Decisions." *The Journal of the New Members Round Table* 1.1 (2010): n. pag. Web. 10 April 2011.

Cultivating a Movement: An Oral History of Organic Farming and Sustainable Agriculture on California's Central Coast. Web. 13 April 2011.

Cunningham Heather, Elah Feder and Isaac Muise. "Paper Cuts Don't Hurt at the Gerstein Library." *Computers in Libraries* 30.2 (2010): 6–10.

Davis, Cindy. "Re: Entrepreneurial Librarian." Message to Anne Less. 28 February 2011. E-mail.

Elkington, John. *Cannibals with Forks: The Triple Bottom Line of 21st Century Business.* New Society Publishers, 1998. Print.

Electronic Green Journal (EGJ). Web. 13 April, 2011.

Ellis, Emily. "Re: Interview questions for Green Entrepreneurial Librarian Book Chapter." Message to Beth Filar Williams 1 March 2011. E-mail.

"Environmentalism: What We Do." Patagonia, 2011. Web. 10 April 2011.

Filar Williams, Beth. "Going Green @Your Library." Web. 13 April 2011.

"Glossary of Terms." Royal Geographical Society. Web. 10 April 2011.

Herzog, Betsy. "Re: collecting Green Librarian stories." Message to Anne Less. 8 March 2011. E-mail.

"Intro—What LEED Is." U.S. Green Building Council, 2011. Web. 10 April 2011.

Jankowska, Maria Anna. "From print to Gopher to Open Journal Systems: A Look Back on the Many Faces of the Electronic Green Journal [Electronic version]." *Electronic Green Journal* 1.25 (2007): 1–12. Web. 10 April 2011.

_____. "Re: Interview questions for Green Entrepreneurial Librarian Book Chapter." Message to Beth Filar Williams. 13 March 2011. E-mail.

_____, and James Marcum. "Sustainability Challenge for Academic Libraries: Planning for the Future College and Research Libraries." *College & Research Libraries* 71.2 (2010): 160–170. Web. 10 April 2011.

Kesselman, Martin A. and Sarah Barbara Watstein. "Creating Opportunities: Embedded Librarians." *Journal of Library Administration* 49.4 (2009): 383–400. Web.

Library Journal. "Rebekkah Smith Aldrich—Community Builders—2010 Movers & Shakers." *Library Journal's Movers and Shakers 2010*, n.d. Web. 10 April 2011.

Mielish, Julia. "Questions for Beth Williams/Green librarians." Message to Beth Filar Williams. 27 February 2011. E-mail.

Merriam-Webster. "Definition of Start-Up." Merriam-Webster, 2011. Web. 10 April 2011.

Newburn, Rebecca. "Re: collecting Green Librarian stories." Message to Anne Less. 22 February 2011. E-mail.

Philis, James A., Kriss Deiglmeier, and Dale T. Miller. "Rediscovering Social Innovation." *Stanford Social Innovation Review* Fall 2008 (2008). Web.

Reti, Irene. "Oral History Summary for Congressman Sam Farr." Web. 30 June 2011.

Reti, Irene. "Oral History Summary for María Inés Catalán: Catalán Family Farm." Web. 30 June 2011.

Reti, Irene. "Re: collecting Green Librarian stories." Message to Anne Less. 22 February 2011. E-mail.

Schwab Foundation for Social Entrepreneurship. "What is a Social Entrepreneur?" Web. 10 April 2011.

Shane, Scott. *A General Theory of Entrepreneurship: the Individual-Opportunity Nexus.* Edward Elgar Publishing. 2004. Print

Sotak, Diane. "Going Green: Libraries and Sustainability." *OLA Quarterly* 2007: 1. *Library, Information Science & Technology Abstracts* 1 (2007). Web. 11 Apr. 2011.

Stoss, Frederick. "Re: Answers: Interview questions for Green Entrepreneurial Librarian Book Chapter." Message to Beth Filar Williams. 1 and 4 March 2011. E-mail.

Stoss, Frederick. "Editorial — Protecting Access to Environmental Information and Saving the Environmental Protection Agency (EPA) Libraries." *Electronic Green Journal*, 1.23 (2006): n. pag. Web. 10 April 2011.

Stoss, Frederick. "Libraries Taking the "LEED": Beyond Leadership in Energy and Environmental Design." *Online*, 34.2 (2010): 20–27. Print.

_____, and Kathleen De La Pena McCook. "Sustainable Communities and the Roles Libraries and Librarians Play." *Reference & User Services Quarterly* 42.3 (2003): 206–211. Print.

Thachappilly, Gopinathan. "What are the Characteristics of an Entrepreneur?" suite101.com, 1 July 2010. Web. 10 April 2011.

Thompson, Kristofer. "RE: [tfoe] Calling all Green Librarians!" Message to Beth Filar Williams. 22 February 2011. E-mail.

Volpe, Sarah. "Re: collecting Green Librarian stories." Message to Anne Less. 28 February 2011. E-mail.

13 — An Interview with Martha Thomas Larson

Amy Archambault

Martha Thomas Larson is the Business Information Specialist at the Greensboro Public Library; she started Future Cents, *a financial literacy program for teens at the Greensboro Public Library in Greensboro, North Carolina. This "free money management program for teens" has grown into a series of workshops that teach financial literacy not only to the community's teens, but frequently, to their parents, as well. In the interview that follows, Ms. Larson describes the genesis of the program, the niche it fills in the community, and how partnerships with community organizations have been essential to the program.*

AA — Martha, tell me about Future Cents, how you got started with it and how you took it from an idea to your first workshop?

ML—Certainly! We were invited by the American Library Association (ALA) to apply for a grant that was being offered by ALA in conjunction with FINRA, the Financial Industry Regulatory Authority. FINRA collects penalties from companies in the financial industry and distributes them to public libraries to support programs about finances and financial literacy.

AA — So when those banking companies pay fines, the money is made available from FINRA as grants to bring it back into a community.

ML—Right.

AA — How was it that the ALA came to you?

ML—I was asked by my assistant director if I was interested in submitting the grant; this was the first grant I had ever done. Fortunately, ALA provided a very good explanation of the grant, and what they needed to see in the proposal. They also provided a template that helped me a great deal. Without these, I don't know that I could have submitted a successful grant proposal on my own, being that was my first try.

We have a teen-centered focus here in this library. Every financial advisor and investment club says that the earlier you teach these principles, the better, so we thought we would generate a program just for youth. That's where the concept of Future Cents originated.

AA—I understand you conducted some focus groups in the course of developing the program; how did that come about?

ML—Well, that was actually a part of the proposal process; a lot of grants require that you involve the target audience in the grant proposal. The grant proposal contained a formal way for us to document that we had generated this concept with input from our target audience. To recruit teens for the focus groups, I approached the YMCA which operates a youth program; following that, I contacted another YMCA program, Black Achievers, and met with each of those groups to assess the need for financial literacy education, talk about the name of the project, how to market it, and what money-related topics would interest them. I met with these two groups which were comprised of very different teens; one of the YMCAs is located in a more affluent part of town while the other has a totally different demographic make-up. From these I got two very different perspectives.

I hadn't been particularly aware of the need for financial literacy programs among teens until I held the focus groups. Among the middle and high school students in the focus groups few had had any exposure to these concepts. Here are some of the things I learned: none of them talked about money at home; none of the students got any exposure to financial education at school; none had had any exposure to concepts related to investments; only 3% had an active savings account; 6% had a checking account; and, only 5% knew how their parents were saving for college. The desperate need for financial literacy programming became obvious to me during the focus groups.

AA — When you found out that you had been awarded the grant, what did you do after that? What were your next steps?

ML— We actually had to move pretty quickly. We were notified in late December that we had won the award, but with the holidays, we didn't hold our first meeting until January. Our plan was to offer the first workshops in June, right after school got out, so we didn't have a lot of planning time.

AA — Did you have help developing the program?

ML— Yes, partners from the community were critical to the program's development during the grant-writing process. Once I had decided to pursue the grant, I formulated my advisory committee and project team. Very early in the process, I turned to a woman who was a middle school teacher and had also worked as a personal coach; she's served as a consultant to the project and filled an important role. Then I happened to attend a Chamber of Commerce event at which a very prominent local financial advisor got a small business award. I just walked up to him and told him what I was doing; he jumped on board and became a member of the advisory committee, too.

I'm a member of Greensboro's Small Business Consortium; through the consortium I have contacts with the Chamber of Commerce, both of the universities and numerous non-profit organizations. It's allowed me to develop a pretty extensive network and I drew from that group in developing my team.

A friend of mine works in the East Market Street Development Corporation, a non-profit organization that is redeveloping and refurbishing the east Market [Street] corridor of Greensboro; the downtown library falls within that corridor. I sought assistance from its members because they know the people in the surrounding churches and neighborhoods.

People have been very willing to volunteer their time and effort. The project team consists of: me, the assistant director who helped me with the proposal, the marketing coordinator here in the library and the consultant. We worked together to develop the concept. The advisory committee consisted of about 8 people who had all different backgrounds, like marketing and finance.

As you can see, members of various community groups joined the effort. Once I had assembled my support groups, we met and developed a plan. At that point, I was able to write the grant proposal.

AA — What role did your community supporters play in forming what *Future Cents* is now?

ML— The consultant I mentioned before played a significant role; she had conducted several workshops in the past and contributed her expertise during the planning phase. The initial focus of the ALA and FINRA grant was a project called "Smart Investing @ Your Library" whose emphasis was investing. It was going to be a primary focus of Future Cents, too, but she said, "No we've got to go all way the way back — we've got to start with banking, and budgeting. We have to start at the very beginning and teach how even to establish a relationship with money and that kind of thing and then move into a more sophisticated realm of money." That gave me the idea of developing a two-tiered curriculum; in the first four sessions we would teach very basic financial concepts, and in the last two we would introduce the investment and savings concepts

AA — What other kinds of partnerships have you established in the community to support the program?

ML—We partnered with A&T [North Carolina Agricultural and Technical State University] because they have a trading room; I thought that would be attractive for young people to be able to experience that with its live ticker running. We're trying to provide our students with experiences as well as educational opportunities; that's why we've pulled in people and partnerships like that. In general, grants like this one expect a lot of community involvement.

AA — Can you describe the program you launched?

ML— For the first week, which we called "orientation," we taught the basics of banking and organizing your finances. We had seven 45-minute sessions. Our presenter gave 7 back-to-back sessions in a day, immediately followed by a second day of 7 more sessions.

On the second day we held a very interactive workshop called the "reality store" where the young people pull out of a hat a mock job, monthly net income, marital status, number of kids, etc. and they have to make their monthly salary last while they pay for things for that month. It's a little like Milton Bradley's game of "Life," but acted out.

AA — How did you recruit students to the program?

ML— We held workshops for two different groups of students and we recruited those groups differently. We ran a set of workshops that were open to the public; we promoted this series to teens and their parents, but mostly to parents. Separately, we approached organizations that were operating summer camps and offered to run their campers through the workshops; we became part of their programming. Some of the groups that participated were JobLink, the YMCA, and the YWCA.

AA — How was your attendance for those early workshops?

ML— It was very good in the summer. I learned in the summer that youth organizations want things for their youth to do. We pulled in the department of social services which had a woman's work group that consisted of young mothers who are looking for work; the organizers wanted them to come in. We had no problem finding groups that were interested in sending their teens through our program. We hope to do more of that and I'm focusing heavily on those captive audiences.

AA — These sessions — are they all free?

ML— Yes and the ones in the future will be, too. That's the crux of the grant ... that's what the funding is for.

AA — After you finished in August, did you run any sessions in the fall?

ML— We did, but recruiting was much more difficult; the summer camps were finished so there were no large groups attending the program. Individual students became much more difficult to attract to the program; we learned that students are very busy during the school year with lots of activities competing for their time. Attracting high school students to our workshops was challenging.

AA — How have you been promoting the program?

ML— We had a great article in the paper, recently. One of the staff reporters of the *Daily News & Record* attended one of our sessions. He talked to a father and son and a mother and daughter who attended the sessions together. It was a great article and because of it we've already had 15 register for the next class.

AA — Have you made any adjustments to the program over time?

ML— Yes. One of the financial advisors said we ought to organize the Finance Q like a college bowl. His idea was for universities to give away scholarships for this. Well, this idea came up before the downturn in the economy. Now the budget cuts are just.... Nobody is giving away anything right now. So instead, I'm organizing a competition where the winning team members will each win a netbook or something that will help them pursue their education, but it won't be on the grand scale that financial advisor had originally envisioned.

AA — Did the grant specify how much of your award should be devoted to the marketing, the materials, and the program?

ML— Yes, as part of the grant proposal, we submitted a budget that was very specific. A large part of it has been set aside for marketing. We're very fortunate in that we have a lot of local business men and women who are willing to volunteer their time so that wasn't that much of an expense and actually conducting the program wasn't that much of an expense, either. The expenses come in enticing people to participate; marketing comprises the largest part of the budget. We're able to offer incentives; for instance, I give away an iPad each year.

AA — What would you say marketing is like ... 75%?

ML—Yes, easily.

AA — What is the breakdown of the rest of the budget?

ML— Materials are a large part of it. Staffing doesn't come into play because the grant can't be used to fund staff. That's what the library is contributing.

AA — How did you use the marketing budget? How did you promote the program?

ML— We hired a public relations firm and with their help, we created a persona and made a video that we posted on YouTube and on our website. We also purchased some pre-movie ads, those little commercials you see before a film. They ran in about 30 local movie theatres, but we they're not generating the hits on the websites that I had expected. They were very expensive and I don't know if we'd do that again.

AA — We talked a little bit about the assessment that you did as you went through each session. Have you revised the program in response to the responses you got?

ML— Yes, our next workshops will definitely include more "on-their-feet" activities. We have to analyze and determine what we think will be most effective with our high school students but I think that with our middle school we'll be successful using the Money Game.

It's a game that we purchased in which the students use fake money to make purchases. I've also developed credit games in which students make purchasing decisions, consider interest rates and things like that. Just things to help keep them engaged so I think they'll be much more interactive. As part of that, we're trying to get our hands on technology because they love it. I had a "Stock Room Café" where they could use the iPad. I also had a laptop they could use to purchase stocks in this money game, working as a group; that worked very well. Anything that I incorporate this year is going to be as interactive as possible.

We learned from the feedback we received in the summer; young people are very honest. We learned which classes worked and which didn't work; we learned that we needed to consolidate several sessions; and we learned that we needed to convert others to a more active learning style. The youth do not like a straight lecture style at all! Based upon evaluations I've made adjustments and am trying to make it very dynamic and interactive.

AA — How would you asses the program's success? What lessons have you learned?

ML—In the plus column I'd include the marketing firm; it was a good idea to build them into the budget. They've made some introductions for us and gotten us on air a lot. We've gotten good results when we appear on the news, whether it's a morning show or they just talked about the program on the evening news. And secondly, from newspaper articles—that's where we've gotten the most results as far as advertising.

I think in the minus column, I'd put that we haven't yet developed a strong presence on the social networks. We need to develop a presence there especially since when the grant ends, we'll lose our marketing budget, but if I can develop some buzz on the social networks, that will help sustain the program and I'll be able to use that as a free marketing tool.

Another weakness is how the website is used. At this point, it's really only used for people to go and look at what programming we have; it's not used as a resource. We built it to look like an arcade with money games, but it's really not used that well.

AA — When will the program end officially?

ML—The grant will end in November 2012, but a part of the grant is to show how it's going to be sustainable and move forward. Now, obviously, it might not be able to move forward in the same fashion with all these elaborate incentives and that kind of thing. But a part of the year-end report will be to show our plans for sustaining this project.

14 — Librarian as Social Entrepreneur

Melody M. Allison

Introduction

As information specialists, librarians organize and manage massive amounts of current information on a broad array of topics and issues for use by their patrons. Generally speaking, librarians are "issue-neutral" when carrying out their professional work. There are times, however, that an issue is so critical, that one needs to take a stand and advocate for it. In my own personal experience, two issues have led to such a stand — the use of pesticides in schools in the early 1990s and more recently the use of medical information generated using men's physiology to treat women. In both cases research information to transform practice was available, but it was not commonly used. Librarians are in a strategic position to connect people with the most up-to-date research and information that can ultimately lead to changes in practice. Librarianship provides numerous tools and opportunities to utilize entrepreneurial methods for the betterment of society with librarians taking on roles as social entrepreneurs.

This chapter defines social entrepreneurship, identifies characteristics of social entrepreneurs, proposes ways librarians are or can be social entrepreneurs and promoters of social entrepreneurship, and provides selected experiences I've had as a social entrepreneur advocating for the translation of research into practice using Integrated Pest Management (IPM) and gender medicine (GM) as examples. Librarians are virtually social entrepreneurs as part of their usual roles. Add an indisputable social cause and they can be an important influence for social change.

Social Entrepreneurship — What and Why?

Change by its nature is disruptive. The road to social change can be perilous as it may shake up firmly entrenched belief systems that form the core of one's identity. Some people readily embrace making changes based on solid facts that raise their consciousness. Others may find change too difficult because they have a great deal invested in their current beliefs and practices. Change requires not only a superb idea but also a formidable leader to influence others and shepherd them through a maze of challenges, both relating to the idea itself and to those who must buy into the idea for its ascendancy.

In recent decades, interest has emerged about how social innovations are transformed into practice. What are the attributes of those who create change against great odds? What are the natures of people who take on great challenges and navigate ideas through the turbulent waters that change often invokes? What are characteristics of innovators and the processes of innovation?

New undertakings can be fraught with challenges and risks. Innovation that has been assimilated into practice can be very rewarding, but even the best ideas may face barriers to implementation, no matter how meritorious. A myriad of obstacles may in the end impede change. It takes a strong and dedicated person to shepherd innovation and change, someone with the drive to tirelessly seek and exploit opportunities, someone with an entrepreneurial mindset. A person who shepherds social innovations from theory to practice shares a number of qualities with business entrepreneurs. Both engage in a new enterprise, venture, or idea; accept accountability for the risks and outcomes; and aim to create value and reward from their undertakings. For the business pursuit, the rewards are economic, and for the social endeavor rewards come from the betterment of society. Thus the term "social entrepreneur" has emerged to describe innovators of social change and "social entrepreneurship" for the act of being a social entrepreneur.

Background of the Concept of Social Entrepreneurship

Social entrepreneurship is a relatively new field. As such, the definition is still evolving. To understand social entrepreneurship, we must understand the meaning of entrepreneurship, the term from which it emanates.

Twentieth century economist Joseph Schumpeter is considered the first to develop entrepreneurship theories. He acknowledges that it is extremely difficult to accomplish change because disrupting routines can be difficult for others to adapt to, perhaps provoking resistance or even physical attack on the proponent. For the entrepreneur to create something that destroys something else requires unusual confidence, aptitudes, and ability to get things done (Schumpeter 132).

Peter Drucker, another 20th century economist, defined an entrepreneur as someone who "always searches for change, responds to it, and exploits it as an opportunity" (28), and stated that innovation is "the specific tool of entrepreneurs, the means by which they exploit change as an opportunity for a different business or a different service" (19). He stated that "[Entrepreneurs] create something new, something different; they change or transmute values" (22).

Arthur C. Brooks, President of the American Enterprise Institute, sees the primary difference between social entrepreneurship and entrepreneurship as "the denomination of rewards sought" (5). Both recognize an opportunity, develop a concept, determine resources needed, launch and grow the venture, and plan for goal attainment (Brooks 5–7). Brooks states that in social entrepreneurship creativity is used to develop bright ideas and also to transform them into opportunities, a process not only dependent on an understanding of what population needs are but also on availability and demand for the ideas.

There is diversity of opinions about what social entrepreneurship is and what it is not. Some scholars see social entrepreneurs as being zealous individuals dedicated wholeheartedly to the mission of change, a zeal which cannot be borne by groups or organizations (Drayton, "The Citizen" 123–4; Dees "Meaning" 4; Light, "Social" 22; Martin and Osberg, "Social" 30–34). Others have a more diluted vision of the social entrepreneur that can be broadened to groups and organizations (Husock; Light, "Reshaping" 50; Mair and Noboa 122; Perrini 14; Wei-Skillern, et al. 4).

Some definitions focus on the person while others focus on ideas or opportunities for change (Bornstein, "How to" 2004, 91–92; Chell, Nicolopoulou, and Karatas-Özkan 486).

Some feel that only nonprofits can practice social entrepreneurship while others feel for-profits and governments can as well (Chell, Nicolopoulou, and Karatas-Özkan 486; Hockerts 145; Husock; Wei-Skillern, et al. 4). There are those who feel the social entrepreneur must invent the innovation, but others who feel this is not necessary, that the act of shepherding the change to fruition is the more important characteristic (Mair and Noboa 122; Martin and Osberg, "Social" 39). There are those who distinguish social entrepreneurship from social enterprises/services and advocacy, and some do not (Hockerts 145–146; Mair and Noboa 122; Martin and Osberg, "Social" 37; Perrini 14; "Social Enterprises" *Wikipedia*).

There may well be no one meta-theory of social entrepreneurship, but many theories (Robinson, Mair, and Hockerts 3). It may be, there are different levels of social entrepreneurship (Light "Driving" 44). Or conceivably we are really talking about different concepts that require different definitions. Future research clarifying the definition of social entrepreneurship needs to continue along with theory development and empirical data to support or disprove assumptions.

Some conceptions of social entrepreneurship mirror my personal experience with social entrepreneurial activity. Bill Drayton, founder of the international organization Ashoka: Innovators for the Public, is credited with creating the term "social entrepreneur" in the early 1980s (Light, "The Search" 4), the same period of time in which he founded Ashoka (Welch xvii) to help individual social entrepreneurs actualize social innovations. He observed a number of similarities between business entrepreneurs and social entrepreneurs. They are driven people; they create innovative revolutionary ideas to solve large-scale problems that society and governments have not resolved or cannot resolve; and they goal-set and problem-solve to reach these solutions. Drayton distinguishes social entrepreneurs from others with innovative ideas, leadership qualities, and other entrepreneurial traits saying that a social entrepreneur "absolutely must change an important pattern across her or his whole society"—a trait he calls "entrepreneurial quality," and one he says few people have (Drayton, "The Citizen" 121–124). Social entrepreneurs "cannot come to rest until their vision has become the new pattern society-wide" (Drayton, "Nothing").

J. Gregory Dees, Professor of the Practice of Social Entrepreneurship and Nonprofit Management at the Fuqua School of Business at Duke University, states: "Social entrepreneurs are one species in the genus entrepreneur. They are entrepreneurs with a social mission ... they create change by engaging innovation for social value, relentlessly pursue new opportunities, and act boldly" ("Meaning" 4). Bloom and Dees liken social systems to ecosystems, and state that for change to be successful the social entrepreneur takes "a holistic approach to understand the synergies between the organisms and the environment" ("Cultivate" 47). They note that social entrepreneurs are not only trying to solve social problems, they are trying to solve the underlying problems that contribute to the social problem, an attribute that differentiates them from other service providers.

Bornstein feels that social entrepreneurship is not just about those who pursue change on a grand scale, but also those individuals who reshape a part of the world in "heroic efforts that take place in front of our noses" (Bornstein, "How to" 2007, xvi). Social entrepreneurs are differentiated from activists. Activists' main objective is to influence decisions and attitudes to create change, while social entrepreneurs do this and utilize other tactics (Bornstein and Davis 37–8). Bornstein acknowledges that change may not be a smooth transitional process, that it may even be fraught with danger. When a new idea threatens the status quo "groups resist change with all the vigor of antibodies attacking an intruding virus" (James O'Toole, "Leading Change" quoted in Bornstein, "How to" 2004, 92). Particularly dangerous are reforms at systems levels.

Characteristics of Social Entrepreneurs

Bornstein describes social entrepreneurs as "transformative forces ... people with new ideas to address major problems who are relentless in the pursuit of their visions, people who simply will not take 'no' for an answer, who never give up until they have spread their ideas as far as they possibly can" (Bornstein "How to Change 2004" 1). So just what are the characteristics of social entrepreneurs that distinguish them from activists, high achievers, and others who indefatigably work toward the betterment of society?

For Drayton, credited with conceiving the term "social entrepreneur," a distinguishing characteristic is "a personality, a temperament that simply can't stop. They are not happy until their ideas have changed the whole society.... People with this temperament are looking for an idea that's important enough, new enough, and ripe enough. When they find it, they will persist because they cannot rest until they have gone all the way and seen the idea change society" (Meehan "15 Minutes" 11).

Bornstein identifies six qualities of successful social entrepreneurs:

- willingness to self-correct
- willingness to share credit
- willingness to break free of established structures
- willingness to cross disciplinary lines
- willingness to work quietly
- a strong ethical impetus

He indicates that social entrepreneurs are "all about" the mission of making the world a better place, not about themselves. Bornstein identifies sharing credit as an example of the selfless intent demonstrated by social entrepreneurs. Social entrepreneurs look at all aspects of the social need and its solution, bringing together whoever and whatever is needed to holistically address the change in a real way. They will then bring people from other areas, work through all angles and "create new social compounds." If something is not working, they will change course, because they are goal focused, not strategy focused (Bornstein, "How to Change 2004" 233–241).

Martin and Osberg observe that social entrepreneurs share similar characteristics with traditional entrepreneurs—they are "attracted to this [a] suboptimal equilibrium, seeing embedded in it an opportunity to provide a new solution, product, service, or process ... [and have a] unique set of personal characteristics he or she brings to the situation — inspiration, creativity, direct action, courage, and fortitude ... [that] are fundamental to the process of innovation" (32–33). Along with characteristics noted in other works, Elkington and Hartigan attribute a unique possible characteristic of social entrepreneurs as being "unreasonable"!

Librarians as Social Entrepreneurs

Creating and implementing innovative solutions to societal problems requires a great deal of information and knowledge. Librarians can be a critical support to those seeking ways to find and implement innovative solutions. They also can become social entrepreneurs by seeking out opportunities to provide access to information, or developing knowledge about particular research, and acting on it.

As information specialists, librarians have access to information in a broad range of areas that can stimulate latent creativity and inspire novel innovative approaches for unresolved problems. These problems may be identified through patron queries, work issues, or personal interests. An important consequence of their work is that they are exposed to information and knowledge in a broad range of areas. Consequently, librarians are well aware of various subject area ecosystems that are vital for creating new ideas and strategies that will make change successful.

Librarians and social entrepreneurs share the same objective of working to improve society through new ideas. Dissemination of up-to-date information is essential to a successful society and to the ability of its members to imagine and carry out pattern-breaking changes. Librarians improve their patrons' lives and society by providing access to information, and they create and utilize innovations to accomplish this. So they are not only making new ideas and information available for others to use, they also create new ideas and innovative methods to make these ideas accessible to users.

Utilizing the latest research findings is especially critical for the health and safety of the individual and society as a whole. Transforming the latest research into actual practice can be fraught with detours, obstacles, and delays. For instance, it can take almost two decades after publication for biomedical research to affect common practice (Balas & Boren 66–67; IOM 364), also known as "bedside to (clinical) practice translation" (Rabin et al. 119). This is an incredibly long time to wait for known improved treatments and medications, even cures, to be available for clinical care. Librarians can make their greatest contributions as social entrepreneurs by helping to promote diffusion of these innovations, including new ideas and research, into practice.

Rogers describes diffusion as "the process in which an innovation is communicated through certain channels over time among the members of a social system ... [it] is a special type of communication in which the messages are about a new idea ... and is a kind of social change, defined as the process by which alteration occurs in the structure and function of a social system" (Rogers 5–6). Some describe diffusion as a passive, unplanned, and uncontrolled process and dissemination as an active, planned process (Rabin et al. 118), but diffusion as used by Rogers includes "both the planned and spontaneous spread of new ideas" (Rogers 6), and his interpretation is used in this discussion. Reference service, cataloging practice, information literacy, liaison, research, and other professional activities are important mechanisms which librarians use to advance the diffusion of information and knowledge (innovation), making these more accessible through word-of-mouth and other entrepreneurial techniques (Allison, "Women's" 434). Librarians not only utilize word-of-mouth to communicate information and knowledge, but they also spread ideas through the print word using what I like to call "word-of-thought." As an example, catalogers analyze items and enter details such as additional subject headings and metadata on the catalog record to make the item more findable and thus more accessible.

Bibliographic instruction can be an opportunity to diffuse innovative ideas. Sessions can be framed around new research findings as examples when teaching how to use specific resources, develop search strategies, and employ other research techniques. Two kinds of learning can be happening at once—the primary how-to-do information resource or research objective as well as a consciousness-raising opportunity to showcase a social innovation.

The librarian's constituents may not be known because they access and use the library resources through its website, social networking, and other Web presences without using the library's physical facility. Thus scalability takes on a new meaning. Access to a library's resources through its web presences are a web search away, and no longer just the purview of a locality. What may seem a local communication can just as readily influence a global community, and selective use of words-of-thought can make it more available for consumption.

These efforts are potentiated when working in an academic and/or research institutions. Using entrepreneurial techniques, librarians can diffuse knowledge about their own innovations and promote innovations of other researchers to increase the scaling of the innovations. Research can be shared through peer-reviewed journals and books, presentations at meetings and conferences, social networking, professional committee and service activities, and other enterprises. New roles in scholarly communication, data curation, and translational research support provide rich and diverse opportunities to develop sophisticated strategies, using word-of-mouth and other techniques to help move research from bench to bedside.

Librarians have many opportunities to enable social entrepreneurs, and also to become social entrepreneurs for new innovations or innovative ideas. When one does not have the time or ability to champion a project, others who have the time and ability can be sought out to help or take on the project (Thompson 429–30). Librarians may be approached by budding or by fully engaged social entrepreneurs seeking information to help create innovative solutions or strategies for pattern change. Librarians may help to identify opportunities to promote innovative ideas or to identify people or organizations that have experience and may be of assistance with their ideas or change in general. Whether as an enabler or entrepreneur, the attention a librarian provides may make the difference in attaining the perfect solution to a societal problem!

Librarian as Social Entrepreneur Enabler: Integrated Pest Management

My first foray into social entrepreneurship began during Earth Week in 1990. My 11 year old daughter came home from school with her knapsack brimming with books. I said to her, "Honey, looks like you have a lot of homework to do!" "No, Mom," she said. "They are going to spray our lockers with pesticides tonight."

Back in the '60s, Rachel Carson's *Silent Spring* launched the environmental movement through a portrayal of the effects that chemicals, specifically DDT, were having on the environment and human health. *Silent Spring* profoundly changed awareness of how human activities can impact nature. After reading this book I vowed to never use synthetic pesticides, and another variable also influenced my reaction to the use of pesticides.

As a registered nurse, I was devoted to protecting people and their health. It is not enough for a nurse to take care of people when they are ill. Finding ways to prevent illness is very much a part of a nurse's holistic training and nature. Over the years various news reports and research publications along with government responses to these reports and publications (e.g., legislation, citizen education, internal policy changes) validated possible short and long term dangers of exposure to pesticides, demonstrating the need to use alternatives to synthetic pesticides and thus to reduce exposure along the chain from production to use.

The news of pesticide spraying in my daughter's school was evidence of an immediate danger to public health and as the bearer of such knowledge, I needed to respond. Although uncertain how to proceed, I was determined to take action. In facing this local challenge, I imagined Rachel Carson would say, "Do what is right for the earth, and the children of the earth." I was convinced that as the project proceeded, someone with the necessary wherewithal would see the merit of the task and take over the project for a quick resolution. In the meantime I would take the plunge.

I saw the problem as follows: Children are mandated to be in school several hours a day. When chemical pesticides are used in buildings, there is increased risk of children breathing in vapors and off-gasses, and perhaps inadvertent contact with residue. Cancers, neurological problems, or immunological problems could be caused by long-term exposure. This was not just an issue for a single locale, but a problem for any child in a school system that used pesticides. Because it was not just a local problem, I planned to utilize a multi-pronged advocacy approach, to change pest control practice as widely as I could.

I decided to begin my strategy with a plan based on a nursing care plan, a tool created for each patient for whom a nurse cares, which maps out all aspects of the plan of care for patients, including all treatments, medications, physician and nursing orders, goals and objectives. Creating one requires doing an assessment, identifying problems/needs/diagnoses, identifying goals, determining interventions, and doing an evaluation of all care plan components. This needs-based approach could be applied to this problem as well in order to begin dealing with the issues involved. I felt that surely someone else would eventually take on this initiative and lead us to a reasonable conclusion: eliminating synthetic pesticides in schools. Until then, this plan would provide an initial strategy.

First, an assessment was necessary to determine what was actually happening and identify any problems with current practices. I called and spoke to the principal who informed me that indeed the school was being sprayed for pests by a local pest control company contracted to spray routinely every month, exceptions being lockers and classrooms which were not sprayed monthly, but periodically as needed. I had never received a notification that this was being done, so parental notifications needed to be addressed in any resolution.

Next, I needed to find out what alternatives were available for pest control in buildings. The very first place I went was my local library. At the time little information was available at the consumer level about alternatives to pesticides for pest control, and when such information was available it was about lawn care, not buildings. The librarian did not despair and located a file she had kept on environmental issues which had the name of an organization, the National Coalition Against the Misuse of Pesticides (NCAMP, now Beyond Pesticides) in Washington, DC, that specialized in pesticide issues and alternatives. I contacted this organization and was very glad to hear that the U.S. Environmental Protection Agency (EPA) was in the process of writing a booklet about the use of Integrated Pest Management (IPM) for schools. IPM is the use of environmental modifications that make it difficult if not impossible for the pest to survive, and when pesticides are needed, the appropriate pesticide with lowest toxicity is used.

NCAMP provided information about every conceivable pesticide issue and alternatives; other environmental groups promoting alternatives (mostly on the East and West Coasts); government agencies involved with programs, regulations, reports; people involved with specific IPM programs for schools and federal government buildings; and research bibliographies, reports, and papers. I immediately began an investigation that led to the local public library, a hospital library, and university libraries in the region to locate research articles. A growing body of evidence was being developed about adverse effects of pesticide exposure at low doses and over longer periods of times, even decades. Finding this information, and alternatives to use of synthetic pesticides, was also a challenge. Librarians assisted with locating needed articles identified in information from pesticide alternative groups. They helped in searching card catalogs and newspaper and journal indexes, and obtaining articles through interlibrary loan. Their help impressed me with the importance of librarians in helping people find information needed to make a profound difference in their lives. This impression influenced me later to become a librarian.

For the next two years, nearly every waking moment was steeped in seeking and finding opportunities to educate and advocate for using IPM in schools. I was becoming active in our county League of Women Voters (LWV). The LWV is a grassroots, nonpartisan organization that encourages and provides resources to help citizens become informed about issues so they can not only make knowledgeable decisions when they vote, but also communicate and advocate positions with government officials. Although our local LWV was very supportive, they had no platform position on the issue of pesticides and alternatives to their use. They provided me with numerous opportunities to educate the members and the public through forums, conferences, and other activities. I began building a foundation for consensus within our local League, and until that goal could be achieved, I founded a local group just for the purpose of advocacy for IPM in schools, including many League members.

In a fortunate development that indicated the growing concern over this issue, the Lake Michigan Inter-League Organization (local LWV of regions around Lake Michigan) had a strong platform about alternatives to pesticides and was planning to move for an LWV of Illinois concurrence with their program at the Illinois annual conference. I came as a local delegate and prepared to support their move as well as advocate for the use of IPM in schools. In the caucuses they asked me to speak about the use of IPM in schools at the business meeting. Our efforts were rewarded, with the organization taking a position supporting the reduction of exposure to pesticides and the use of non-toxic alternatives. Illinois leagues at the local and state level were now in position to lobby and support efforts to promote alternatives to pesticides.

Other groups also took an interest. The Illinois Sierra Club had previously proposed legislation in the Illinois State Assembly for the use of IPM in schools that failed to pass. In part because of various activities I was instigating, they resumed their efforts to get a bill on pesticide use passed into law. The Illinois Environmental Council (IEC) was another group with which I was in frequent contact, each supporting the other concerning IPM for schools.

At the time the U.S. General Services Capital Region had just finished a pilot using IPM for all federal buildings, including the White House and Capital, with plans to broaden the program to all federal buildings in the U.S. The program head, Dr. Albert Greene, agreed to speak and provide a workshop session on environmental analysis with IPM solutions for selected sites. Our local university agreed to donate lodging in campus housing as well as a room for the meeting. Campus buildings were made available for a walk-through "hands-on" consultation for the workshop session of the presentation. Invitations were sent out to regional state universities, regional pest control businesses, state environmental groups, LWVs across the state, local newspapers, and regional elected government officials, including the sitting governor. The meeting was co-sponsored by the local LWV and the pesticide group, and the local university's housing office. Attendees included the local state representative and local school pest control contractors.

The work that took place through these synergistic efforts over two dizzying years on various angles to educate and advocate did culminate in a change to IPM in the state's schools as well as a state law requiring the state health department prepare and provide IPM training for interested schools. The local school's pest control contractor developed IPM protocols for schools, which were offered as an option for their franchise locations in five states. The IEC worked with other entities toward the creation of a state pesticide group, the Safer Pest Control Project (SPCP), which is a strong advocate and lobbyist for IPM in schools and other environments. The SPCP led and won the charge for changing the Illinois school IPM law from one of voluntary use of IPM in public schools to one mandating use. This experience was a truly collaborative phenomenon, made possible by a multitude of players. Evidence-based research and protocols won out, improving safety for the school children of Illinois and beyond. Because of my experiences with librarians, I went back to school and became a librarian. Later while doing research on another issue, I would find out that this experience was social entrepreneurship and provided definition to the compelling focus and dedication that possessed me through this endeavor.

An interesting side note is that although I have not been active on the IPM front in some time, recently our university library preservation unit wanted to do IPM in our departmental library at the University of Illinois. I am coordinating our library's participation in the program. How different, and satisfying, it is to know that the use of IPM has translated to our university setting, and is now a routine option.

Gender Biology: Librarian as Social Entrepreneur

WOMEN'S HEALTH MOVEMENT OF THE 1970S

In 1973 the first edition of the book *Our Bodies, Ourselves* (OBOS) was published. I happened upon it as an undergraduate in nursing school, and it had a profound influence on me over the years as a nurse and as a woman. Alexander notes that this book changed the medical landscape for women and helped create the women's health movement and also helped foster the notion of patient as team member. Women began to increasingly question societal views and expectations concerning a myriad of issues. Women were not only questioning traditional roles that restricted their rights to participate as full, equal, and autonomous constituents in society, they were organizing to raise political, sexual and reproductive awareness. Women began to scrutinize the medical care system and its provision of services for their reproductive and other health issues.

As these institutional adaptations developed, a new sense of the role of the patient began to evolve, from passive to active participant. Women were gaining a new awareness and confidence. What they began to see is that for some conditions they may have different physical experiences than men, experiences that were not listed in the textbooks. Why was their experience different, and why was it not described in the standard textbooks?

SOCIETAL AND GOVERNMENT INTERVENTION

During this time women were expanding their roles outside traditional areas, including expansion into medicine and government, introducing these issues into high level discussions and policy. Coincidentally, in 1977 FDA guidelines were made to exclude "women of childbearing potential" (U.S. HEW 7). This action was partially to protect unborn children and also because normal hormone fluctuations made it more difficult to control the physiological environment and interpret outcomes. While well intended, the resulting biomedical research was done with men and thus medical care was based on the male physiology.

In 1983 a Public Health Services Task Force on Women's Health Issues was formed (U.S. HHS PHS NIH ORWH 1). In 1985 it proposed several recommendations in its report "Women's Health: Report of the Public Health Service Task Force on Women's Health Issues," including the recommendation that "biomedical and behavioral research should be expanded to ensure emphasis on conditions and diseases unique to, or more prevalent in, women in all age groups" (U.S. HHS PHS Task Force 76). In 1987 the National Institutes of Health (NIH) urged grant applicants to consider women to be included in biomedical research (U.S. HHS NIH, "NIH Guide" 2).

A growing number of medical professionals, researchers, and health advocates were becoming concerned about the gender inequities in biomedical research. The Society for Women's Health Research (SWHR) was formed in 1990 and has been a leader in bringing attention to sex differences in health and illness, a concept coined "sex-based biology" by SWHR founder Dr. Florence Haseltine. It has also promoted advocacy for the inclusion of women in clinical research. In 1990 the SWHR and the Congressional Caucus for Women were both concerned that research bias was still occurring and became allies in advocating that the General Accounting Office (U.S. GAO, now General Accountability Office) perform an audit to ascertain current status of the 1987 NIH guideline recommendations (SWHR "History"). The report found that the policy was not applied consistently nor implemented adequately (U.S. GAO, "Statement" 1). Soon after the report, the NIH created its Office of Research on Women's Health (ORWH) with the mandate to support biomedical research for all conditions that can affect women, to make sure they are adequately represented in biomedical research, and to proactively promote enlistment of women in biomedical research (IOM "Women and Health," 44).

Several government initiatives and regulations evolved with advocacy from others such as the Society for Women's Health Research (SWHR), to support the study of sex-differences for biomedical applications. Despite efforts of the federal government, various agencies and other entities, including the three major federal women's health offices, there continues to be research without proportionate representation of women, underrepresentation of sex and gender differences in medical care, and lack of sex-specific reporting of data (Melloni et al. 135–142; Beery and Zucker 565,571). As of 2010, NIH Phase I and Phase II research did not mandate female representation. The SWHR submitted comments to the FDA urging closer FDA and NIH collaboration (perhaps a joint NIH/FDA council), with recommendations to mandate appropriate representation of both sexes in all phases of research supported by the NIH, and also that the FDA mandate and insist on sex-based analysis all along the continuum —from submission for drug approval to follow-up after the drug has been marketed (Greenberger).

For a comprehensive look at the history and events leading up to the inclusion of women in biomedical research, I recommend beginning the journey with these books: *Bodies of Knowledge: Sexuality, Reproduction, and Women's Health in the Second Wave* (Kline); *Women and Health Research* (IOM, "Women and Health"); *Exploring the Biological Contributions to Human Health: Does Sex Matter?* (IOM, "Exploring"); and *Women's Health Research: Progress, Pitfalls, and Promise* (IOM, "Women's Health"). Additional background resources (e.g., History, Government Documents) can be found at <www.GenderBiology. net>.

The journey for inclusion of females in biomedical research and analysis of results based on sex differences has been long and arduous, demonstrating an unacceptable delay in translating research to practice — a delay that librarians are quite suited to assist in reducing.

TRANSFORMATION FROM SPECTATOR TO INSTIGATOR

As a young woman I noticed times when the experiences of myself, family members, and friends did not fit a traditional mold and thus were not validated by the establishment. In practice as a nurse, I also saw times that symptoms did not fit the standard textbook examples and thus went unheeded. I could not understand these discrepancies at the time, but hoped that someday their legitimacy would be established. How exciting it was in 1997 to see a nearly full page article in a local newspaper entitled "What a Surprise! Men and Women are Medically Different" (Shelton C1).

More has been published about gender biology and medicine in scholarly journals and books as well as consumer publications in recent years. In the role of academic librarian and liaison to a number of biomedical areas, I also developed research and service agendas relating to biomedical interests. In keeping up with biomedical developments as a medical librarian, I was always pleased to see gender-specific publications. However, when I and my loved ones go to the doctor or medical facility, all too often the care prescribed is not what is indicated in research results. What could a librarian do to foster gender-specific research findings into practice? As a result, my interest in gender differences in health and disease treatment evolved to include ways librarians could help propel research into practice.

Normally librarians don't advocate for particular positions on specific issues. We utilize expert resources, teach others about them and how to use them, and use them to assist others in their queries. But now and then, there are research results that are overwhelmingly obvious, even essential, and need to be disseminated. Gender-specific biomedical research is an area in which such dissemination is lacking. Women are not receiving evidence-based care for many clinical conditions because the research has not been based on their unique physiology. That is a major problem, and librarians are in a perfect position to help get the word out to biomedical researchers, clinical professionals, healthcare consumers, and other librarians.

My mission became to work at promoting this issue until gender-specific medicine was part of standard practice. As I learned from my IPM journey, when an idea is right the outcome *will* be right. Both problems were experienced locally, but both problems were universal. Therefore, solutions should be achieved locally and universally.

Opportunities to extend knowledge are available in the everyday practice of librarianship. The review of newly purchased books acquainted me with new titles, some relating to gender biomedical research, such as *The Y Chromosome and Male Germ Cell Biology in Health and Diseases* (Lau and Chan) and *Sex and the Brain* (Einstein). One milestone publication was *Principles of Gender-Specific Medicine* (2004), by leading women's research advocate Dr. Marianne J. Legato, founder of the Partnership for Gender-Specific Medicine at Columbia University <partnership.hs.columbia.edu/> and founder/editor of *The Journal of Gender-Specific Medicine* and *Gender Medicine*.

Bibliographic instruction on life sciences resources afforded me an opportunity to use gender research as search examples. Using an exciting and timely topic as an example can also acquaint the attendee about the kinds of research which may be useful personally or professionally, perhaps even inspiring someone to pursue gender-specific research as a career.

My first formal forte was a presentation in 2005 at a state library association conference about the history of gender-specific research entitled *Women's Health: History in the Making*. The presentation was a basic overview of the evolution and progression of gender-specific research, and included common terms from the literature. Other topics covered were examples of physiological differences and their presentation in health and disease, and the role of government and other players in establishing the field of gender-specific medicine.

To share the history and other gender-specific information I had culled over the years, the blog hosting services seemed the perfect solution. Thus was born GenderBiology.net, a news blog for healthcare professionals and consumers and library and information professionals to learn about and keep up with news and resources about gender biology and medicine. Content includes bibliographies of related news, books, periodicals, government documents, history sources, listservs, and institutions. News items link to the original source of the news as well as related primary research articles in PubMed biomedical literature database from the National Library of Medicine (NLM). I created a business card and magnets for GenderBiology.net to disseminate when appropriate at library conferences and doctors' offices and hospitals as an opportunity to spread the word.

I had used my growing files and book collection to prepare this presentation. News of my interest in gender biology was spreading, which led to an invitation to publish an article in a *Library Trends* themed issue on gender issues in information needs and services. This resulted in the article I wrote called "Women's Health: Librarian as Social Entrepreneur." This paper provided an introduction to gender-specific research and the barriers to its translation into practice, and explored ways that librarians could become players in translating this information into clinical applications.

Throughout my IPM adventure I was told by a number of people that one person could not make a difference, a change in how things were done. While researching the concept of change for the paper, I happened upon Gladwell's *The Tipping Point* and Bornstein's *How to Change the World*. Reading these books I came to realize that my near obsession was social entrepreneurship. There actually was a term for it! Identifying myself as a social entrepreneur invigorated me to identify and pursue opportunities to move gender-specific research to a position of prominence.

The Medical Library Association's member publication *MLA News* has a column "Internet Resources" which focuses on resources for specific topics and provided a chance to disseminate information about core resources for biomedical research on sex differences to librarians who provided biomedical and health information support to consumers and professionals. I submitted a column on gender biology resources that was published in May of 2008 (Allison, "Internet" 12).

Another fortuitous opportunity came to me in writing the chapter "U.S. Government Documents and Technical Reports" in *Introduction to Reference Sources in the Health Sciences* (Allison, "U.S. Government"). Government information and agencies have been a big part of the gender-specific research story so writing a chapter about government resources provided a chance to use related issues as examples. For instance, when discussing publications distributed by the Government Printing Office (GPO), an example of access to information was "the inclusion of women in biomedical research and drug analysis by the U.S. Food and Drug Administration can be important for both healthcare consumers and professionals" (Allison, "U.S. Government" 92). Another example came when describing how challenging, even confusing, finding government information can be when government entities charged with overseeing and disseminating gender specific research have very similar names, including the HHS Office on Women's Health (OWH), the NIH Office of Research on Women's Health (ORWH), and FDA Office of Women's Health (OWH) (Allison, "U.S. Government" 94–95).

Opportunities that may seed knowledge about gender medicine into the fertile soil can always be found. Tipping points will eventually occur, and a web of librarians will make it happen sooner, for gender biology and any number of other important evidence-based changes that will enhance society. Where government and other organizations have failed, social entrepreneurs can succeed.

Conclusion

Social entrepreneurs, as seen by many scholars in the field, are themselves solutions to society's intractable problems; problems that government, charitable, and other institutions have failed to resolve (Dees, "Taking"; Bornstein and Davis; Light, "Driving"). Their *energy, passion, drive, persistence* to see solutions through are needed to shepherd change to successful implementation. Society is not the only place where there are seemingly intractable problems. The exponential growth in technological change over recent decades has caused many disruptions in library and information services, resources, and management. These disruptions are not necessarily caused by negative or malicious forces. Massive changes require time for assimilation of the change itself, and normalization of the other affected components. These disruptions have been potentiated by economic realities which have enormously affected society and libraries. Both are in desperate need of innovative solutions.

The future holds hope as more and more elements of society, government, and business recognize the need for social entrepreneurs and are identifying ways to support them. Many Next Gen librarians are exhibiting a social entrepreneurial spirit. Indeed, at the ACRL (Association of College and Research Libraries) 2011 conference, a presentation, *In the Spirit of Ben Franklin: 13 Virtues of Next Gen Librarians*, focused on virtues next-gen librarians need to flourish. The presenters named nine virtues and then asked the audience to come up with four more (Howard). Included were a number of characteristics that distinguish social entrepreneurs including: creative [outside the box], adventurous, passionate, persistent, and courageous with ability to take risks (Howard). So the "Next Gen Librarians" are expressing an entrepreneurial spirit as a natural synergism with their work!

Librarians are in an ideal position to become social entrepreneurs and to enable social entrepreneurs to address these intractable problems. Librarians need to be cognizant about cultivating a working environment that fosters social entrepreneurial activity. We must find ways to support "blue-sky" and "out-of-the-box" thinking for others and for ourselves. That "unreasonable" (Elkington and Harrington, "The Power" 6–24) colleague in their midst may just have a pattern-changing idea that advances librarianship to a whole new level. We should not be dissuaded from action when we come up with the perfect solution simply because others tell us that we don't know what we are talking about. We work in environments where we can easily become or find experts that will help us along the social entrepreneurship continuum. From creating the perfect solution to disseminating the innovation, we can move new ideas forward and nurture them once they are diffused. We are not only keepers of knowledge; we can be movers of knowledge, influencing change in our roles as social entrepreneurs.

Works Cited

Alexander, Ruth Bell, et al. "A Letter from the Founders." *Our Bodies, Ourselves: Health Resource Center.* Boston Women's Health Book Collective, 2005–2008. Web. 2 Feb. 2011 <http://www.ourbodiesour selves.org/book/inside/letter.asp>.

Allison, Melody M. *GenderBiology.net.* 2006. Web. 23 Apr. 2011. <http://www.genderbiology.net/>.

_____. "Internet Resources: Gender Biology." *MLA News,* May 2008, 406: 12. Print.

_____. "U.S. Government Documents and Technical Reports" *Introduction to Reference Sources in the Health Sciences.* 5th ed. Eds. Huber, Jeffrey T., Jo Anne Boorkman, and Jean C. Blackwell. New York: Neal-Schuman, 2008. 91–110. Print.

_____. "Women's Health: Librarians as Social Entrepreneurs." *Library Trends.* 56.2 (2007): 423–448. Print.

Balas, E. Andrew, and Suzanne Austin Boren. "Review Paper: Managing Clinical Knowledge for Health Care Improvement." *Yearbook of Medical Informatics 2000.* Eds. Van Bemmel, J. H., & A. T. McCray; New York: International Medical Informatics Association, 2000. 65–70. Print.

Beery, Annaliese K., and Irving Zucker. "Sex Bias in Neuroscience and Biomedical Research." *Neuroscience and Behavioral Reviews* 35.3 (2011): 565–72. SciVerse. Web. 4 Apr. 2011.

Bornstein, David. *How to Change the World: Social Entrepreneurs and the Power of New Ideas.* Oxford: Oxford UP, 2004. Print.

_____. *How to Change the World: Social Entrepreneurs and the Power of New Ideas.* Updated ed. Oxford: Oxford UP, 2007. Print.

_____, and Susan Davis. *Social Entrepreneurship: What Everyone Needs to Know.* Oxford: Oxford UP, 2010. Print.

Bloom, Paul N., and J. Gregory Dees. "Cultivate your Ecosystem." *Stanford Social Innovation Review* 6.1 (Winter 2008): 47–53. *ABI/INFORM Global, ProQuest.* Web. 28 Mar. 2011.

Brooks, Arthur C. *Social Entrepreneurship: A Modern Approach to Social Value Creation.* Upper Saddle River, NJ: Pearson Prentice Hall, 2009. Print.

Carson, Rachel. *Silent Spring.* Boston: Houghton Mifflin, 1962. Print.

Chell, Elizabeth, Katerina Nicolopoulou, and Mine Karatas-Özkan. "Social Entrepreneurship and Enterprise: International and Innovation Perspectives." *Entrepreneurship & Regional Development* 22.6 (2010): 485–493. *Business Source Elite, EBSCOhost.* Web. 14 Apr. 2011.

Changing the Face of Medicine: Marianne J. Legato. Bethesda, MD: National Library of Medicine. Web. 23 Apr. 2011 <http://www.nlm.nih.gov/changingthefaceofmedicine/physicians/biography_197.html>.

Drayton, Bill. *Entrepreneur for Society.* YouTube Video. Ashoka, n.d.. Web. 21 Mar. 2011 <http://www.ashoka.org/entrepreneurforsociety>.

_____. *Nothing More Powerful.* YouTube Video. Ashoka, n.d. Web. 21 Mar. 2011 <http://www.ashoka.org/nothingmorepowerful>.

Drayton, William. "The Citizen Sector: Becoming as Entrepreneurial and Competitive as Business." *California Management Review* 44.3 (Spring 2002): 120–132. *Business Source Elite, EBSCOhost.* Web. 21 Mar. 2011.

Dees, J. Gregory. "The Meaning of 'Social Entrepreneurship.'" Durham, NC: Center for the Advancement of Social Entrepreneurship, The Fuqua School of Business, Duke University, 31 Oct. 1998; 30 Mar. 2001 rev. 1–5. Web. 7 Mar. 2011 <http://www.caseatduke.org/documents/dees_sedef.pdf>.

_____. "Taking Social Entrepreneurship Seriously." *Society* 44.3 (2007): 24–31. *Academic Search Premier, EBSCOhost.* Web. 7 Mar. 2011.

Drucker, Peter F. *Innovation and Entrepreneurship: Practice and Principles.* New York: Harper & Row, 1985. Print.

Einstein, Gillian, Ed. *Sex and the Brain.* Cambridge, MA: MIT Press, 2007. Print.

Elkington, John, and Pamela Hartigan. *The Power of Unreasonable People: How Social Entrepreneurs Create Markets That Change the World.* Boston, MA: Harvard Business Press, 2008. Print.

GenderBiology.net. *History*. Web. 23 June 2011 <http://www.genderbiology.net/genderbiologynet/his
tory/>.

Gladwell, Malcolm. *The Tipping Point: How Little Things Can Make a Big Difference*. New York: Little,
Brown, and Co., 2002. Print.

Greenberger, Phyllis; Society for Women's Health Research. Letter. [*Comments Submitted on FDA NIH
Collaboration to the Food and Drug Administration*.] FDA Division of Dockets Management (HFA-
305). 26 May 2010. Web. 29 Apr. 2011 <http://www.womenshealthresearch.org/site/DocServer/SWHR_
Comment_on_FDA_NIH_Collaboration_05.26.10.pdf?docID=5548>.

Hockerts, Kai. "Entrepreneurial Opportunity in Social Purpose Business Ventures." *Social Entrepreneurship*. Eds. Mair, Johanna, Jeffrey Robinson, and Kai Hockerts. Houndmills, England: Palgrave
Macmillan, 2006. 142–154. Print.

Howard, Jennifer. "College Librarians Look at Better Ways to Measure the Value of Their Services." *The
Chronicle of Higher Education*. 1 Apr. 2011. The Chronicle. Web. 1 Apr. 2011.

Husock, Howard. "New Ideas People." *Philanthropy Magazine* 1 July 2004. Web. 23 Mar. 2011 <http://
www.philanthropyroundtable.org/article.asp?article=816&paper=1&cat=148>.

Institute of Medicine. Board on Health Sciences Policy. Committee on Understanding the Biology of
Sex and Gender Differences. Wizemann, Theresa M., & Mary-Lou Pardue, Eds. *Exploring the Biological
Contributions to Human Health: Does Sex Matter?* Washington, DC: National Academy Press, 2001.
Print.

Institute of Medicine. Committee on Quality of Health Care in America. *Crossing the Quality Chasm:
A New Health System for the 21st Century*. Washington, DC: National Academy Press, 2001. Print.

Institute of Medicine. Division of Health Policy. Committee on the Ethical and Legal Issues Relating to
the Inclusion of Women in Clinical Studies. Mastroianni, Ruth Faden, and Daniel Federman. Eds.
Women and Health Research: Ethical and Legal Issues of Including Women in Clinical Studies. Washington, DC.: National Academy Press, 1994. Print.

Institute of Medicine of the National Academies (IOM). Board on Population Health and Public Health
Practice. Committee on Women's Health Research. *Women's Health Research: Progress, Pitfalls, and
Promise*. Washington, DC.: The National Academies Press, 2010. Print.

"Joseph Schumpeter." *Wikipedia, The Free Encyclopedia*. Wikimedia Foundation, 6 Jan. 2011. Web. 18
Mar. 2011 <http://en.wikipedia.org/wiki/Joseph_Schumpeter>.

Kline, Wendy. *Bodies of Knowledge: Sexuality, Reproduction, and Women's Health in the Second Wave*.
Chicago: University Of Chicago Press, 2010. Print.

Lau, Yun-Fai, and Wai-Yee Chan, Eds. *The Y Chromosome and Male Germ Cell Biology in Health and
Diseases*. Singapore: World Scientific, 2007. Print.

Legato, Marianne J., Ed. *Principles of Gender-Specific Medicine*. Amsterdam; Boston: Elsevier Press, 2004.
Print.

Light, Paul C. *Driving Social Change: How to Solve the World's Toughest Problems*. Hoboken, NJ: Wiley,
2011. Print.

_____. "Reshaping Social Entrepreneurship." *Stanford Social Innovation Review* 4.3 (Fall 2006): 47–51.
ABI/INFORM Global, ProQuest. Web. 21 Mar. 2011.

_____. *The Search for Social Entrepreneurship*. Washington, DC: Brookings Institution Press, 2008. Print.

_____. "Social Entrepreneurship Revisited." *Stanford Social Innovation Review* 7.3 (2009): 21–22. *ABI/
INFORM Global, ProQuest*. Web. 21 Mar. 2011.

Mair, Johanna, and Ernesto Noboa. "Social Entrepreneurship: How Intentions to Create Social Venture
are Formed." *Social Entrepreneurship*. Eds. Mair, Johanna, Jeffrey Robinson, and Kai Hockerts. Houndmills, England: Palgrave Macmillan, 2006. 121–141. Print.

Martin, Roger L, and Sally Osberg. "So·cial en·tre·pre·neur·ship: the case for def·i·ni·tion." *Stanford
Social Innovation Review* 5.2 (Spring 2007): 30–39. *ABI/INFORM Global, ProQuest*. Web. 24 Mar.
2011.

Meehan, Bill. "15 Minutes with Bill Drayton, CEO of Ashoka." *Stanford Social Innovation Review* 1.4
(Spring 2004): 11–12. *ABI/INFORM Global, ProQuest*. Web. 5 Apr. 2011.

Melloni, Chiara, et al. "Representation of Women in Randomized Clinical Trials of Cardiovascular Disease Prevention." *Circulation: Cardiovascular Quality and Outcomes* 3.2 (2010): 135–142. Web. 31 Mar.
2011. <http://circoutcomes.ahajournals.org/content/3/2/135.long>.

Perrini, Francesco. "Social Entrepreneurship Domain: Setting Boundaries." *The New Social Entrepreneurship: "What Awaits Social Entrepreneurial Ventures?"* Ed. Perrini, Francesco. Cheltenham, UK:
Edward Elgar, 2006. 1–25. Print.

Rabin, Borsika A., et al. "A Glossary for Dissemination and Implementation Research in Health." *Journal
of Public Health Management and Practice* 14 .2 (2008): 117–23. *OvidSP. Web*. 12 Apr. 2011.

Robinson, Jeffrey A., Johanna Mair, and Kai Hockerts, eds. *International Perspectives on Social Entrepreneurship*. Hampshire, England: Palgrave Macmillan, 2009. Print.

Rogers, Everett M. *Diffusion of Innovations*. 5th ed. New York: Free Press, 2003. Print.

Schumpeter, Joseph A. *Capitalism, Socialism, and Democracy*. 3rd ed. London: George Allen & Unwin, 1950. Print.

Shelton, Deborah L. "What a Surprise! Men and Women are Medically Different." *Mid-Illinois Newspapers* Monday, June 16, 1997: C1. Print.

Society for Women's Health Research (SWHR). *History*. Washington, DC.: SWHR, n.d. Web. 3 Apr. 2011. <http://www.womenshealthresearch.org/site/PageServer?pagename=about_history>.

Thompson, John L. "The World of the Social Entrepreneur." *The International Journal of Public Sector Management* 15.4/5 (2002): 412–431. *ABI/INFORM Global, ProQuest*. Web. 28 Mar. 2011.

"The Times They Are a-Changin'." *Wikipedia, The Free Encyclopedia*. Wikimedia Foundation, Inc., 03 Mar. 2011. Web. 03 Apr. 2011.

United States. Department of Health and Human Services. National Institutes of Health. *NIH Guide for Grants and Contracts*. 16.30 (4 Sept. 1987): 1–6. Web. 3 Apr. 2011. <http://grants.nih.gov/grants/guide/historical/1987_09_04_Vol_16_No_30.pdf>.

United States. Department of Health and Human Services. Public Health Service. National Institutes of Health. Office of Research on Women's Health. Office of the Director. *Report of the National Institutes of Health: Opportunities for Research on Women's Health, September 4–6, 1991, Hunt Valley, Maryland*. NIH Publication No. 92-3457. Bethesda, MD: U.S. NIH, 1992. Print.

United States. Department of Health and Human Services (HHS). Public Health Service. Task Force on Women's Health Issues. [Special Section.] "Women's Health: Report of the Public Health Service Task Force on Women's Health Issues, Vol. 1." *Public Health Reports*. 100.1 (1985): 73–106. Web. 3 Apr. 2011. <http://www.ncbi.nlm.nih.gov/pmc/articles/PMC1424718/pdf/pubhealthrep00101-0075.pdf>.

United States. Department of Health, Education, and Welfare. Public Health Service. Food and Drug Administration (FDA). *General Consideration for the Clinical Evaluation of Drugs*. HEW Publication no (FDA) 77-3040. Feb. 1977. Web. 3 Apr. 2011. <http://www.fda.gov/downloads/ScienceResearch/SpecialTopics/WomensHealthResearch/UCM131196.pdf>.

U.S. Environmental Protection Agency. *Integrated Pest Management (IPM) in Schools*. 16 Feb. 2011. Web. 14 Mar. 2011. <http://www.epa.gov/pesticides/ipm/>.

United States. General Accounting Office. *Major Management Challenges and Program Risks: Department of Health and Human Services*. Publication No. GAO-03-101. Jan. 2003. Web. 29 Apr. 2011. <http://www.gao.gov/pas/2003/d03101.pdf>.

United States. General Accounting Office. *Statement of Mark V. Nadel, Associate Director, National and Public Health Issues, Human Resources Division, Before the Subcommittee on Health and Environment Committee on Energy and Commerce, House of Representatives*. 18 June 1990. GAO/T-HRD-90-38. Print.

United States. General Accounting Office. *Women's Health: NIH Has Increased its Efforts to Include Women in Research*. Publication No. GAO/HEHS-00-96. May 2000. Web. 29 Apr. 2011. <http://www.gao.gov/archive/2000/he00096.pdf>.

United States. General Accounting Office. *Women's Health: Women Sufficiently Represented in New Drug Testing, but FDA Oversight Needs Improvement*. Publication No. GAO-01-754. July 2001. Web. 29 Apr. 2011. <http://www.gao.gov/new.items/d01754.pdf>.

United States. General Services Administration. Integrated Pest Management. 21 Dec. 2010. Web. 01 May 2011. <http://www.gsa.gov/portal/category/21654>.

Wei-Skillern, et al. *Entrepreneurship in the Social Sector*. Los Angeles: Sage, 2007. Print.

Welch, Wilford. *The Tactics of Hope: How Social Entrepreneurs Are Changing the World*. San Rafael, CA: Earth Aware, 2008. Print.

About the Contributors

Melody M. **Allison** is the agricultural, consumer, and environmental sciences librarian, and an associate professor of library administration, at the Funk Library of the University of Illinois at Urbana–Champaign. She holds a MSLIS from the University of Illinois at Urbana–Champaign and a BS in nursing from Angelo State University in Texas. Recent publications include the chapter "U.S. Government Documents and Technical Reports" in *Introduction to Reference Sources in the Health Sciences*, 5th ed. and the *Library Trends* article "Women's Health: Librarian as Social Entrepreneur."

Molly C.A. **Anderson** works as a library paraprofessional in monographic acquisitions and material donations management with the Collection Development Team at Montana State University Library. She holds an MA in public administration from Montana State University at Bozeman and a BA in interdisciplinary environmental studies from the Evergreen State College in Olympia, Washington. Her research interests include environmental stewardship in public sector agencies and the use of new media to communicate policy narratives.

Amy **Archambault** is a freelance designer and information architect. She holds a BA in communications/journalism from Loyola University in Maryland and a MA degree in instructional technology from Bloomsburg University. She has worked as an instructional designer for Syracuse University and as an information architect for Wachovia (now Wells Fargo). She is pursuing her MLIS degree in library and information studies at the University of North Carolina at Greensboro.

Mary Ellen **Bates**, president and founder of Bates Information Services, is a thought-leader in info-entrepreneurship. Since 1991, she has provided strategic business research for business professionals and info pros. The author of seven books and numerous articles on the information industry, she received her MLIS from the University of California, Berkeley.

Shakeela **Begum** is the director of development for the University of British Columbia where her team has won national awards for innovative marketing, communications and fundraising initiatives. She holds a law degree from the University of British Columbia and a BA degree in criminal justice from Thames Valley University in England. Her research interests include fundraising on the web and visionary mindsets. Her book *The AUL Guide to Fundraising* is to be published in 2012.

Andrea D. **Berstler** is the branch manager of the Henrietta Hankin Branch of the Chester County Library. She holds a BS degree in bible studies and a Pennsylvania State Teacher's Certification, as well as an MLS from Kutztown University. She is a member of the Association for Rural & Small Libraries, Inc., serving on the Board of Directors since 2008. Her professional interests include library management, strategic planning with a focus on preparing for changes within an organization, and designing libraries around a customer service model.

Manuela **Boscenco** has been part of the Library Development team at the University of British Columbia since 2008, actively promoting the library's online image gallery — the Vault — and coordinating donor activities. She holds a MA degree in archival, library and information science from the University of British Columbia and a BA degree in English and German from Universitatea de Vest, Romania. Her research interests include philanthropy and marketing libraries in the digital age. Her article in the 2009 summer issue of *Feliciter* on digital image copyright issues won the Canadian Library Association Student Article Contest in 2009.

Sharon K. **Curtis** works as a library paraprofessional in serials management at Montana State University Bozeman. She holds a BA degree in history from the University of Texas at Arlington and a MA degree in history and a professional certificate in museums and field studies from the University of Colorado at Boulder. She earned her MLIS from the University of Wisconsin–Milwaukee. Her research interests include the history of libraries in society and serials management in academic libraries.

Stephen H. **Dew** is collections and scholarly resources coordinator, University of North Carolina at Greensboro. He is the libraries' point person for issues related to scholarly communication and open access. During his 34 years of professional employment, Dew has worked in a variety of public service and technical service positions in five academic libraries. His MLS is from the University of Texas, and his PhD in history is from the University of Arkansas. He is the former editor of the *Journal of Library and Information Services in Distance Learning* and the author of *The Queen City at War: Charlotte, North Carolina, During World War II, 1939–1945*.

Sarah B. **Dorsey** has served as head of the Music Library at the University of North Carolina at Greensboro since 1994. She holds a BA degree in music from Stetson University, an MA degree in music from Boston University and an MLS degree from the University of Arizona (Tucson). She has presented at the International Association of Music Libraries.

Gail Z. **Eckwright** serves as program director for INSIDE Idaho at the University of Idaho Library. She is a research librarian and library liaison, and has held a number of other positions at the UI library over the past 33 years. She holds an MLS degree from the University of Wisconsin–Madison and an MA in literature from the University of Idaho. Her research interests include collection development, and library faculty and their place within the university.

Beth **Filar Williams** serves as the coordinator of library services for distance learning at the Jackson Library, University of North Carolina at Greensboro. She holds a MA degree in library and information science from the University of Maryland and a BA degree in geography from Johns Hopkins University. She blogs at Going Green @ your library and published on the topic in the book *Greening Libraries* and in the *Electronic Green Journal*. She presents on this topic, on distance and online learning, instructional design for e-learning and other technology trends at library conferences and consortium workshops.

Bruce **Godfrey** earned his BA degree from the University of Virginia in 1996 and his MS degree from the University of Idaho in 2000. Since then, he has worked as the GIS specialist at the University of Idaho Library, where he manages INSIDE Idaho, the Idaho Geospatial Data Clearinghouse. His professional interests include designing and implementing applications that facilitate the use of geospatial data. He works as part of Idaho EPSCoR's cyberinfrastructure team.

Christy **Groves**, MSLS, is coordinator of user services and an assistant professor at the James E. Walker Library, Middle Tennessee State University. For 16 years, she has been directly involved with recruitment, supervision, and development of library faculty and staff. She has headed a number of service excellence initiatives. She is committed to embracing trends and technologies germane to sustainability and relevance in libraries.

Peter **Hesseldenz** serves as the academic liaison for business and economics at the University of Kentucky Libraries. He holds a BA degree from the University of Wisconsin and a MA degree from the University of Kentucky, both in English literature. He also earned a MLS degree from the University of Kentucky. His research interests include business librarianship, information literacy, and reference models. A recent publication is "Library Resources and Services in 21st Century Online Education" (coauthored with Heath Martin) published in *Computer-Mediated Communication*, edited by Sigrid Kelsey and Kirk St. Amant.

Mary **Krautter** serves as head of reference and instructional services at the Jackson Library, University of North Carolina at Greensboro. She holds MA and BA degrees in English from Virginia Tech and an MLS degree from the University of North Carolina at Chapel Hill. Her research interests include information literacy and management of reference collections in the digital age. Recent publications include a co-authored chapter in *Middle Management in Academic and Public Libraries* published in 2011 and a chapter scheduled in the upcoming proceedings of the Reference Renaissance conference.

Heather **Lambert** is emerging technologies librarian and an assistant professor at the James E. Walker Library, Middle Tennessee State University. She possesses MA degrees in library science and anthropology. She oversees the Library's Digital Media Studio and is an advocate for connecting with users at their points of need. She has significant experience with trending technological applications in libraries, as well as with project management, connecting with users through social media, and gathering feedback from users to sustain library relevance.

Martha Thomas **Larson** received her undergraduate and post-graduate degrees from the University of Alabama. She graduated with a degree in law in 1987 and a MA in library sciences in 1989. She serves as the business librarian at the Greensboro Public Library and heads the business and nonprofit specialties.

Anne M. **Less** develops collaborative knowledge-sharing systems, in order to ensure that teams efficiently and effectively achieve rigorous sustainability goals. She serves as a consultant to Google Inc., creating and implementing resources that support the company's design and construction teams with healthy building material selection. Anne is a LEED Green Associate and holds an MLS degree from the University of North Carolina at Chapel Hill.

Mary Beth **Lock** is director of access services at the Z. Smith Reynolds Library at Wake Forest University in Winston-Salem, North Carolina. She earned her BS degree in biology from Wayne State University and her MLS degree from North Carolina Central University. She served on both steering committees, in 2009 and in 2011, that planned and executed *The Entrepreneurial Librarian Conference*. A recent publication is a chapter, "Ethical Uses of Information: The Good, the Bad, the Confusing," for an upcoming open source information literacy textbook.

Erik **Mitchell** is an assistant professor at the University of Maryland College of Information Studies and senior research fellow in iPAC, the Information Policy & Access Center. He received a PhD from the School of Information and Library Science at the University of North Carolina at Chapel Hill and an MLIS degree from the University of South Carolina. His research focuses on the roles of metadata and cloud computing in personal and organizational contexts.

Doralyn **Rossmann** serves as collection development librarian at the Montana State University Library. She holds a MSLS degree and a BA degree in political science and English from the University of North Carolina at Chapel Hill and a MA degree in public administration from Montana State University. Her research focuses on public budgeting, Web scale discovery tools, and managing e-book collections. Recent publications include an article on e-books and MARC records in *Serials* and an article on participatory budgeting processes in *Public Administration Review*.

Mary G. **Scanlon** serves as research and instruction librarian for business and economics at the Z. Smith Reynolds Library, Wake Forest University in Winston Salem, North Carolina. She served on the steering committees for both Entrepreneurial Librarian conferences in 2009 and 2011. She earned an MBA degree from the Weatherhead School of Management at Case Western Reserve University and an MLIS degree from Kent State University. Publications include "Re-conceiving Entrepreneurship for Libraries: Collaboration and the Anatomy of a Conference." She has been active on the executive committee of Business Librarians in North Carolina (BLINC) and currently serves as chair.

Susan Sharpless **Smith** is associate dean at the Z. Smith Reynolds Library, Wake Forest University in Winston-Salem, North Carolina. Smith received a MA degree in library and information studies from the University of North Carolina–Greensboro and a MA degree in educational technology leadership from George Washington University. She is enrolled at UNCG working toward a PhD in higher education. The third edition of her monograph *Web-Based Instruction: A Guide for Libraries* was published in 2010.

Tim **Spalding** is creator and developer of *LibraryThing*, the social cataloging website for booklovers. Beyond cataloging personal libraries, *LibraryThing* enables people to share their insights, identify similar titles that others might want to read, and come together electronically, connected by a love of books. He earned his BA degree in history and classics from Georgetown University. He now works with libraries to help bring the features of social media, like tagging and reviews, to library catalogs.

Jeff **Tiberii** is currently a bureau chief at WUNC 91.5 North Carolina Public Radio in Greensboro, previously working at WFDD 88.5 in Winston-Salem. He has served as a morning show host, news reports and sports commentator. Jeff he has covered a presidential inauguration, the criminal case of former Senator John Edwards, three ACC Men's Basketball Tournaments, and an Orange Bowl. He holds a BS degree in broadcast journalism from Syracuse University. His broadcasting work has earned him more than 20 state and regional awards.

Kristin **Whitehair** serves as the electronic resources selector for Johnson County Library in Kansas. She holds a BA degree in history from Kansas State University and an MLIS degree from Louisiana State University. She is completing an MA degree in public administration at the University of Kansas. Her research interests include performance management, digital copyright, and digital user services. Publications include a co-authored chapter in *Computer Mediated Communication: Issues and Approaches in Education* and an article published in the *Journal of Library and Information Services in Distance Learning*.

Joe M. **Williams** is head of access services, University Libraries, University of North Carolina at Greensboro. He received his MSLS in 2000 from University of North Carolina at Chapel Hill and was selected as a 2001–2003 NCSU Libraries Fellow. Since 2000, he has presented widely on issues related to learning spaces and public services in academic libraries, co-editing *Teaching with Technology: An Academic Librarian's Guide* in 2007.

Index